GALLA PLACIDIA

WOMEN IN ANTIQUITY

Series Editors: Ronnie Ancona and Sarah B. Pomeroy

This book series provides compact and accessible introductions to the life and historical times of women from the ancient world. Approaching ancient history and culture broadly, the series selects figures from the earliest of times to late antiquity.

Cleopatra
A Biography
Duane W. Roller

Clodia Metelli
The Tribune's Sister
Marilyn B. Skinner

Galla Placidia
The Last Roman Empress
Hagith Sivan

GALLA PLACIDIA

THE LAST ROMAN EMPRESS

Hagith Sivan

OXFORD
UNIVERSITY PRESS

OXFORD
UNIVERSITY PRESS

Oxford University Press, Inc., publishes works that further
Oxford University's objective of excellence
in research, scholarship, and education.

Oxford   New York
Auckland   Cape Town   Dar es Salaam   Hong Kong   Karachi
Kuala Lumpur   Madrid   Melbourne   Mexico City   Nairobi
New Delhi   Shanghai   Taipei   Toronto

With offices in
Argentina   Austria   Brazil   Chile   Czech Republic   France   Greece
Guatemala   Hungary   Italy   Japan   Poland   Portugal   Singapore
South Korea   Switzerland   Thailand   Turkey   Ukraine   Vietnam

Published by Oxford University Press, Inc.
198 Madison Avenue, New York, New York 10016

www.oup.com

Oxford is a registered trademark of Oxford University Press

Library of Congress Cataloging-in-Publication Data
Sivan, Hagith,–
Galla Placidia: the last Roman empress /Hagith Sivan.
p.   cm.—(Women in antiquity)
Includes bibliographical references and index.
ISBN 978-0-19-537912-9—ISBN 978-0-19-537913-6
1. Galla Placidia, Empress, ca. 386–450. 2. Rome—History—Valentinian III, 425–455.
3. Rome—History—Germanic Invasions, 3rd–6th centuries. 4. Empresses—Rome—Biography. I. Title.
DG338.S58   2011
937′.09092—dc22 [B]   2010041076

1 3 5 7 9 8 6 4 2

Printed in the United States of America
on acid-free paper

To Jim Seaver
whose passing on March 14, 2011, has made us all poorer;
he will be long remembered.
And to
Albert Noyer,
Author and Galla fan,
with thanks for shared hilarity

Contents

Abbreviations

ACO.	*Acta Conciliorum Oecumenicorum*
ACW.	Ancient Christian Writers
Agnellus, LPR.	Agnellus of Ravenna, *The Book of Pontiffs of the Church of Ravenna*, trans. D. M. Deliyannis (Washington 2004)
AJP.	*American Journal of Philology*
AT.	*Antiquité Tardive*
Blockley. R. C.	Blockley, *The Fragmentary Classicising Historians of the Later Roman Empire: Eunapius, Olympiodorus, Priscus and Malchus* (Liverpool 1983)
BMCR.	*Bryn Mawr Classical Review* (online)
Byz.Z.	*Byzantinische Zeitscrift*
CA.	*Collectio Avellana* (CSEL 35)
CIL.	*Corpus Inscriptionum Latinarum* (available online)
CJ.	*Codex Justinianus*
CLRE.	R. S. Bagnall et al., *Consuls of the Later Roman Empire* (Atlanta 1987)
CM.	*Chronica Minora* (Mommsen)
Colman-Norton.	P. R. Colman-Norton, *Roman State and Christian Church: A Collection of Legal Documents to AD 535*, 3 vols. (London 1966)
CP.	*Classical Philology*
CSEL.	*Corpus Scriptorum Ecclesiasticorum Latinorum*
CTh.	*Codex Theodosianus* (Mommsen-Meyer-Krueger, available online)
DOP.	*Dumbarton Oaks Papers*
G&R.	*Greece and Rome*
HSCP.	*Harvard Studies in Classical Philology*
ICUR.	*Inscriptiones Christianae ad Urbem Romam pertinentes*
ILCV.	*Inscriptiones Latinae Christianae Veters*
ILS.	*Inscriptiones Latinae Selectae*
IRC.	*Inscriptions Romaines de Catalogne*
JAC.	*Jahrbuch für Antike und Christentum*

JECS.	*Journal of Early Christian Studies*
JEH.	*Journal of Ecclesiastical History*
JHS.	*Journal of Hellenic Studies*
Jones, *LRE.*	A. H. M. Jones, *The Later Roman Empire 284–602*, 2 vols. (Norman, Okla 1964)
JRA.	*Journal of Roman Archaeology*
JRS.	*Journal of Roman Studies*
JTS.	*Journal of Theological Studies*
LCL.	Loeb Classical Library
LP (Davis).	R. Davis, *The Book of the Pontiffs (Liber Pontificalis): The Ancient Biographies of the First Ninety Bishops to AD 715* (TTH 6, rev. ed.) (Liverpool 2000)
LP (Duchesne).	L. Duchesne, *Le Liber Pontificalis, texte, introduction et commentaire*, 2 vols. (Paris 1886–1892)
MGH AA.	*Monumenta Germaniae Historica. Auctores Antiquissimi*
MM.	*Madrider Mitteilungen*
NPN.	Nicene and Post-Nicene Fathers
Orosius.	M-P. Arnaud-Lindet (ed., trans., comm.), *Orose, Histoires*, 3 vols. (Paris 1991)
PBSR.	*Papers of the British School at Rome*
PL.	*Patrologia Latina*
PLRE II.	J. R. Martindale, *The Prosopography of the Later Roman Empire II, AD 395–527* (Cambridge 1980)
RAN.	*Revue archéologique de Narbonnaise*
REAug.	*Revue des Etudes Augustiniennes*
REByz.	*Revue des Etudes Byzantines*
REL.	Revue des études latines
Seeck, Regesten.	O. Seeck, Regesten der Kaiser und Päpste für die Jahre 311 bis 476 n.C. (Stuttgart 1919)
SCh.	Sources Chrétiennes
TAPA.	*Transactions of the American Philological Association*
TTH.	Translated Texts for Historians (Liverpool)
VM.	E. A. Clark, *The Life of Melania the Younger: Introduction, Translation, and Commentary* (New York 1984)

Introduction

> What might have been is an abstraction
> Remaining a perpetual possibility
> Only in a world of speculation

T. S. ELIOT, "BURNT NORTON," FOUR QUARTETS

This book was born from pure temptation. I could not resist the offer to write a monograph centering on so colorful a character as Galla Placidia. The project presented an opportunity to recapture my interest in the genre of biography, in which I had experimented with Ausonius of Bordeaux, and to return to my Western roots whence I had diverged in recent years in search of a biography of a land.[1] Nor is this book my first foray into Galla's realm. In 2002 at Kalamazoo I had the pleasure of presenting Galla's secret diaries in the session of the Pseudo Society. These, of course, were a figment of my imagination, much aided by the excellent nonfictional monograph that Stewart Oost dedicated to the same subject, which I had purchased long ago.[2]

Herein, too, was a dilemma that I had to face at the dawn of the project. No sooner had I reread, with pleasure and admiration, Oost's book than I knew that I had no interest in producing an updated life and times along the same laudable lines. Oost's basic narrative of the first half of the fifth century, the era that coincides with Galla's life span, remains sound in spite of a plethora of more recent studies on barbarians and Romans, ethnogenesis, ethnicity and identity, and a host of

1. H. Sivan, *Ausonius of Bordeaux: Genesis of a Gallic Aristocracy* (London 1993); H. Sivan, *Palestine in Late Antiquity* (Oxford 2008).
2. S. I. Oost, *Galla Placidia Augusta: A Biographical Essay* (Chicago 1968).

other fashionable or slightly outmoded themes and terminologies employed to further our understanding of the decades of Roman "decline and fall" and of the birth of the Middle Ages.[3] The book in front of you is, therefore, not a conventional biography, like those woven around Galla's contemporaries, be they emperors like Theodosius II, Constantius III, and Valentinian III; military men like Stilicho and Aetius; female saintly figures like Melania the Younger; empresses like Pulcheria; or even a single year like 428.[4] Lacking a contemporary biographer, like Melania's Gerontius, Galla's life had to be reconstructed piecemeal from a handful of direct references and plenty of comparative material.

How, then, at the dawn of the twenty-first century, can one write of an ancient woman, without repetition, and without transforming the subject into an abstract? How does one tackle simultaneously the fixity of the life cycle of women (upbringing, marriage, motherhood) and the changeable in what they are and what they say? To appreciate Galla's impact in full, I deemed it vital to provide clear articulation of the vagaries of women's lives in late antiquity (c. 250–750), so evocatively outlined in masterful depictions like Peter Brown's *The Body and Society in Late Antiquity* and in many other studies by scholars like Anti Arjava, Joelle Beaucamp, Gillian Clark, Kate Cooper, Judith Evans Grubbs, and Aline Rousselle, to mention but a few.[5] Contextualizing Galla's life in

3. R. Collins, "Review Article: Making Sense of the Early Middle Ages," *English Historical Review* 124 (2008), 641–65, surveys five recent books on the Roman roots of the Middle Ages.

4. For Theodosius II, F. Millar, *A Greek Roman Empire*; for Constantius III, W. Lütkenhaus, *Constantius III: Studien zu seiner Tätigkeit und Stellung im Westreich 411–421* (Bonn 1998); for Stilicho, S. Mazzarino, *Stilicone: la crisi imperiale dopo Theodosio* (Milan repr. 1990); for Aetius, G. Zecchini, *Aezio: L'ultima defesa dell'Occidente romano* (Rome 1983), and D. Coulon, *Aetius* (Villeneuve d'Ascq 2003); G. Traina, *428 AD: An Ordinary Year at the End of the Roman Empire* (Princeton 2009). There are no biographies, to the best of my knowledge, of either Honorius or Arcadius. Rather, their courts were presented in studies such as A. Cameron, *Claudian: Poetry and Propaganda at the Court of Honorius* (Oxford 1970); M. Dewar, *Claudian: Panegyricus de sexto consulatu Honorii* (Oxford 1996); A. Cameron and J. Long, *Barbarians and Politics at the Court of Arcadius* (Berkeley 1993); and J. H. W. G. Liebeschuetz, *Barbarians and Bishops: Army, Church and State in the Age of Arcadius and Chrysostom* (Oxford 1990). Pulcheria has a fair share of the market relating to imperial women, with several monographs, from A. B. Teeten, *The Life and Times of the Empress Pulcheria* (London 1907), through M. J. Borowski, *Pulcheria, Empress of Byzantium: An Investigation of the Political and Religious Aspects of Her Reign 414–453* (PhD, University of Kansas 1979), to K. Holum, *Theodosian Empresses* (Berkeley 1982); V. Limberis, *Divine Heiress* (London 1994); and C. Angelide, *Pulcheria: la castità al potere* (Milan 1998). The Italian series *Donne d'Oriente e d'Occidente* includes biographies of imperial women including Helena, Pulcheria, Galla Placidia, Melania the Younger, Amalasuntha, and even Serena; A. Magnani, *Serena: l'ultima romana* (Milan 2002).

5. P. Brown, *The Body and Society: Men, Women, and Sexual Renunciation in Early Christianity* (New York 1988); A. Arjava, *Women and Law in Late Antiquity* (Oxford 1996); A. Arjava, "A

this manner, I believe, highlights current approaches to women, women's bodies, marriage, family, and law in late antiquity. While the sources used were, with few notable exceptions, invariably written by men, they provide patterns that assist in assessing both the usual and the exceptional in Galla's biography.

We need to recognize that to bring to light the lives of Roman women in a manner congenital to our concerns entails a movement against the current of memory. To write a biography of an ancient woman is an exercise in remembering what has been forgotten and relegated to a place outside the mainstream of society. Such is the paradox that I confronted when faced with the task of composing a biography of a woman who had been a celebrity in her own time. Daughter and granddaughter of Roman emperors, sister of more emperors, wife of a barbarian chieftain as well as of a Roman general, mother of another emperor—such distinctions, one presumes, would guarantee a viable historical narrative. Yet the facts that constitute the life and career of Galla Placidia (c. 390–450 C.E.) hardly lend themselves to a detailed reconstruction of her personality, preferences, or pleasures. Nonetheless, there has been no dearth of modern attempts. Barring those that verge on the fantastic, a good number offer sober accounts, primarily in the life and times genre, in which emphasis must be placed on the temporal framework rather than on the individual.[6]

Bibliography on Women and the Family in Late Antiquity and the Early Middle Ages (2nd to 7th Century AD)" (online, http://www.nipissingu.ca/department/history/muhlberger/orb/arjava3. htm); J. Beaucamp, *Le statut de la femme à Byzance, 4e–7e siècle*, 2 vols (Paris 1990–1992); G. Clark, *Women in Late Antiquity: Pagan and Christian Life-Styles* (Oxford 1993); K. Cooper, *The Virgin and the Bride: Idealized Womanhood in Late Antiquity* (Cambridge, Mass. 1996); K. Cooper, *The Fall of the Roman Household* (Cambridge 2007); J. Evans Grubbs, *Law and Family in Late Antiquity: The Emperor Constantine's Marriage Legislation* (Oxford 1995); J. Evans Grubbs, *Women and the Law in the Roman Empire: A Sourcebook on Marriage, Divorce and Widowhood* (London 2002); A. Rousselle, *Porneia: On Desire and the Body in Antiquity*, trans. F. Pheasant (New York 1996).

6. Recent crop of the former include H. Gourdin, *Galla Placidia: impératrice romaine, reine des Goths: biographie (388–450)* (Paris 2008). Gourdin is a prolific composer of biographies ranging from Delacroix to Walt Disney and from Geiseric to Pushkin and Audubon. S. Sorrell, *Galla Placidia: Empress of Rome in a Time of Turmoil (389–450)* (New Orleans 2006), an attractive and artful mixture of fact and fiction; G. Herzhaft, *Galla Placidia* (Paris 1987) (the book appears in a series titled Les romanesques, and the author also has the distinction of compiling an encyclopedia of the blues); and A. A. Oliviero, *A Time of Rome: The Empress Galla Placidia* (Bloomington 2006), its jacket graced with a lurid image of a scantily clad luscious woman. Among scholarly biographies of Galla, V. A. Sirago, *Galla Placidia: la nobilissima (392–450)* (Milano 1996), a revised and abbreviated version of V. A. Sirago, *Galla Placidia e la trasformazione politica dell'Occidente* (Louvain 1961), with the indispensable review by L. (Cracco) Ruggini, "Fonti, problemi e studi sull'età di Galla Placidia," *Athenaeum* 40 (1962), 373–91; A. Collaci, *Galla Placidia: la vita e i giorni* (Florence 1995); P. Caffin,

I could not make up for the reticence of ancient historians but I could compensate for the aridity of the sources by bringing to life occurrences modalized by participation of women, and situations that molded women of Galla's class and upbringing. One emphasis of my study, therefore, has been on the experiences of women from the cradle to death. Here the repetitive tenor of life cycles, punctuated by Galla's exceptional record, invariably engaged themes of virginity, marriage, childbearing, and widowhood. Here, too, the changes that the coming of Christianity entailed required a refinement of the generalized metaphors used for women.

Exceptionally, it is also possible to hear Galla's own voice. We have several letters written by her on two occasions, both involving ecclesiastical politics. In spite of the dictates of the genre, be it letters of invitation to attend church councils or letters to imperial relatives on church matters, these prose compositions remain crucial as a reflection of the rarely heard voice of women. Issued at two junctions of her career (419 and 449, respectively), these documents are also closely associated with Galla's recasting of the self. They accompanied a transformation of what I call "female orthodoxy," from an orthodoxy of legal marriage and childbearing, the inevitable fate of women, to a new orthodoxy of demonstrable religious piety.

I begin with a wedding (chapter 1) in Narbonne, an important city in southern Gaul (now France) along the road leading from Italy to Spain. In 414 the city hosted a curious ceremony—the wedding of a Roman princess (Galla), captive of the Goths, with a Gothic king (Athaulf), her captor. In the unpredictability that fashioned the intersections of Romans and barbarians, the Gallic wedding of Galla and Athaulf conjured up a motley crowd in the city that had been the earliest of all Roman colonies north of the Alps. The ceremonies bore no echoes of the groom's heretic ("Arian") or ethnic (barbarian) affiliation. To grasp such rituals I

Galla Placidia: la dernière impératrice de Rome (Paris 1977); L. Mazzolani Storoni, *Galla Placidia* (Milan 1975; repr. 1981). Assunta Nagl's century-old biography, *Galla Placidia: Studien zur Geschichte und Kultur des Altertums* (Paderborn 1908), which is also available via the Web, remains a useful overview of traditional approaches and an interesting counterpart to the most recent overviews of Galla's life; M. Harlow, "Galla Placidia: Conduit of Culture?" in *Women's Influence on Classical Civilization*, ed. F. McHardy (London 2004), 138–50; and C. L. Connor, "Female Imperial Authority: Empresses of the Theodosian House: Galla Placidia," in *Women of Byzantium* (New Haven 2004), 45–72, but only pages 64–72 are devoted to Galla. Note the different dates provided for Galla's birth, from 388 to 392. For discussion see ch. 1.

explore nuptial poems, a traditional genre at weddings of scions of eminent families. Analyzing their themes, I review the predictable and the modifications, the appropriation and the colonization of subjects long entrenched in this genre. Through the projection of these poems I present the protagonists: Galla and her ancestry; Athaulf and his connections; as well as the individuals who pronounced, perhaps even composed, the wedding paeans.

Let me be clear to avoid possible confusion. We do not have the actual wedding compositions that directly addressed the audience at Galla's Gallic wedding. But we do have other such compositions, as well as guidelines conveniently assembled under the name of Menander Rhetor for anyone with serious ambitions in this compositional department.[7] What I conjure is, therefore, deductive, plausibly based on contemporary works that did survive, like Claudian's nuptial poems, as well as on information regarding such ceremonies and rituals. Similarly, excavations at Narbonne have not pinpointed the mansion where Galla's wedding was held, but we know enough of contemporary houses to venture into a reconstruction of Galla's nuptial venue.

Casting the net back to Galla's decade at Rome (400–410 C.E.), I consider the options that Christianity unfolded to young women. Did Galla entertain the assumption of perpetual virginity, a not unfashionable choice endorsed by eminent theologians? Was she a reluctant or willing bride? How did her presence in the Gothic camp, her desirability, or lack of it, interject a variation into the close circuit of negotiations between Roman governments and barbarian monarchs?

Chapter 2 ("Funerals in Barcelona") follows Galla's meandering in Gothic company as the Goths decamp from Gallic Narbonne to Spanish Barcelona. Here I introduce a city in transition, with a new Christian center built in the heart of Barcelona's industrial installations, modifying the landscape of this thriving commercial port. This is a period of transformation that, exceptionally, modern spectators can share through the spectacular site of Plaça del Rei, nowadays in the heart of the most cheerful part of Barcelona. At Barcelona, where Galla bore to Athaulf a son lost in infancy, I take the time to meditate on the theme of death.

7. D. A. Russell and N. G. Wilson, *Menander Rhetor: Translation and Commentary* (Oxford 1981); M. Heath, *Menander: A Rhetor in Context* (Oxford 2004); L. Pernot, *La rhétorique de l'éloge dans le monde gréco-romain* (Paris 1993).

How was death inscribed, described, and experienced? Here I bring into the discourse a fellow Roman aristocrat, Paulinus (of Nola), for whom Spain and Barcelona represented likewise a loss (of his child) and a sense of profound displacement. Like Galla, Paulinus knew well the western provinces in ways that aped, yet also severed from, the past. He hailed from Gaul (where his family owned vast properties), lived in Italy (as governor of a province), married a Spanish heiress and moved to Spain, and was acclaimed priest in Barcelona, but moved back to Italy to become bishop of a town in Campania. The paths taken by Paulinus and by Galla linked indirectly in Spain. In Italy, during a schism over papal elections, they would link again.

Chapter 3 ("The Making of an Empress") begins with Galla's second wedding, this time in the imperial capital of Ravenna in 417, to Constantius, the general on whose services Galla's brother, Honorius (emperor of the western provinces, 395–423 C.E.) depended. Once again a word of warning. We do not have the orations or poems that would have been delivered on so august an occasion, especially in the presence of the emperor. Nor do we possess the funeral orations that would have been composed in honor of either her dead child or her husbands. Applying a deductive method, I conjure the words that such situations would have generated to re-create the mood and the manners.

Galla's second marriage produced two healthy children and imperial titles for herself and her spouse, both seemingly ingredients of a happy ending. Not quite. As I trace Galla's early years at the imperial court (417–423), I examine the ways in which she carved a role for herself at the court, how and why she intervened in the affairs of the papacy, and how her involvement reconnected her with Paulinus, by then a venerable bishop in Italy. Here I rely on the precious testimony of Galla's own letters to the bishops of Africa and to Paulinus. The chapter further delves into her fall from grace and exile, episodes that invite brief reflections on the complexity (or perhaps confusion) of contemporary power structures.

Chapter 4 ("Restoration and Rehabilitation") begins with an analysis of an inscription at Rome and a double-pronged investigation of two senatorial projects, one the rehabilitation of a dead and disgraced senator, the other a literary banquet. These two enterprises, I maintain, strikingly illustrate the ambiguity of Galla's position as regent. In neither text is Galla directly named. Yet both set up a system of internal cross-references that assist in comprehending Galla's relations with the powerful senate of Rome. Both underline the skills with which she navigated between poles of power—the senate, the army, and the church. I end the chapter with a consideration of patterns of relations between the court and the capital's bishop and how these contributed to Galla's reincarnation as a pious matriarch.

Chapter 5 ("A Bride, a Book, and a Pope"), accompanies the nuptials of Valentinian III, Galla's son, in 437 with Licinia Eudoxia, his relative and daughter of the eastern emperor Theodosius II and his wife Eudocia. Here I embark not on an exchange of vows but rather on an exchange of texts, and of ideologies. I follow the course of two weighty books, the Theodosian Code, the authoritative gift of the bride's father to the new realm of his daughter, and a luxurious Pentateuch, the Law of ancient Israel, a matching gift from Galla to her daughter-in-law. I end the chapter with an examination of contending orthodoxies through an exchange of letters, prompted by Pope Leo, between women of the western court and the imperial family of Constantinople.

Admittedly, some may regard the connections I forge between Galla, the Theodosian Code, and an illustrated Pentateuch as especially speculative. Galla's imprint on such weighty projects remains elusive. Only rarely do the dedications of codices survive, like the one gracing the so-called Calendar of 354. Pictorial Bibles, especially those beginning with the Creation, are hardly likely to preserve a dedication to the mortal who paid for the work. More serious is the fact that in the absence of hard criteria for dating, art historians tend to rely on paleographic, stylistic, and iconographical analyses to endow a codex with a sponsor or a season. Valid as such methods are, in the absence of dated comparative material, such analyses must be treated with extreme caution.

Chapter 6 ("Between Rome and Ravenna") begins with the belated internment in 450 of the child Galla had lost in Barcelona in 415. The funeral, conducted by Leo the pope, provides an occasion to examine Rome's funerary landscape, the chapel and the cemeteries that spelled a new Christian city within the panorama of pagan Rome. The occasion further allows reflections on the fate of individual senators who held office under Galla's auspices in the late 420s and 430s. I further use the internment to introduce vagaries of memory, the public remembrance of a long-gone child, and attempted forgetfulness of a wayward living daughter. I close the chapter with an inconvenient journey, at least as I experienced it in 2008, between Rome and Ravenna. Here, with my pen rather than with a slow train, I depart from St. Peter's at Rome to reach Ravenna, where I end this journey at the church Galla dedicated to John the Evangelist, the saint whose mercy had saved her and her children from the stormy sea in 423. Without John, I suppose, this book would not have been possible.

The conclusion briefly meditates on surprising statistics—in spite of child emperors, numerous usurpers and civil wars, endless barbarian invasions, considerable loss of territory, and a court that appeared all but detached from provinces and frontiers, the Valentinian-Theodosian dynasty, of which Galla and her son were the last representatives in the west (and Theodosius II and Pulcheria the last in the east), lasted nearly as long as the Julio-Claudians, the first imperial dynasty of Rome. Was the sixth-century senator Cassiodorus, then, correct in his wholly negative assessment of Galla's reign?[8]

8. See ch. 7.

CHAPTER ONE

A Wedding in Gaul
(414)

Narbonne: The Nuptial Venue

The year is 414. The month is January. A wedding takes place in the city of Narbonne, the oldest Roman foundation on Gallic soil. The city is a major station along the Via Domitia, the road that links Italy with Spain. Its harbor faces the Mediterranean; in the back loom the Pyrenean mountains. The bride, Galla Placidia, is decked in abundant royal silks. She is, after all, a princess of imperial blood, granddaughter and daughter of Roman emperors, Valentinian I (364–375) and Theodosius I (379–395), respectively, sister of one reigning emperor, Honorius (395–423), and aunt of another reigning monarch, Theodosius II (408–450). None of the bride's relatives is in attendance, neither her brother nor her nephew or nieces. Honorius had remained in Italian Ravenna, his capital since 402; Theodosius II and his sisters in Constantinople, capital of the Eastern Roman Empire. Of the bride's family at Rome, once consisting of her cousin and adopted sister Serena, Serena's husband Stilicho, and their three children, only a young daughter was left. But she had been packed off to a nunnery in 410 after the execution of her parents and brother. Another relative, Laeta, widow of Gratian (375–383), Galla's assassinated uncle, had been living at Rome with her mother, not too old perhaps to travel but hardly inclined to traverse the troubled Italian peninsula to attend a wedding of a little-loved relative.[1]

---

1. Zosimus 5.39.4 on Laeta, second wife of Gratian, and her mother helping to relieve the hunger ushered in by the Gothic siege of Rome in 408–410 by disbursing their own resources. This gesture, unusual enough to be recorded by Zosimus's source, followed the execution of Serena, who had been suspected of assisting the Goths (Zos. 5.38–39), and below. It is unclear whether Laeta's act was meant to counterbalance Galla's share in Serena's death. Zosimus's deliberate juxtaposition of these two dramatically different reactions to the horrid state of affairs in the city under siege hints at strained relations between Laeta and Galla.

Narbonne may appear an odd choice for a wedding celebration of a Roman imperial princess. Her presence in Gaul, rather than at Rome, Ravenna, or Constantinople, reflects the chaotic conditions that had prevailed in the western provinces of the Roman Empire in the early years of the fifth century.[2] Even less predictable than the nuptial venue was the groom, a Gothic king named Athaulf. On this solemn occasion he donned the military garb of a Roman officer. The position had been conferred on him by a man whose credentials as an emperor of the Roman realm were never recognized by the bride's imperial relatives. The guests were a motley assembly of local Gallic notables, Roman opportunists, and barbarians, the latter followers of Alaric, king of the Goths (Tervingi) for fifteen years (395–410) and the groom's deceased brother-in-law.[3]

Marital alliances of members of the Valentinian-Theodosian dynasty (364–455) to which Galla belonged received an inordinate amount of contemporary coverage, not untinged with a touch of romance. The beauty of Galla, Galla Placidia's mother, was reputed to have won over the heart of the widower Theodosius I in the course of a melodramatic interview conducted by her mother, Justina.[4] The latter, herself a noted belle of impeccable lineage, had weathered the death of one husband, a usurper (Magnentius, 351–353), to marry some dozen years later a legitimate emperor (Valentinian I).[5] Arcadius, Galla's half brother and emperor of the Eastern Roman Empire (395–408), had fallen in love with the beautiful Eudoxia, sight unseen, on the basis of a portrait painting.[6]

2. G. Halsall, *Barbarian Migrations and the Roman West 376–568* (Cambridge 2007) for one recent survey.

3. H. Sivan, "Alaricus Rex: Legitimizing a Gothic King," in *The Construction of Communities in the Early Middle Ages*, ed. R. Corradini et al., Transformation of the Roman World (Leiden 2003), 109–21; H. Sivan and R. W. Mathisen, "Forging a New Identity: The Kingdom of Toulouse and the Frontiers of Visigothic Aquitania," in *The Visigoths: Studies in Culture and Society*, ed. A. Ferreiro (Leiden 1999), 1–60. On the Goths see also the ample bibliographies compiled annually by Alberto Ferreiro.

4. Eunapius, fr. 58 (Blockley).

5. Ibid., without naming the woman herself. She is identified as daughter of Iustus, wife of Magnentius and later of Valentinian I. For Justina's connections with the Constantinian dynasty, J. Rouge, "La pseudo-bigamie de Valentinien I," *Cahiers d'histoire* 3 (1958), 5–15; and J. Rouge, "Justine la belle Sicilienne," *Latomus* 33 (1974), 676–79, with the stemma presented in F. Chausson, "Une soeur de Constantin: Anastasia," in *Humana Sapit: Études d'antiquité tardive offertes à Lellia Cracco Ruggini*, ed. J.-M. Carrié and R. Lizzi Testa (Turnhout 2002), 134. See now in greater detail and length Chausson's thesis, *Stemmata aurea: Constantin, Justine, Théodose: revendications généalogiques et idéologie impériale au IV s. ap J.-C.* (Rome 2007).

6. Zosimus 5.3.3; W. Treadgold, "The Bride Shows of the Byzantine Emperors," *Byzantion* 49 (1979), 395–413.

A few years after Galla Placidia's own 414 wedding, her nephew, Theodosius II, married the Athenian Athenais who had been chosen as bride by his sister.[7]

Precedents for odd, not to say irregular and highly politicized, matrimonial procedures, therefore, had been evident. Of the brides' ethnic affiliation it may be noted that Arcadius's bride was half Frank. Honorius's two wives, neither probably his own choice, were one-quarter Vandal. Of the bridal religious affiliation it may be noted that Athenais had been a pagan who had to undergo both baptism and change of name prior to her admission to the imperial bedchamber. Beauty was a basic requirement, at least as articulated by an eager young man about to be presented with a bride. Thus Athenais-Eudocia was evidently "so exceedingly comely that no other woman in Constantinople, even one of imperial blood, possessed such beauty."[8]

Not one of these royal weddings was hailed by contemporaries in terms that verged on prophecy, and even eschatology, as were the 414 nuptials of Galla and Athaulf. Philostorgius, an Arian anti-Nicene historian from Cappadocia (Asia Minor), and Hydatius, an orthodox clergyman from Galicia (Spain), borrowed from the Bible, using Daniel 2:31–45 and Daniel 11:6, respectively, to convey the novelty of the matter:[9]

> Then the daughter of the king of the south shall come to the
> king of the north to ratify the agreement. But she shall not
> retain her power and his offspring shall not ensure. She shall
> be given up, she and her attendants and her child and the one
> who supported her. (Daniel 11:6)

Another Spanish theologian of Hydatius's Nicene conviction, Orosius, reporting words pronounced by the bridegroom himself, captured the moment as the apex of Romanization. According to Orosius, it had been no less than a divine scheme (*iudicium divinum*) that threw Galla in the path of the marauding Goths so that, united in marriage to such a powerful barbarian king, she would be rendered highly useful to the

---

7. *PLRE II*, 408–9 (Eudocia 2).

8. *Chronicon Paschale* s.a. 420, trans. M. Whitby and M. Whitby (TTH 7) (Liverpool 1989), 66 (slightly modified).

9. Philostorgius 12.4 (Bidez), Eng. trans. P. R. Amidon, *Philostorgius' Church History* (Leiden 2007), 158, in a fragmentary passage that alludes to the famous vision of the metallic cycle of empires; Hydatius, *Chron.* s.a. 414, referring to the progeny of the daughter of the king of the south and the king of the north, although Daniel is rather pessimistic about the outcome of the marital arrangment.

Roman state.[10] During the wedding itself, Orosius further alleged, the groom swore eternal allegiance to Rome and to everything that Rome stood for, forswearing his previous intention to destroy the empire. The words of his bride on the occasion were not preserved. For the polytheist historian Olympiodorus of Thebes (Egypt), the marriage of a Roman princess with a Gothic chieftain provided a potential prelude to a new phase in Roman-barbarian relations.[11]

Such perceptions, crafted in light of later events, ignored a crucial question—was Galla a willing or coerced bride? Did the wedding represent the culmination of a tragic process that had begun with the storming of her residence at Rome in 410 and ended in prolonged captivity and marriage to her captor? Or should we succumb to a more romantic view that has been beautifully advanced by fictional tales woven around Galla falling for a handsome barbarian (and vice versa)?[12] In 410 Galla was about twenty years old.[13] Already in 400, hints were dropped regarding approaching nuptials between her and Eucherius, son of Serena and Stilicho and Galla's second cousin.[14] Yet, the ambitious parents did not manage to reach even the stage of betrothal.[15] The murder of Stilicho and Eucherius in 408 sealed these marital designs for good. Should one detect behind the abortive attempt Galla's reluctance to enter the state of matrimony? We know little of her movements at that point beyond two facts: her birth in Constantinople

10. Orosius 7.40.2.

11. Olympiodorus, fr. 24 (Blockley).

12. S. Sorrell, *Galla Placidia: Empress of Rome in a Time of Turmoil (389–450)* (New Orleans 2006), for one recent example. Galla's ongoing inspiration is worth a separate study.

13. Galla's date of birth has been a matter of controversy. S. I. Oost, *Galla Placidia Augusta: A Biographical Essay* (Chicago 1968), 48, advanced 388/389 as her birth year, being the eldest child of Theodosius and Galla. S. Rebenich, "Gratian, a Son of Theodosius, and the Birth of Galla Placidia," *Historia* 34 (1985), 372–85; and S. Rebenich, "Gratianus Redivivus," *Historia* 38 (1989), 376–79, postpones her date of birth to 392/393, allowing for an older child of Galla and Theodosius (Gratian), attested by Ambrose's *Epistula extra collectionem* 11.17, where Theodosius was addressed as *Gratiani pater* (unless the allusion is to metaphorical paternity of the emperor Gratian), and in Ambrose's *de obitu Theodosii* 40 that refers to Gratian and Pulcheria as Theodosius's *pignora*. Galla may have been born to Theodosius I and Galla, following the birth of John (Iohannes), a boy, perhaps stillborn, whose existence can be only surmised from an inscription in a church honoring John the Evangelist that Galla Placidia later dedicated at Ravenna, see chs. 3 and 6.

14. Claudian, *Stil.* II, 341ff.; A. Cameron, *Claudian: Poetry and Propaganda at the Court of Honorius* (Oxford 1970), 47, 54, 154. Note the description of the unnamed bride as *progenitam Augustis Augustorumque sororem*, a forerunner of the way in which Galla would describe herself, prior to her elevation to the rank of Augusta, in letters addressed to ecclesiastical dignitaries, see ch. 3.

15. This would appear a striking failure of the couple's plan, especially in view of Galla's later success in affiancing two infant princes in 424, her own five-year-old son with his toddler cousin, daughter of Theodosius II, see ch. 5.

and her residence in Rome about a decade later.[16] Since Honorius resided mostly in Milan (395–401) and Ravenna (401–423), it appears that Galla did not join the imperial court.[17] Whether by choice or not is unclear. Another question remains: how did she manage to avoid marriage?

It has become customary to maintain that upper-class women, especially members of the imperial family, had little choice when it came to marriage or to the selection of future husbands. Aristocratic alliances often depended on the trading of female members to partners carefully chosen to promote the interests of their male relatives.[18] Christianity, it is often asserted, allowed a modicum of choice, especially if both parents and daughters opted for the course of perpetual virginity.[19] This was an option that theologians like Jerome counted as the height of female noble achievements:

> Who has set a better example of courage than Eustochium,
> who by resolving to be a virgin has breached the gates of the
> nobility and broken down the pride of a consular home? The
> first of Roman ladies, she has brought under the yoke the first
> of Roman families.[20]

Even widows with wealth, education, and excellent theological connections could adopt a Christian form of "virginal fertility," providing they avoided remarriage.[21] Galla's distance from the imperial court would have been instrumental in allowing her to forge a filiation outside the

---

16. Oost, *Galla Placidia*, 53–94, for speculative reconstruction. I would assign her Roman period to 395–410. It is unclear how and when Galla was placed in the hands of the Goths. Orosius 7.40.2 connects the transfer with the 410 sack of Rome, claiming that she had been captured by Athaulf as his potential bride. She may have been taken prisoner already in one of the earlier sieges of the city, in either 408 or 409, Zosimus 6.12.3, or even traded as part of the negotiations between Honorius's government and Alaric, or Athaulf. For discussion see H. Sivan, "From Athanaric to Ataulf: The Shifting Horizons of 'Gothicness' in Late Antiquity," in *Humana Sapit* (above n. 5), 56–57.

17. A. Gillett, "Rome, Ravenna and the Last Western Emperors," *PBSR* 69 (2001), 137–38 [131–67].

18. Cf. matrimonial schemes of late Republican generals, and most strikingly of the first emperor of Rome, Octavian-Augustus, who married off his only daughter, Julia, four times to men whom he carefully selected, E. Fantham, *Julia Augusta* (Milton Park 2006), passim.

19. H. Sivan, "On Hymen and Holiness in Late Antiquity: Opposition to Aristocratic Female Asceticism at Rome," *Jahrbuch für Antike und Christentum* 36 (1993), 81–93.

20. Jerome, *Ep.* 66.3 (Eng. trans. NPN).

21. To use the expression of P. Brown, *The Body and Society: Men, Women, and Sexual Renunciation in Early Christianity* (New York 1988), 369. See also his comments on the educated widows of Rome of Jerome's circle, Ibid., 366–86, and on the same circle, E. Clark, *Jerome, Chrysostom and Friends: Essays and Translations* (New York 1979); and E. Clark, "Theory and Practice in Late Ancient Asceticism: Jerome, Chrysostom, and Augustine," *Journal of Feminist Studies in Religion* 5 (1989), 25–46.

confines of all sexuality. In Rome of Galla's youth the influence of Jerome's vigorous promotion of virginal asceticism in the early 380s must have continued to reverberate. Celebrating rather than berating Galla's choice, Jerome's rhetoric would have prepared the ground for a princess vowed to virginity.

In Galla's Roman world of the early years of the fifth century, the torments of sexuality collided with the canonical image of the good wife who bears children. The fatality of fertility was strikingly reflected in the incessant pregnancies, miscarriages, and early death of Galla's own mother. Ingredients of resistance to parental plans had been sown by Galla's contemporary, Melania the Younger, who, at least according to her admiring biographer, strenuously objected to marriage, albeit in vain.[22] In Galla's own maternal family two aunts, sisters of the emperor Valentinian II were consecrated (or doomed) to perpetual virginity already in the early 390s.[23] The combination of virginal piety and politics would have been further inspired by developments at the court in Constantinople. Upon the sudden death of the emperor Arcadius in 408, his daughters, urged no doubt by the eldest, Pulcheria, renounced sex in favor of chaste life in the palace. In this light the possibility that in 414 Galla would have been a reluctant, if not a battered, bride need not be wholly discounted. Such a stance would serve to explain, in part, why she had spent several years in the Gothic camp before donning a bridal gown in Narbonne.[24]

Notwithstanding bridal scruples and adverse circumstances, the atmosphere in Narbonne must have been festive, helped and abetted by the warm wine that the guests imbibed:

> [The bride], dressed in royal raiment, sat in a hall decorated in the Roman manner. By her sat [the groom], wearing a Roman general's cloak and other Roman clothing. Amidst the celebrations, along with other wedding gifts [the groom] gave [the bride] fifty handsome young men dressed in silk clothes,

22. E. A. Clark, *The Life of Melania the Younger* (New York 1984). She was married at fourteen in 399.

23. See ch. 2 for Ambrose's address to the two princesses in the funeral oration pronounced over the corpse of Valentinian II in 392. Ambrose is the sole ancient source to refer to these two women.

24. For other reasons, above all the uneven course of Gothic-Roman negotiations, see below. In addition, Athaulf had been married before but no information regarding his wife's death is disclosed. She may have passed away only in 413.

each bearing aloft two very large dishes, one full of gold, the other full of precious, or rather priceless stones which had been carried off by the Goths at the sack of Rome. Then nuptial hymns were sung. . . . Then the ceremonies were completed amidst rejoicing and celebrations by both barbarians and Romans.[25]

Guests fortunate enough to have been invited to the wedding assembled in the reception rooms at the house of the Narbonese Ingenius (Ingenuus). His villa would have boasted several reception rooms of various shapes and sizes, a diversity due to seasonal changes, as well as to a desire to maintain and promote social distinctions among guests and, of course, to impress.[26] In the 109 villas excavated and meticulously catalogued in the neighboring provinces of Septimania and Aquitania, reception rooms varied in size from 40 square meters to 300 square meters, ranging in form from a simple square through rectangles, apsidal, multiapsidal, and cruciform to octagonal shape.[27] Participants in Galla's wedding would have been spread, according to rank, and perhaps to ethnicity, across several such rooms, coming together only for the ceremony itself. Gatherings of this sort were staged scenes of solidarity of rank and class.

The home that Ingenius provided for Galla's nuptials most likely resembled the excavated suburban home of another Narbonese magnate, dubbed the Porticoed House (Maison à Portiques).[28] The mansion was substantial, measuring some 1,000 square meters, its size and decoration

25. Olympiodorus, fr. 24 (Blockley) (slightly amended). A water heater, shown under dining tables and designed to mix wine with hot water during meals, was a fixture in aristocratic dwellings; K. M. D. Dunbabin, "Wine and Water at the Roman Convivium," *JRA* 6 (1993), 116–41.

26. L. Bek, "'*Quaestiones conviviales*': The Idea of the Triclinium and the Staging of Convivial Ceremonies from Rome to Byzantium," *Analecta Romana* 12 (1983), 81–107; K. M. D. Dunbabin, "Triclinium and Stibadium," in *Dining in a Classical Context*, ed. W. J. Slater (Ann Arbor 1991), 121–48; and K. M. D. Dunbabin, "Convivial Spaces: Dining and Entertainment in the Roman Villa," *JRA* 9 (1996), 66–79; S. P. Ellis, "Power, Architecture and Décor: How the Late Roman Aristocrat Appeared to His Guests," in *Roman Art in the Private Sphere: New Perspectives on the Architecture and Décor of the Domus, Villa and Insula*, ed. E. Gazda (Ann Arbor 1991), 117–34; and S. P. Ellis, "Late Antique Dining: Architecture, Furnishings and Behaviour," in Domestic Space in the Roman World: Pompeii and Beyond, ed. R. Laurence and A. Wallace-Hadrill (*JRA* supp. 22) (Portsmouth 1997), 41–51; E. Morvillez, "Les salles de réception triconques dans l'architecture domestique de l'Antiquité tardive en Occident," *Histoire de l'Art* 31 (1995), 15–26; J. Rossiter, "Convivium and Villa in Late Antiquity," in Slater, *Dining*, 199–214.

27. C. Balmelle, *Les demeures aristocratiques d'Aquitaine: Société et culture de l'Antiquité tardive dans le Sud-Ouest de la Gaule* (Bordeaux-Paris 2001), 155–77.

28. M. Sabrié, R. Sabrié, D. Rouquette, and Y. Solier, *La maison à portiques du Clos de la Lombarde à Narbonne et sa décoration murale* (RAN supp. 16) (Paris 1987); M.Sabrié and R. Sabrié (eds.), *Le Clos de la Lombarde à Narbonne: Espaces publics et privés du secteur nord-est* (Montagnac

mirroring the aspirations, resources, and standing of its owners. It had a long history. Constructed originally in the late first century (B.C.E.), the building underwent numerous modifications and two phases of abandonment.[29] Around 200 C.E. the reception rooms were covered with wall paintings conceived and executed with dramatic panache. They included an aedicule elaborately drawn around figures of armed men flanking Plenty and Victory.[30] Their size and style seemed more suitable to a public monument than to a private home. The decor apparently projected messages of loyalty to the emperors and to imperial ideology. When the Porticoed House was abandoned in the first half of the third century, the paintings were still fresh. At the end of the fourth century a modest church was planted atop the house. It too was abandoned, apparently around the middle of the fifth century.[31] Beyond that date the structure functioned solely as a locale for funerary services. The precise fate of the paintings remains unclear. They may have been completely covered by the time Galla and Athaulf arrived.

To glimpse further into the Narbonese setup in 414, one has to turn to the city of Toulouse, northwest of Narbonne, where a monumental residence recently discovered had been constructed around 400 C.E. atop an old pottery atelier.[32] It boasted palatial dimensions of some 90 by 30 meters, an imposing size for an urban dwelling. One of its walls leaned against the city wall, facing the gracious river Garonne. Its rooms were arranged around a vast apsidal court calculated to inspire visitors with a sense of awe upon approaching the enclosed reception rooms. At Toulouse, perhaps as in Ingenius's home, weather permitting, entertainment

2004); M. Sabrié and R. Sabrié, *Le Clos de la Lombarde: Un quartier de Narbonne dans l'Antiquite* (Narbonne 2002), exhibit catalog; G. Sanchez and M. Sirventon (eds.), *Narbonne 25 ans d'archeologie: Catalogue d'exposition* (Narbonne 2000). In general on urban housing: J.-P. Sodini, "Habitat de l'Antiquité tardive," *Topoi* 5 (1995), 151–218, and 7 (1997), 435–577. On Gallic dwellings, *La maison urbaine d'époque romaine en Gaule Narbonnaise et dans les provinces voisines,* Actes du colloque d'Avignon, novembre 1994 (Avignon 1996). On Gallic porticoes in general, J. F. D. Frakes, *Framing Public Life: The Portico in Roman Gaul* (Wien 2009).

29. On the paintings of this phase, A. Barbet, *La peinture murale en Gaule romaine* (Paris 2008), 263–66.

30. Ibid., 266. Cf. the contemporary series of statuettes that embellished the great villa of Chiragan, including a series of twenty-eight imperial portrait busts of emperors from Augustus to Gallienus, D. Cazes, *Le Musée Saint Raymond: Musée des Antiques de Toulouse* (Toulouse 1999), 79–147.

31. Y. Solier et al., *La basilique paléochrétienne du Clos de la Lombarde à Narbonne: Cadre archéologique, vestiges et mobiliers* (Paris 1991).

32. Balmelle, no. 62, with R. de Filippo, "Le grand bâtiment du site de Larrey: la question palatiale," *Aquitania* 14 (1996), 23–29. The site awaits further excavations and publications. It has been conjectured that the house provided royal residence for the Visigothic kings of Aquitania in the fifth century.

took place outdoors in carefully laid-out courts with space designed for comfortable eating.

The image of nuptial gaiety in Narbonne, dictated by visions of reconciliation between Goths and Romans, masked profound tensions in the Gothic camp that led, two years after the wedding, to the murder of the groom and the rejection of the bride by his people. But in January 414 the matrimonial spectacle operated at several levels. In the minds of the noble Gallo-Roman participants, Athaulf's self-conscious effort to pose as a Roman military leader inspired hopes of imminent reinvigoration of Roman might. Athaulf's own reputed and much-quoted words on serving Rome as the only way to rule lawless barbarians lent substance to this expectation.[33] The dancing Goths may have understood this Romanized flavor of their chief's nuptials as an illustration of their ultimate acceptance. Since 376 the Goths had been wandering between East and West, prey to broken and mended treaties between their leaders and various Roman governments. During Alaric's reign the Goths had wandered from the Balkans to Italy and thence to Gaul in search of a permanent home. Even an eastern interpreter, like Olympiodorus, echoed the hopes of western observers regarding a new era in the relationship between Romans and barbarians. Yet the optimism generated by the wedding spectacle was not shared by the imperial government itself. Nor did it inspire confidence in a group of Goths within Athaulf's own camp as to his ability to negotiate favorable terms for them.

Missing from the wedding was a religious ceremony.[34] By modern calculations the bride was Catholic (or Nicene), the groom Arian, a mode of Christianity linked with Arius of Alexandria and condemned as heresy already in the 325 council of Nicaea. The Gallic informer who told Jerome about the marriage and disclosed Athaulf's innermost desire was a man whom Orosius (who was in Bethlehem at that point) praises for his Nicene religiosity.[35] This praise and the association with Jerome strongly suggest that Athaulf's Gallic connections extended to

33. Orosius 7.43.4–6.

34. Admittedly, marriage was not yet a sacrament of the Catholic Church nor a fixed ritual. Paulinus of Nola's attempt to Christianize the traditional epithalamium evidently failed. Nor is it clear what a Gothic wedding would be like. That of Fravittas (below) appears to have spurred a bloody clash.

35. For the identity of Orosius's informer, the pious Theodosian officer, D. Frye, "A Mutual Friend of Athaulf and Jerome," *Historia* 40 (1991), 507–8; and D. Frye, "Rusticus: Ein gemeinsamer Freund von Athaulf und Hieronymus? A Response," *Historia* 43 (1994), 504–6. In general, A. Marchetta, *Orosio e Ataulfo nell'ideologia dei rapporti romano-barbarici* (Rome 1987); and M. Cesa, "Il matrimonio di Placidia ed. Ataulfo sullo sfondo dei rapporti fra Ravenna e i Visigoti," *Romanobarbarica* 12 (1992–1993), 23–53.

former Gallo-Roman officials with remarkable Catholic credentials. Through this Gallic guest at the wedding the news traveled on the wings of piety and pilgrimage along the east-west axis from Gallic Narbonne to Palestinian Bethlehem, and from the court of an Arian king to the cell of an orthodox monk. The absence of Sigesarius from the wedding is another curious omission of the sources. He is identified as the Arian bishop in Alaric's camp, a cleric loyal to Alaric's house who later tried to save the lives of Athaulf's children by Alaric's sister.[36]

Public festivities of this sort, ostensibly the epitome of tranquillity and ethnic harmony, operated in reality as catalysts for sharpening conflicting identities and agendas. This is seen in a similar spectacle that had taken place about a generation before the memorable marriage of Galla and Athaulf.[37] The occasion was a banquet that the emperor Theodosius arranged, possibly to honor the nuptials of Fravittas the Goth with an unnamed Roman woman. The emperor's presence and sponsorship functioned as a live stamp of approval of a marriage that, in theory at least, transgressed an imperial law that had banned Roman-barbarian marriage.[38] Besides the Gothic groom, the list of invitees included an unspecified number of Goths. In the course of making merry and drinking, one Gothic group left the hall in protest. The groom then drew a sword and stuck it into the body of Eriulfus, the leader of the secession. According to Eunapius, the bone of contention revolved on the correct attitudes toward Rome. Its two extremes hinged on an alleged Gothic desire to take violent possession of the entire imperial realm on the one hand, and on Gothic wholehearted acceptance of the status quo as dictated by the recent treaty with the imperial government on the other. The latter found an eloquent expression in the wedding of Fravittas; the former in Eriulfus's vociferous antagonism. This is, at least, how Roman historians viewed the events over which the emperor Theodosius, Galla's father, apparently presided with equanimity, and their perceptions of fragmentation and dissension may correctly reflect the prevailing moods among the Goths.

36. Sozomen 9.9; Olympiodorus, fr. 26, B.

37. Eunapius, fr. 59 (Blockley) for what follows. The date is unclear but I would assign it to the early 380s since Eunapius specifically refers to "the early years of Theodosius" at the opening of the fragment. In his account the link between the imperial banquet and a wedding is unclear but I do not think I err in associating the imperial patronage of the event with the wedding, which the emperor also used as a demonstration of his power and benevolence.

38. H. Sivan, "Why Not Marry a Barbarian? Marital Frontiers in Late Antiquity (CTh 3.14.1)," in Shifting Frontiers in Late Antiquity, ed. H. Sivan and R. Mathisen (Aldershot 1996), 136–45.

Whether the emperor further fostered such rivalries by providing spacious venues and plenty of food is unclear, but Zosimus, for one, believed that this indeed had been the case.[39]

Athaulf's own march from Italy to Gaul signaled divisions in the Roman camp itself. By the early fifth century the close affinity between the Narbonese aristocracy and their Italian overlords had been badly shaken. Gaul, Britain, and Spain became breeding grounds for pretenders to the imperial throne. The sudden appearance of the Goths in southern Gaul in 412, a bonus (if helping locals) and a bane (if assisting remote Ravenna or acting in their own interests), deepened the wedge between Italy and Gaul.[40] Narbonne's nobility played a central role in the frequent changes of regime that took place during the first two decades of the fifth century. Only a few months before the 414 wedding, Narbonne had been the scene not of nuptial celebrations but of a bloodbath. A Gallic noble named Jovinus had made a bid for the imperial throne in 411 with the assistance of Burgundians and Alans whom he recruited beyond the Rhine. Somewhat reluctantly Jovinus also attached to his camp the followers of Athaulf who had been wandering somewhat aimlessly throughout Italy since their abortive attempt to cross over to Africa in 410. But relations between the Gaul and the Goth soured when Jovinus elected his own brother as a coemperor, an honor to which Athaulf himself may have aspired. Athaulf promptly offered his services to the Ravenna court, turned to besiege Jovinus at Valence, and upon its capture he dispatched Jovinus to Narbonne, presumably with a promise to spare his life. At Narbonne Jovinus was executed, with many other nobles, on the command of Dardanus, the Gallic praetorian prefect who had remained loyal to Honorius throughout chaos and confusion.[41] Their severed heads were sent to Honorius in Ravenna.[42]

39. Zosimus 4.56–57, who presents the events as an excursus relating to the early years of Theodosius.

40. J. Drinkwater, "The Usurpers Constantine III (407–411) and Jovinus (411–413)," *Britannia* 29 (1997), 269–98; Halsall, *Barbarian Migrations*, 222–24.

41. The list of those executed included, besides Jovinus, his brother Sallustius, his praetorian prefect Decimius Rusticus and his chief secretary Agroetius. Olympiodorus, fr. 20 (Blockley); *Chron. Gall.* 70; Hydatius, *Chron.* 54. Dardanus's initiative gained him lasting notoriety among his fellow aristocrats, who never forgave him, as Sidonius's words decades later suggest (*Ep.* 5.9.1).

42. The Annals of Ravenna record their arrival at the capital on August 30, 412 (a mistake for 413?); B. Bischoff and M. Koehler, "Eine illustrierte Ausgabe der spätantiken Ravennater Annalen," in *Medieval Studies in Memory of A. Kingsley Porter*, ed. W. Koehler (Cambridge Mass. 1939), I, 125–38.

That Dardanus chose Narbonne to witness the execution of local Gallo-Roman notables shows how entangled were the strands that were to determine the stability or instability of the Theodosian dynasty in the west. Jovinus had close ties with the nobility of Narbonne.[43] Dardanus's power base and property were in the neighboring province of Narbonensis Secunda, near Sisteron and the Alpine region of Gaul.[44] The family was well connected. Dardanus's brother, Claudius Lepidus, held the governorship of Germania Prima, the region where Jovinus had been elevated. Whether the grim sight of severed aristocratic heads inspired other local aspirants with dread remains unclear. It took only four decades to produce another short-lived Gallic contender to the imperial throne (Avitus in 456). Dardanus's orchestrated executions left lasting impressions on the recorders of Gallic history, who bitterly resented, or endorsed, his drastic actions.[45]

Galla's wedding feast may have helped to assuage a few of these recent and bitter memories. In the inexorable game of power in Gaul of the early 410s, a wedding could create illusions of harmony and understanding, an opportunity to display rare unanimity between migrants and locals. Such illusions were enhanced by the delivery of wedding verses. A poem praising the occasion could have extolled the city of Narbonne in Virgilian terms as the potential producer of ethnic connectivity, a nodal point to test the ideology of peaceful coexistence between Romans and barbarians.[46] Narbonne, it could be claimed, bridged the great Roman past and its projected great future. The city had harbored the earliest Roman colony, and it could, with luck, develop into a Gothic-Roman capital of a new and vigorous realm. Other themes of these traditional nuptial compositions, like the bride's and groom's physical attributes and ancestry, lent themselves to a compelling presentation. In January 414, however, many of these topics called for an adroit hand, ready to reveal as much as to conceal.

43. J. F. Matthews, *Western Aristocracies and Imperial Court AD 364–425* (Oxford 1975), 321. R. Scharf, "Iovinus-Kaiser im Gallien," *Francia* 20 (1993), 1–13, suggests that Jovinus spearheaded a Gallic aristocratic separatist movement, a suggestion opposed by Halsall, *Barbarian Migrations*, 223.

44. *CIL* 12,1524 = *TCG*, 54, an inscription commemorating Dardanus's founding of a fortified estate that he piously named Theopolis (the City of God).

45. Rutilius Namatianus 1.293f.; Sidonius, *Ep.* 5.9.1; vs. *Chro. Min.* 1.654; Matthews, *Western Aristocracies*, 322 n. 1.

46. P. Hordern and N. Purcell, *The Corrupting Sea: A Study of Mediterranean History* (Oxford 2000), 392, on connectivity of Mediterranean ports in general.

Wedding festivities of well-placed individuals like Galla and Athaulf called for epithalamia and fescennine verses, compositions designed to honor bride and groom, and the occasion, as well as to cheer and impress the select guests. In 414 these were pronounced, perhaps even composed, by three men, none a professional poet but all three well-educated Roman dignitaries. One, Attalus, had been prefect of the city of Rome (Praefectus Urbis Romae) in 409, an emperor raised to the purple by Gothic courtesy, and an inmate at the Gothic camp since 410.[47] Two Gallo-Romans, Phoebadius and Rusticus, assisted Attalus with the delivery. Rusticus left Gaul soon after the wedding. Arriving in the Holy Land, he imparted his impressions of the memorable wedding to an audience of two theologians, Jerome and Orosius, in the former's cell in Bethlehem. The words that Orosius heard on that occasion were later inscribed in his account of the contemporary troubles that beset the empire between 406 and 417.[48]

Attalus, Phoebadius, and Rusticus, three improvised poets, would have added to a sense of incongruity, if such prevailed during the Narbonese nuptial proceedings. Marriage songs in late antiquity were ordinarily composed and delivered by professional poets. In 398 the talented Alexandrian Claudian was selected to compose both epithalamium and fescennina in honor of the wedding of the emperor Honorius with Maria. Claudian's patron at the court, Stilicho, father of the bride, entrusted the delicate task to an ingenious and enormously creative poet.[49] Bound by classical traditions although performed at a Christian court, these wedding compositions inevitably featured a benign Venus, a cheerfully active Cupid, and a host of other pagan divinities regardless of the religious affiliation of either bride or bridegroom.[50] Epithalamia would describe the couple in glowing terms,

47. *PLRE II*, 180–81 (Attalus 2) and below.
48. The identification of Rusticus, the nuptial panegyrist, with the unnamed Narbonese whom Orosius met in Jerome's cell in Bethlehem is based on the arguments presented by Frye, "Mutual Friend," and Frye, "Rusticus" (above n. 35). On Orosius in Palestine in 415, J. Vilella, "Biografia crítica de Orosio," *Jahrbuch für Antike und Christentum* 43 (2000), 94–121, esp. p. 106.
49. Cameron, *Claudian*, 98f. and 193f.
50. On the licentious character of these compositions, whether pronounced in Republican or Christian times, Ibid., 98; W. G. Holmes, *Age of Justinian and Theodora* (London 1912), 117 n. 4, for relevant passages. On the sole, and failed, attempt to convert the genre of epithalamium, by Paulinus of Nola (*Carmen* 25, 406/407 C.E.), Cameron, *Claudian*, 194–95.

referring to their ancestry and to achievements of their forebears, extolling places of birth and upbringing, and looking forward to an equally distinguished progeny.

One theme requiring multiple manipulations would have been that of wedding preliminaries, or the unromantic entanglement that had led to the marriage. When the Goths entered Narbonne in late summer 413 at the time of the vintage, Galla had been in the Gothic camp for three years. Even then Athaulf required the intercession of Candidianus as promoter of the union.[51] Candidianus may have been a member of Jovinus's extended Narbonese family, or an opportunist who tried to improve fortune and position through serving the Goths. He would have argued that the continuing presence of an unattached princess of marriageable age in the camp introduced a sense of unwonted incongruity into Roman-Gothic relations.

Within the larger context of contemporary western history between 402 and 414, when Honorius's throne was continuously threatened by unexpected moves of barbarians, court intrigues, and provincial usurpation, the vicissitudes of a single princess as captive and possibly coerced bride reflected the unrecorded lot of women.[52] We know next to nothing about barbarian women on the move, in spite of sophisticated modern analyses of barbarian migrations in late antiquity. The scant attention paid to women invariably has focused on gender discussion, and specifically on feminine-masculine stereotypes.[53] The result invariably reads in familiar terms: "the female status remained exclusively defined in terms of sex: marriage and childbearing," coupled with "a subtle change in the political importance of women."[54]

Migrations and perpetual warfare cast a shadow on the activities of women, sharply contrasting with the amount of information that we have regarding women in the semisedentary Gothic society that preceded the move from Gothia (formerly Dacia, north of the Danube) to Roman

51. Jordanes, *Get.* 160 places the marriage in Italy. Oost, *Galla Placidia*, 106, interprets this as a declaration of intent on Athaulf's part in order to pressure Honorius's government. On the stages of the negotiations in which Galla's name was raised, see above. Jordanes's statement may reflect the rising fortunes of Constantius, who became *magister utriusque militiae* (chief commander of both the infantry and the cavalry troops) in 411 and whose interest in Galla may have been declared as early as that year.

52. On Galla's capture, Jordanes, *Get.* 159, with an emphasis on Honorius's inability to assist. On this decade, Matthews, *Western Aristocracies*, 307–28; M. Cesa, *Impero tardoancico e barbari: La crisi militare da Adrianopoli al 418* (Como 1984), passim.

53. Halsall, *Barbarian Migrations*, 482–88.

54. Ibid., 483.

territory in 376.[55] In Gothic martyrologies, women feature prominently as victims of religious persecutions in the early 370s.[56] A Gothic queen by the name of Gaatha, noted for Christian orthodoxy (as opposed to the Goths' later Arianism), even gathered the remains of martyrs, carrying them to Roman territory to deposit them in a church at Cyzicus (north-western Asia Minor), a fair way from Gothic territory.[57] The lot of female slaves who willingly joined the Gothic camp together with their menfolk can only be guessed at.[58] Some were sold back to Romans as slaves.[59] Free women taken captive by barbarian invaders were often prevented from returning home freely; when they did, they did not receive the support needed to restore their health and to provide their basic needs.[60]

Naturally no wedding praise poem was likely to hark back to Galla's capture in 410. Having shared the experience of Gothic captivity, Attalus, the wedding panegyrist, could display considerable empathy toward the bride. His shifting fortunes were duly noted by contemporary historians. Between 410 and 414 Attalus had been raised to the purple (by Alaric the Goth with the collusion of the Roman senate), deposed (with Alaric sending his diadem to Honorius as token of reconciliation), taken out of his home with his son, and forced to join the meandering Gothic camp as it wandered across Italy and southern Gaul.[61] Had Attalus elected to compare his recent history with that of Galla, he could have stated, as Zosimus did, that "although only a hostage, Galla enjoyed every honour and attention due to a member of the imperial family."[62] Had Attalus possessed a romantic bent, a characteristic notable in its absence among members of the Roman senatorial aristocracy of late antiquity, he could have further

55. And they contrast sharply with the central role of women in the Frankish court in the fifth and sixth centuries as recorded by Gregory of Tours in the *Historia Francorum* and in the Ostrogothic court of Ravenna as recorded by Cassiodorus, Ennodius, and Procopius. J. Nelson, "Queens as Jezebels: The Career of Brunhild and Bathild in Merovingian History," in *Medieval Women: Studies in Honor of Rosalind Hill*, ed. D. Baker (Oxford 1978), 31–77; S. F. Wemple, *Women in Frankish Society: Marriage in the Cloisters* (Philadelphia 1981).

56. P. Heather and J. Matthews, *The Goths in the Fourth Century* (TTH 11) (Liverpool 1991), 126–27.

57. Ibid., 127.

58. Zosimus 5.42 numbers no fewer than 40,000 slaves who deserted to Alaric's camp during the siege of Rome.

59. Sirm. 16 excerpted in *CTh* 5.7.2 (*de postliminio*); J. F. Matthews, *Laying Down the Law: A Study of the Theodosian Code* (New Haven 2000), 134–37.

60. Ibid. G. D. Dunn, "The Validity of Marriage in Cases of Captivity: The Letter of Innocent I to Probus," *Ephemerides Theologicae Lovanienses* 83 (2007), 107–21.

61. Zosimus 6.6–12.

62. Zosimus 6.12.3 (Eng. trans. R. T. Ridley).

claimed, as Jordanes the Gothic historian did a century later, that it was Galla's nobility, beauty, and chaste purity that attracted Athaulf.[63]

In the collection of fragments that constitute, or rather construct, Galla's story between 410 and 414, the emergence of Constantius in 411 as Honorius's new *magister utriusque militiae* (commander in chief) generated a new discourse of mutual Roman-Gothic blackmail with Galla as centerpiece. In spite of the fundamental separation of women from this kind of diplomatic exchange, the demands regarding Galla's return broke up the familiar monotony of the negotiations:

> Athaulf was asked to return Placidia at the urging especially of Constantius, who later married her. But when the promises to Athaulf, especially that to supply grain, were not met, he did not hand over Placidia, and prepared to break the peace and make war.

Such may have been Constantius's opening gambit in 411.[64] Honorius, well tried in the art of resisting Gothic requests, even at the cost of Rome and his sister, was hardly inclined to trade corn for Galla. His own subjects in Italy had as great a need to be fed as did the Goths.[65] The renewed negotiations between Goths and Romans placed deceit at the heart of the exchange and predictably floundered:

> When Athaulf was asked to return Placidia, he demanded the grain which had been promised. Although they could not fulfil their promises, they nevertheless swore to deliver it, if they received Placidia. The barbarian pretended to agree and advanced to the city named Marseilles, which he hoped to capture by treachery. There he was wounded . . . and retired to his own tent.

The equation of Galla with grain in the cold terms of diplomacy would allow a learned and imaginative panegyrist to resort to a comparison of woman with earth, two life-giving sources conferring legitimacy on male ownership of land and of wife.

63. Jordanes, *Get.* 160.

64. Olympiodorus, fr. 22.1 (Blockley) usually dated to 413 to correspond with Heraclius's African usurpation in order to account for the government's refusal to provide corn. Yet land, grain, and Roman commands had been the Goths' main demands since Alaric became king in 395 and possibly before. H. Wolfram, *History of the Goths*, trans. T. J. Dunlap (Berkeley 1988), 140–68, esp. 156–57; H. Sivan, "Alarico tra Pollenzo et Roma," in *Romani et Barbari: Incontro e scontro di cultura,* ed. S. Giorcelli Bersani (Torino 2004), 259–69, and H. Sivan, "Alaricus Rex," 109–21.

65. Jordanes, *Get.* 159; Rutilius Namatianus 1.21, on the ravaged Italian countryside, the result of Gothic presence between 402 and 412.

By 413, after the Romans ejected Athaulf and his Goths from Marseilles, Galla's presence achieved new prominence:

> Athaulf was preparing to marry Placidia and, since
> Constantius was demanding her return, he increased his
> demands so that when those were not met, he might seem to
> have acted reasonably in detaining her.[66]

Behind the uneven progression of negotiations between Honorius and Athaulf between 410 and 413, it is possible to discern forgetfulness and ambition. In the first round the promise of Galla's return failed to secure for the Goths the much-needed edible provisions. In the second round it is alleged that Athaulf embarked on negotiations fully prepared to renege on his assurances. In the third round Athaulf apparently demanded too high a price for Galla's return in the full knowledge that he would be refused and hence be free to marry her himself. In reality, the presence of Galla in the Gothic camp, as a hostage or as a bride, prevented any sort of accommodation with Honorius's government.[67]

To represent Athaulf as a man smitten by love for a woman who had been living under his auspices for several years might stretch credulity. Using Claudian's fanciful imagery, Attalus could have essayed a depiction of Athaulf, a man possibly in his thirties, as one burning with love for a captive princess in her early twenties, just as in 398 Claudian had described the fourteen-year-old Honorius's pining to wed his younger cousin Maria.[68] Venus and Cupid, perhaps more mature than usual, could have been engaged in consultation how to subsume Athaulf's failed diplomacy vis-à-vis Honorius into arrows carefully aimed to capture Honorius's virginal sister. Rooted in time and tradition, the theme of love would have glossed over the fact that the bride was well above the average age at which aristocratic girls, whether pagan or Christian, usually married.[69]

66. Olympiodorus, fr. 22.1, 22.2, 23 (Blockley). The precise chronology is unclear.

67. Oost, *Galla Placidia*, 135; Matthews, *Western Aristocracies*, 317.

68. Claudian, *Epithalamium* 8–10. Claudian's homage to the occasion of the wedding of Honorius and Maria consisted of no less than four fescennine poems and a lengthy epithalamium (the Loeb text and translation are now available via the Internet).

69. K. Hopkins, "The Age of Roman Girls at Marriage," *Population Studies* 18 (1965), 309–27; C. Carletti, "Aspetti biometrici del matrimonio nelle iscrizioni cristiane di Roma," *Augustinianum* 17 (1977), 39–51; B. D. Shaw, "The Age of Roman Girls at Marriage; Some Reconsiderations," *JRS* 77 (1987), 30–46. The average seems to have been somewhere between fourteen and twenty. Melania's forced marriage at fourteen and Licinia Eudoxia's at fifteen suggest that in such circles political and economic factors weighted toward a lower age range.

Preliminaries, then, had to be carefully tailored to suit the occasion, navigating a safe course between the demands of literary genres and of realities. Turning to elements of bridal praise, Galla's physical attributes and genealogy were subjects that could fire the imagination. The beauty of the bride, a banal yet vital element of epithalamia, invariably depicted brides as beautiful spectacles for the pleasure of both intimates and outsiders. Here the panegyrist could rely on his own eyes as well as on rumor and romantic tales. Galla, he could assert, inherited her good looks from Galla and Justina, her mother and grandmother, women whose loveliness captivated the hearts of emperors.[70] These two stood at the intersection of complex relationships that formed the underpinning of the Valentinian-Theodosian dynasty. Yet, besides recognition of Galla's fertility, the bearing of two dead boys and one live girl, there would be little else to record about her.

The memory of Justina, Galla's grandmother, by contrast, would have evoked a double deviance. She married twice in spite of social and ecclesiastical stigma that expected widows to remain *univira*, and she was a staunch supporter of Arianism, the form of Christianity that Theodosius I, Galla Placidia's father, later outlawed but that the Goths wholeheartedly embraced. Had Attalus elected to enter the fray of faiths, he could have enlisted Justina to speak on behalf of Athaulf's creed.[71] In view of the religious affiliation of the panegyrists of 414, one suspects that allusions to religious matters were tactfully omitted. Attalus was a recent convert from polytheism to Arianism; Rusticus was a man with excellent credentials of orthodoxy, to judge by his association with Jerome and Orosius, two outspoken orthodox theologians.[72] Galla herself professed, like her father, unflinching orthodoxy. An official wedding discourse would have forged the commonality of comeliness between Galla and Justina while prudently ignoring the religious convictions that separated them.

Matching bridal beauty with the groom's good looks, another prominent theme of epithalamia, would have been an easy enough task. According to a sixth-century historian, Athaulf was a "man of imposing beauty and great spirit. Although not tall of stature he was distinguished for beauty of face and form."[73] Athaulf's genealogy, on the other hand, called for radical fantasies. His most famous relative was Alaric, who in turn

---

70. Zosimus 4.43.2–44.4 (387) and above.
71. Matthews, *Western Aristocracies*, 188–90.
72. Sozomen 9.9.1 on Attalus's baptism; below on Rusticus.
73. Jordanes, *Get.* 158 (trans. Mierow), a description matched by Jordanes's depiction of Galla as noble, chaste, and beautiful, *Get.* 159.

claimed descent from the Balthi royal family.[74] The relationship between Alaric and Athaulf, however, rested not on blood but on matrimony. Alaric had married Athaulf's sister.[75] That Athaulf's claim to royalty rested on the prestige of the Goth who had sacked Rome and ravaged Italy reeked of a flagrant imbalance—unsavory to Italian ears, like Attalus's own, but perhaps pleasing to Gallic ears after the brutality that Dardanus had practiced in Honorius's name. To extol the genealogy of Athaulf, whose relationship with Attalus was fraught with tension, to praise his affiliation with a man depicted as Rome's eternal foe, were tasks that would have baffled even an experienced panegyrist.[76] Some in the audience would have remembered Stilicho's victories over Alaric in the early years of the century. The entire Gothic camp would have recalled how just a year before the wedding Stilicho's successor, Constantius, ejected the Goths from Marseilles, driving them to Narbonne. A few may have regretted not handing Galla over to her ardent Roman suitor in exchange for corn.

Asymmetries would have taken a new shape with the recital of the bride's illustrious connections. On both sides Galla boasted Roman emperors. Through both Justina, her maternal grandmother, and Gratian, her uncle, Galla's claim to imperial nobility harked all the way to Constantine (306–337), the first Christian emperor of Rome. Gratian had married a granddaughter of Constantine, posthumous daughter of his son Constantius II (337–361).[77] Had Attalus desired to poke fun at Honorius, whom he and his senatorial colleagues shunned in favor of an alliance with Alaric the Goth, he could have compared, to Honorius's detriment, the emperor's purely paternal lineage with Galla's, who alone held impeccable imperial credentials on both maternal and paternal sides.[78] The prestige of Galla's birth, it would seem, could be celebrated with pomp.

74. Jordanes, *Get.* 146. Alaric's royal origins have been debated and doubted, Wolfram, *History of the Goths*, 32, as is the date of his assumption of royalty. Ibid., passim, for Alaric's career. Sivan, "Alaricus Rex" (above n. 64).

75. Zosimus 5.37 on the Alaric-Athaulf connection. The sister remains unnamed as is Athaulf's first wife, his children, and even his brother, the last surfacing after Athaulf's assassination, Olympiodorus, fr. 26 (Blockley). Alaric's own wife is alluded to in Claudian, *de bello gothico* 626–29 as a crazy woman expecting her invincible husband to deck her with jewelry removed from the necks of Roman matrons.

76. Claudian, *de bello gothico* 518–49; Cameron, *Claudian*, 156–88.

77. Amm. Marc. 21.15.6, 29.6.7.

78. Here Attalus would have created a new historiography as well. Flaccila, Theodosius's first wife, mother of Arcadius and Honorius, had been honored with the title Augusta, a title rarely conferred on fourth-century empresses. She acquired a reputation for Nicene orthodoxy mixed with anti-Arian zeal (Gregory of Nyssa, *oratio funebris in Flaccillam*; Sozomen, *HE* 7.6.3). On her coinage and imagery, M. Marcos, "Política dinástica en la corte de Teodosio I: Las Imágenes de

Yet had Honorius deigned to attend his sister's wedding with a barbarian monarch, he would have cut a ridiculous figure, as imagined by the Victorian novelist Wilkie Collins:

> Nothing could be more pitiably effeminate than the appearance of this young man. His eyes were heavy and vacant; the forehead low and retiring; his cheeks sallow; and his form curved as if in premature old age. An unmeaning smile dilated his thin, colourless lips . . . with just enough intellect to be capricious, and just determination enough to be mischievous, he was an instrument fitted for the uses of every ambitious villain who could succeed in gaining his ear.[79]

Other poetic casualties of the wedding's praise poems would have been Galla's cousin Serena and her husband, the half Vandal Stilicho, the latter Honorius's regent for more than a dozen years (395–408). Deceased, the circumstances of their deaths would have precluded more than a passing allusion to Galla's adolescence. Both Serena and Galla had been living in Rome, the former clearly the dominant social figure in Rome's aristocratic circles. When the noble Melania the Younger desired to liquidate her vast Roman holdings in the face of familial opposition, the ascetic aristocrat turned for help to Serena, and not to Galla.[80] Championing Melania may have cost Serena her life.[81] Galla's collusion in the senatorial decision to put her relative and erstwhile guardian to death (409) was vouchsafed by Zosimus.[82] It was believed, he claimed, that Serena was ready to admit Alaric and his Goths into starving Rome. The rumor, as Zosimus punctiliously added, proved fatally misplaced. Serena's death not only failed to engineer a Gothic withdrawal from Rome but rather

Aelia Flacia Flaccilla," in *Congreso internacional La Hispania de Teodosio 1995* (Salamanca 1997), I, 155–64. She was the sole female member of the imperial family to whom Ambrose directly alluded in his funeral oration on the death of Theodosius I (*de obitu Theod.* 40). See also below ch. 2. By contrast, Galla's status as stepmother of two young Augusti appeared vulnerable. During Theodosius's lengthy absence in the west, she remained in Consantinople, where a quarrel with Arcadius resulted in her expulsion from the palace in 390, Marcellinus Comes, s.a. 390; Oost, *Galla Placidia*, 48–50.

79. W. Collins, *Antonina: Or the Fall of Rome* (London 1875), 21–22.

80. *Vita Melaniae* 11–12; Clark, *Melania*, 100–109.

81. Oost, *Galla Placidia*, 85, n. 159, denies Galla any share in the proceedings leading to the execution. A. Demandt and G. Brummer, "Der Prozess gegen Serena im Jahre 408 n. Chr.," *Historia* 26 (1977), 479–502, regard the assistance Serena rendered to Melania as the main cause of her downfall, but see the comments of Clark, *Melania*, 106–7; Magnani, *Serena*, 113–14.

82. Zosimus 5.38.

hastened its sack.[83] A year before Serena's execution, Stilicho had been murdered (408). Neither his imperial connections nor his spectacular record of service, nor the fact that both his daughters were married off to Honorius while his son was expected to marry Galla, saved him from rivals at the court. Instead of a paradigm of conjugal affection, the marriage of Stilicho and Serena would have been implicitly contrasted with that of Athaulf and Galla.

Completing the chart of the complex web of genealogies, a wedding composition would have included a topographical guide of respective upbringing. With Galla the panegyrist could embrace Constantinople, Ravenna, and Rome as cities befitting her birth and background. Cities had long been favored subjects of panegyrics.[84] Contantinople, the emperor Constantine's "Second Rome" and Galla's birthplace, had become the permanent imperial residence under Galla's father, a city noted for its own senate, palaces, and monumental architecture.[85] Its imposing walls warded off a Gothic siege in 378.[86] The episode was not likely to have been recounted in 414. Moreover, most of the wedding invitees were not familiar with the capital of the Eastern Roman Empire. Galla's own familiarity with Constantinople would have been limited to the earliest memories of childhood. Paradoxically, a few among the very old Goths at the wedding would have been witnesses of the grandeur of the eastern capital. These were men who had accompanied the Gothic king Athanaric in 381 when he came to Constantinople at the invitation of Theodosius I. The same elderly Goths would have marched in the extravagant funerary proceedings that the emperor staged in honor of the dead Gothic monarch.[87]

Ravenna and Rome, the new and the old imperial capitals, the latter Galla's residence, the former Honorius's, both worthy sites of praise,

83. Rumors of noble ladies ready to open the gates of Rome to Alaric extended also to Proba who, prompted by piety and pity for the sufferings of the besieged, did what Serena had been suspected of; see Sivan, "Anician Women, the Cento of Proba, and Aristocratic Conversion in the Fourth Century," *Vigiliae Christianae* 47 (1993), 140–57.

84. A. Cameron, "Wandering Poets: A Literary Movement in Byzantine Egypt," *Historia* 14 (1965), 470–509.

85. G. Dagron, *Naissance d'une capitale: Constantinople et ses insitutions de 330 à 451* (Paris 1974); R. Krautheimer, *Three Christian Capitals: Topography and Politics* (Berkeley 1983).

86. Amm. Marc. 31.16.3–7.

87. Zosimus 4.34.3–5, referring to the enrollment of Athanaric's followers in the ranks of the *limitanei* (border troops) along the Danube as well as to the return home of others. Some may have joined Alaric later.

could potentially present a problem. Should Ravenna be praised for its impregnable position, a factor that emboldened Honorius to object strenuously to Gothic demands? Should it be lauded as a city of seas and suburbs, fortified by the presence of the imperial navy (in nearby Classe), an asset that the Goths never possessed?[88] Was Attalus aware of Ravenna's saintly patron, Apollinaris, a well-educated Antiochene like Ampelius, Attalus's own father, who had migrated, like St. Peter himself, from the east to Rome?[89]

Rome, the Eternal City, would have featured prominently in the rhetoric surrounding the wedding. The chief panegyrist at the wedding had been the prefect of the city, an elevated office that constantly thrust its holder into the public eye.[90] Nor did he have to exert extraordinary inventiveness. Countless works, in verse and prose, had provided rich configurations of exaltation.[91] Fourteen years before the wedding, Claudian constructed a memorable image of Rome as a

> city greater than any that upon earth the air encompasses, whose amplitude no eye can measure, whose beauty no imagination can picture, whose praise no voice can sound, who raises a golden head amid the neighbouring stars and with her seven hills imitates the seven regions of heaven, mother of arms and of law ... the city that ... fought a thousand battles ... never yielding to her losses nor showing fear at any blow. ... She alone has received the conquered into her bosom and like a mother, not an empress, protected the human race with a common name ... drawing together distant races with bonds of affection. To her rule of peace we owe it that the world is our home.[92]

Yet, while praising the glorious and rather remote past of the pagan city, its more recent Christian history provided material for aggravation rather than acclaim. Should one then refer to Rome as the city of Romulus and Remus, or as that of Peter and Paul?[93] Should Roma the goddess be hailed

---

88. Agnellus, *LPR* praef. 47 (Eng. trans. Deliyannis).
89. Agnellus, *LPR* 1.
90. Matthews, *Western Aristocracies*, 18–23, on the power and prestige of the office.
91. F. Paschoud, *Roma Aeterna: études sur le patriotisme romain dans l'occident latin à l'époque des grandes invasions* (Rome 1967).
92. Claudian, *De cons. Stil.* 3.131–55 (trans. Platnauer, LCL).
93. M. Roberts, "Rome Personified, Rome Epitomized: Representations of Rome in the Poetry of the Early Fifth Century," *AJP* 122 (2001), 533–65, esp. 560.

as the city's divinity and divine source of protection or merely as a per-
sonification of Rome's greatness?[94] Should one allude to the city's recent
misfortunes, the result of prolonged yet fruitless Gothic wanderings in
Italy (402–411), in the presence of the Goths, not to mention the conspicuous display of the loot from Rome as gifts of the groom to his bride?[95]

Galla's childhood and adolescence at Rome, if projected as an ideal
curriculum, would have dispelled disequilibrium.[96] Since Galla had
been brought up by Serena, the description of Maria's list of reading
would have been apt:

> Imbibing maternal traditions, she studies the models of
> exemplary chastity. Nor does not cease, with her own mother
> as a guide, to unroll Greek and Roman tomes—venerable
> Homer, Thracian Orpheus and Sappho beating a Lesbian lyre.
> In just such a manner Latona had instructed Diana. In just
> such a manner gentle Mnemosyne in her cave transmitted
> instructions to docile Thalia.[97]

Had the wedding panegyrists elected to introduce elements of Christian
education as well, they could have used the material that Jerome had put
at parental discretion. To acquire the alphabet Jerome recommended
the use of ivory carved letters:

> Get for her a set of letters made of boxwood or of ivory and
> call each by its proper name. Let her play with these so that

94. Ibid., 561–62.

95. Olympiodorus, fr. 24 (Blockley).

96. Children and childhood (with the attendant theme of family and parents) in the ancient
world have become a growing industry, especially since the publication of P. Ariès, *Centuries of
Childhood: A Social History of Family Life*, trans. R. Baldick (New York 1962). To mention but a few,
S. Dixon (ed.), *Childhood, Class and Kin in the Roman World* (London 2001); J. K. Evans, *War,
Women and Children in Ancient Rome* (London 1991); D. I. Kertzer and R. P. Saller (eds.), *The Family
in Italy from Antiquity to the Present* (New Haven 1991); M. Harlow and R. Laurence, *Growing Up
and Growing Old in Ancient Rome* (London 2002); B. Rawson and P. Weaver (eds.), *The Roman
Family in Italy: Status, Sentiment, Space* (Oxford 1997); J.-P. Neraudau, *Etre enfant à Rome* (Paris
1984); B. Rawson, *Marriage, Divorce and Children in Ancient Rome* (Oxford 1991); E. Scott, *The Archaeology of Infancy and Infant Death* (Oxford 1999); T. E. J. Wiedemann, *Adults and Children in the
Roman Empire* (New Haven 1989). On children and Christian upbringing, C. Horn and J. W. Martens, *"Let the Little Children Come to Me": Childhood and Children in Early Christianity* (Washington, DC 2009); and C. Horn and R. Phenix (eds.), *Children in Late Ancient Christianity* (Tübingen
2009).

97. Claudian, *Epith.* 231–35—"maternosque bibit mores exemplaque discit / prisca pudicitiae
Latios nec volvere libros/desinit aut Graios, ipsa genetrice magistra, / Maeonius quaecumque senex
aut Thracius Orpheus / aut Mytilenaeo modulator pectine Sappho / sic triviam Latona monet, sich
mitis in antro / Mnemosyne docili tradit praecepta Thaliae." Cf. the list in *Laus Serenae* (Claudian,
C. 30), 146–58, emphasizing Homer and Virgil.

even her play may teach her something. Make her grasp the right order of the letters and see that she forms their names into a rhyme. Also, constantly disarrange their order and put the last letters in the middle and the middle ones at the beginning so that she may know them all by sight as well as by sound. . . . Offer prizes for good spelling and draw her onwards with little gifts such as children of her age delight in.[98]

In a letter to a concerned mother on the upbringing of an aristocratic girl, Jerome, who had a great deal to say about the education of chaste noble ladies, insisted on initiation into language and literature through Psalms, and into correct pronunciation through Genesis.[99] The proposed biblical reading list had to be gradually ingrained, beginning with Psalms and carefully culminating with the salacious Song of Songs. Nor were the traditional occupations of women of rank, like spinning wool, to be neglected.

> Let her begin by learning the Psalter, and then let her gather rules
> of life out of the proverbs of Solomon. . . . Then let her pass on to
> the gospels never to be laid aside when once they have been
> taken in hand. Let her also drink in with a willing heart the Acts
> of the Apostles and the Epistles. As soon as she has enriched the
> storehouse of her mind with these treasures, let her commit to
> memory the prophets, the Heptateuch, the books of Kings and of
> Chronicles, the rolls also of Ezra and Esther. When she has done
> all these she may safely read the Song of Songs, but not before.[100]

Jerome did concede the implausibility of such a rigorous program of education and isolation in the heart of aristocratic Rome.

Yet the literary activities of the noble Proba who married Virgil with Genesis show that the combination of Rome, classical education, and female immersion in biblical culture could result in ingenious if somewhat insipid literary enterprises.[101] By the late fourth century even

98. Jerome, *Ep.* 107.4 (NPN Eng. trans.). Cf. Quintilian, *Inst. Orat.* 1.1.26. Dolls, too, were carved of ivory; C. Horn, "Children's Play as Social Ritual," in Burrus, *Late Ancient Christianity* (2005), 104.

99. Jerome, *Ep.* 107, dated to 403. Cf. *Ep.* 128 to a concerned father on the upbringing of a small girl, full of advice that would have been rather impractical in the environment of the court.

100. Jerome, *Ep.* 107.12 (NPN trans.).

101. E. A. Clark and D. F. Hatch, *The Golden Bough, the Oaken Cross: The Virgilian Cento of Faltonia Betittia Proba* (Chico 1981). Sivan, "Anician Women." Among recent contributions, S. McGill, "Virgil, Christianity, and the *Cento Probae*," in *Texts and Culture in Late Antiquity: Inheritance, Authority, and Change,* ed. J. H. D. Scourfield (Swansea 2007), 173–94.

Christian women from the provinces could have been well versed in biblical and extrabiblical texts.[102] Remarkably, the Bible generated not only a comprehensive program of literacy but also a new kind of physical mobility that enabled women to embark on long-distance journeys of their own volition.[103] Pilgrimages to destinations like Egypt, Syria, and especially Palestine had become something of a vogue in the wake of the well-publicized journey of piety undertaken in the late 320s by Helena, the emperor Constantine's aged mother. A charismatic heretic, like the Spaniard Priscillian of Avila, attracted to his ranks female supporters who joined his journeys, as well as learned women who were willing to wield their erudition to promote Priscillian's ascetic if heretical piety.[104]

To bridge the blatant gaps between the backgrounds of bride and groom, Attalus would have resorted to the Aeneid, rather than the Song of Songs, to conjure a wandering warrior who won the heart of a princess. Such flight of fancy would have enabled the panegyrist to gloss over the meager record of Attalus's military career unless he wished to recite Alaric's achievements:

> Alaric had laid waste Greece and the coasts of Thrace
> And in the mad pride of his many victories
> And the arrogance inspired by his crossing of the Alps
> Had laid siege to the trembling cities of Liguria
> With winter as his ally,
> A season that favours a race accustomed to inclement skies.[105]

Equally light of touch would have been another conventional theme of wedding compositions, that of the good wife, an ideal creature and an idea without a body. What would a good Roman wife do with a barbarian in bed? She could facilitate an exchange of ideologies, initiating her savage spouse into the mysteries of Roman law and order. She could mediate between the barbarian's alleged bestiality and civilization, Rome's major gift to humanity. She would have been the reason to extol heterogeneity, rather than separation between Romans and barbarians.

---

102. J. Wilkinson, *Egeria's Travels to the Holy Land* (Jerusalem 1981), 151–52, on collating the correspondence of Abgar of Edessa with Jesus; and passim on Egeria's biblical culture.

103. E. D. Hunt, *Holy Land Pilgrimage in the Later Roman Empire 312–460* (Oxford 1982), passim.

104. H. Chadwick, *Priscillian of Avila* (Oxford 1978); V. Burrus, *The Making of a Heretic: Gender, Authority and the Priscillianist Controversy* (Berkeley 1995), passim.

105. Claudian, *VI Cons. Hon.* 440–45 (trans. Platnauer, LCL).

Entrusting the articulation of such propositions to a wedding panegyrist, the epithalamium would have ended on an upbeat note, delineating future marital concord and predicting the joyful arrival of an heir. In 414 such rhetoric would have extended beyond the perimeters of the individual couple to celebrate the greater goal, that of infusing Rome's veins with Gothic blood. Herein lies the celebrated image of Athaulf as a converted barbarian, a man sobered by experience and marriage, and ready to harness Gothic energy in Rome's service. In words reported by Orosius, who had heard them from Rusticus, one of the wedding panegyrists,

> Athaulf had first ardently desired to eradicate the Roman name
> and to make all the Roman territory an empire of the Goths in
> fact as well as in name, turning Romania into Gothia, with
> himself as Augustus, presiding over the empire. But when he
> discovered from long experience that neither were the Goths
> capable of obeying laws because of their unbridled barbarism,
> nor could a state exist without laws, he elected to seek the glory
> of restoring the Roman name through the might of the Goths.[106]

Such noble sentiments, claimed Orosius, had been inspired by the prudent advice of Galla, "a woman of surpassing intellect, and of faith above reproach."[107] Were Athaulf's words a Gothic joke, as has been recently suggested, a ridiculous ambition without foundation?[108] Or were these the reflection of a sober policy statement, somewhat overly optimistic but not entirely misplaced, an expression of Athaulf's own ambition to succeed Stilicho? Sincerely uttered or in mockery, Athaulf's memorable pledge to restore Rome's dwindling fortunes echoed Attalus's grandiloquence upon his own elevation to the imperial throne by Alaric in 409. At Rome Attalus had promptly announced his intention to restore to the senate its ancient rights and to make Rome once again the capital of the entire empire, west and east.[109] In 414 he could only reflect on Claudian's rosy vision, nearly two decades before, of imperial unity:

---

106. Orosius 7.43; J. M. Wallace-Hadrill, "Gothia and Romania," *Bulletin of the John Rylands Library* 44 (1961), 213–37.

107. Orosius 7.43.7: "Feminae sane ingenio acerrimae et religione satis proba(ta)e."

108. Halsall, *Barbarian Migrations*, 225, with Athaulf echoing Roman stereotypic views of barbarians. See also J. F. Matthews, "Roman Law and Barbarian Identity in the Late Roman West," in *Ethnicity and Culture in Late Antiquity*, ed. S. Mitchell and G. Greatrex (London 2000), 31–44.

109. Sozomen, *HE* 9.8.2; Sozomen 6.7.3; Matthews, *Western Aristocracies*, 297.

> Let east and west, the two brothers' [Honorius and Arcadius]
>   realm,
> Join in their applause, and peace and joy fill the cities
> illuminated by the sun at rising and at setting.[110]

A brief honeymoon would have followed the wedding. It would have been spent in the tranquil and beautiful Gallic countryside, momentarily away from crowds and cares. Ingenius, Galla's Narbonese host, probably owned, besides his suburban home, a villa in the countryside, as did many Gallic notables. Of the few surviving examples from the province of Narbonensis Prima, of which Narbonne was the capital, the villa of Loupian provides an exemplary case of survival and modification.[111] Like the Narbonese porticoed villa, Loupian had been constructed originally in the first century B.C.E. Unlike the Narbonese house, Loupian weathered troubled times to achieve its heyday around 400 C.E., when the Goths arrived in Gaul. At this stage the residential space was modified to achieve grandiose, even monumental dimensions, with several apsidal reception rooms overlooking a large courtyard. One reception room alone measured 160 square meters. A newly installed heating system kept owners and guests cosily warm on cold and humid nights. The garden areas also underwent expansion, perhaps to provide space for summer gatherings. Simultaneously, the wine cellar lost its storage capacity, due to either a different system of storing or different imbibing tastes.[112] Whoever owned Loupian around 400 also trod on beautifully appointed mosaic floors with distinct floral, vegetal, and geometric motifs.[113] The artists commissioned to execute the mosaics hailed from the neighboring province of Aquitania as well as from the distant shores of the eastern Mediterranean.[114]

110. *Fescennine verses* II.36–40 (trans. Platnauer, LCL).

111. C. Pellecuer and H. Pomaredes, "Crise, survie ou adaptation de la villa romaine en Narbonnaise Première? Contribution des récentes recherches de terrain en Languedoc-Roussillon," in P. Ouzoulias et al. (eds.), *Les campagnes de la Gaule a la fin de l'Antiquité*. Actes du colloque Montpellier, mars 1998 (Antibes 2001), 503–32. I have not seen C. Pellecuer, *La villa des Prés Bas (Loupian, Hérault) dans son environnement: Contribution à l'étude des villae et de l'economie domaniale en Narbonnaise* (thesis, Université de Provence 2000); an English abstract is available online.

112. Pellecuer and Pomaredes, "Crise, survie," 518–22.

113. H. Lavagne, "Deux mosaïques de style orientaisant a Loupian (Hérault)," *Monuments Piot* 61 (1977), 61–86; and H. Lavagne, D. Rouquette, and R. Prudhomme, "Les nouvelles mosaïques de la villa gallo-romaine de Loupian," *Revue archéologique de Narbonnaise* 14 (1981), 173–203. On many Aquitanian parallels and Aquitanian sources of artistic inspiration, Balmelle, *Les demeures*, passim.

114. Lavagne, "Deux mosaïques"; and Lavagne et al., "Les nouvelles mosaïques."

At Loupian the owners added a church at the beginning of the fifth century at a discreet distance of one kilometer from the house itself.[115] Measuring some 35 by 9 meters, the design of the church, a rectangle with an apse, echoed the architecture of the villa itself. Its size suggests a space for a number of worshippers well beyond the nuclear family of the owners, allowing a measure of social mingling. The sanctuary further contained a baptistery. Church and baptistery reflected an extension of economic and social activities of the villa owners.[116] Loupian had become a microcosm, well capable of complete autarchy and accommodating demanding guests. Had they spent the early days of their marriage at Loupian, Galla and Athaulf would have had at their disposal everything needed for a highly satisfying honeymoon, from a place of worship to private baths and wine cellar. The match seemed poised to bring about the long-delayed concord between Goths and Romans.

115. Pellecuer and Pomaredes, "Crise, survie," 529.

116. I. Bermond and C. Pellecuer, "Recherches sur l'occupation des sols dans la région de l'étang de Thau: son apport à l'étude de la villa et des campagnes de Narbonnaise," *Revue archéologique de Narbonnaise* 30 (1997), 63–84; and in general on the intersection of private and public piety, K. Bowes, *Private Worship, Public Values, and Religious Change in Late Antiquity* (Cambridge 2008), 149–50 (on Loupian) and passim. Cf. the manipulation of water sources by Gallic estate owners, H. Sivan, "Town, Country and Province in Late Antique Gaul: The Example of CIL XIII 128," *Zeitschrift für Papyrologie und Epigraphik* 79 (1989), 103–113.

CHAPTER TWO

Funerals in Barcelona
(414–416)

Spain: A Theodosian Cradle

Less than two years after the wedding in Gaul, Galla lost her firstborn son and her husband, the former of natural causes, the latter a victim of assassination. Both were buried in Spanish Barcelona.[1] How and why the Gothic camp had to decamp from Gaul is a narrative that has been often rehearsed.[2] To begin with, whatever Athaulf had hoped to achieve by marrying the emperor's sister, be it an appointment to an elevated position in the Roman army or perhaps even a share of the imperial throne itself, failed to materialize. At Honorius's court the new strong man, Constantius, reacted to the news of the nuptials by blockading Narbonne. The sea no longer bore the victuals that the Goths so desperately and habitually needed. Nor did they have a navy to counterattack the ships that Constantius had mustered. Even the natural fertility of the Gallic soil could not recover sufficiently swiftly to support the Gothic camp after a decade of barbarian invasions, repeated usurpation, marauding bands, and countless clashes between various groups vying for supremacy.

The Gothic departure from Gaul, like their arrival, had been under duress, a factor amply manifested in acts of looting local properties.[3] In the words of a disillusioned Gallo-Roman nobleman,

1. I am very grateful to Julia Beltrán de Heredia Bercero for her generous help and the prompt dispatch of important and useful material relating to recent excavations at Barcelona.
2. Wolfram, *History of the Goths*, for one standard narrative. The information is based primarily on Orosius 7.43 and on the lengthy poem of Paulinus of Pella, written nearly half a century after the events it traces. Matthews, *Western Aristocracies*, 307–28.
3. Jordanes, *Get.* 163 claims that Athaulf planned to save Spain from the Vandals, mixing, in all probability, the activities of Valia with those of Athaulf. See below.

At the behest of their king Athaulf,
On the verge of departing from our city
[The Goths], men whom we had welcomed in peace,
burnt down the city to cinders
not without subjecting us to hardships as though by
    right of war.[4]

Why Spain? The Spanish provinces hardly offered a haven either for barbarian refugees seeking sustenance or for an imperial princess who had contracted an alliance that the court refused to countenance.[5] By 414 Spain had experienced half a decade of barbarian dominance over much of its territory, spearheaded by Vandals, Alans, and Sueves who had crossed the Pyrenean mountains in 409. Nor was the lot of the Hispano-Roman locals lightened by a series of self-proclaimed defenders, or usurpers, depending on one's point of view, men who regarded Spain primarily as a launching pad for gaining a foothold in Gaul and, with luck, in Italy. One contemporary historian summed up the swift pace of events between 406 and 414 in the western provinces as an inextricable chain of adversities composed of "barbarians running wild" and the rise and fall of local aspirants to the imperial throne.[6]

Among the men who rose and fell were two of Galla's Spanish relatives, the brothers Didymus and Verinianus, young, rich, and noble, who undertook, according to the Spaniard Orosius, not "to assume tyranny [=usurpation] against a tyrant but rather to defend, in the name of the legitimate emperor [Honorius], their homeland [*patria*] and their own against tyrant and barbarians."[7] Relying on slaves from their holdings whom they armed, the brothers headed north in an attempt to bar the Pyrenean passes from Gaul to Spain. They were swiftly defeated by Constans, son of Constantine. The latter had been raised to the purple by the troops stationed in Britain in 407; the former had been defrocked of his monkish attire and vocation to command an army against the Theodosians in Spain (409 C.E.). The captured Didymus and Verinianus,

4. Paulinus of Pella, *Eucharisticon*, 311–14; S. M. Perevalov, "Bazas 414: la rupture de l'alliance alano-gothique," *Dialogues d'histoire ancienne* 26 (2000), 175–94.
5. In general, M. Kulikowski, *Late Roman Spain and Its Cities* (Baltimore 2004); and M. Kulikowski and K. D. Bowes (eds.), *Hispania in Late Antiquity: Current Perspectives* (Boston 2005).
6. Orosius 7.40.4.
7. Orosius 7.40.5, hastening to add that the brothers' intention was made abundantly clear as events developed.

with their families, did not share Galla's good fortune.[8] They were executed rather than ransomed. Other members of the Theodosian clan managed to escape the carnage in Spain, one heading to Italy, the other to the east. Galla may have met the former. One lesson to be derived from the fate of her relatives in Spain would have been sad and simple. Common paternity and common interests did not always provoke the imperial court to send much-needed assistance. Put crudely, one was on one's own with Honorius on the throne.

For the meandering Goths following Athaulf's lead, the relative remoteness of Spain from the Ravenna court, coupled with the ever-alluring African shores beyond the pillars of Hercules (Gibraltar), suggested freedom of action. The province of Tarraconensis, south of the Pyrenees, had been the least ravaged of all the Spanish provinces and remained, nominally at least, under the control of the imperial government. A truce with that government could follow, with luck. Athaulf had been adept at offering his services to the highest bidder. The presence of the Vandals, the Goths' old enemies in Spain, apparently provided another incentive. A unique and exceptionally garbled Gothic version of the same events casts Athaulf as the savior of the suffering Spaniards.[9] No sooner had he reached Barcelona, it was alleged, than the Goths set out against the Vandals.

For Galla, Spain represented autochthony and orthodoxy. It was the land of her ancestors, the origins of her paternal family. In 389 the effusive praise of the Gallic panegyrist Pacatus described Theodosius's Spanish motherland as

> [a] land blessed above all other lands [*terris omnibus terra felicior*] . . . Exposed neither to the heat of the south nor subject to arctic cold. Enclosed on one side by the mountains of the Pyrenees, on another by the billows of the ocean . . . it is shut off by the genius of cunning nature like another world [*alter orbis*]. A land boasting a large number of splendid cities [*egregiae civitates*], in addition to fields, cultivated and fallow, full of crops and herds. Add the wealth of its gold-bearing

---

8. Zosimus 6.4–5.

9. Jordanes, *Get.* 163. The war that the Goths waged on the Vandals is usually dated slightly later, after Athaulf's death. It did little to alleviate the situation. In general see the series of articles by E. A. Thompson, "The End of Roman Spain," *Nottingham Mediaeval Studies* 20–23 (1976–79), repr. in E. A. Thompson, *Romans and Barbarians* (Madison 1982), 137–229.

rivers, its mines of gleaming jewels. . . . It is Spain that spawns the toughest soldiers, the most experienced generals, the most eloquent orators, the most famous poets. She is the mother of judges, and the mother of emperors. She gave the empire the great Trajan, and then Hadrian. To her the empire is indebted for you [Theodosius].[10]

Theodosius had hailed from Cauca in the northwest of Spain (province of Gallaecia) and his ascension to the imperial throne resulted in substantial increase of the wealth, mobility, and prestige of the Spanish aristocracy.[11] Cauca and its territory experienced something of a building boom in the late fourth century, due most likely to the rise to imperial prominence of the Theodosian clan.[12] The regime of another Spaniard, Magnus Maximus (383–388), whom Theodosius fought and killed, produced other opportunities for local advancement. Maximus apparently elevated Tarraconensis to the rank of a consular province.[13]

By the time Galla arrived in Spain (414/415), two decades after Theodosius's demise, Gallaecia had fallen under the control of the Suevi, whose presence rendered the region dangerous and uninviting.[14] Prudent Gallaecian ecclesiastics, like Bishop Avitus of Braga, who had left Gallaecia on a pilgrimage to the Holy Land in 409, elected to stay in Palestine indefinitely. In 416 Avitus dispatched letters and relics to his

10. Pacatus, "Panegyric of Theodosius," 4, in C. E. V. Nixon and B. Saylor Rodgers, *In Praise of Later Roman Emperors: The Panegyrici Latini* (Berkeley 1994), 252 (Eng. trans., slightly modified), 649 (Mynor's Latin text).

11. K. F. Stroheker, "Spanische Senatoren der spätrömischen und westgotischen Zeit," *MM* 4 (1963), 107–32; A. Chastagnol, "Les Espagnols dans l'aristocratie gouvernementale de Théodose," in *Les empereurs romains d'Espagne* (Paris 1965), 269–307. The increased wealth of the family is further reflected in the ability of the two young brothers, Didymus and Verinianus, to marshal an army composed of their own slaves, above. The prominence of Spaniards in the imperial and ecclesiastical administration antedates Theodosius's accession in January 379, as the careers of Bishop Ossius of Cordoba and of Theodosius Comes, Theodosius's father, demonstrate. There is, however, hardly a doubt that such a process was accelerated under the regime of Theodosius. On Spain under Theodosius, see the various articles assembled byR. Teja and C. Pérez (eds.), *Actas Congreso internacional La Hispania de Teodosio 1995*, 2 vols. (Salamanca 1997). In general on Spanish wealth and trade, P. Reynolds, *Hispania and the Roman Mediterranean, AD 100–700: Ceramics and Trade* (London 2009).

12. J. Arce, "The Urban Domus in Late Antique Hispania: Examples from Emerita, Barcino and Complutum," in *Housing in Late Antiquity*, ed. L. Lavan et al. (Leiden 2007), 321 (305–36).

13. *CIL* II 4911, commemorating the restoration of a road damaged by floods and the new title of the provincial governor.

14. E. A. Thompson, "The Suevic Kingdom of Galicia," in *Romans and Barbarians: The Decline of the Western Empire* (Madison 1982), 161–87.

successor, Palchonius of Braga.[15] Neither reached their intended recipient in the remote Spanish province, no doubt to the chagrin of locals, who stood in dire need of miracle-working bones. Orosius, the priest entrusted with their delivery, traveled only as far as the Mediterranean island of Minorca.[16] Failing to brave the dangerous roads from Tarraconesis to Gallaecia, Orosius deposited his precious cargo in the hands of the local Minorcan bishop before hastening to join Augustine in Africa.

A journey to Cauca to pay homage to her ancestors would have been a foolhardy enterprise in 414/415, had the pregnant Galla chosen to travel in Spain at all. Had she still desired to see with her own eyes imperial imprints in the Iberian peninsula, she could safely head to Centcelles, a locality near the city of Tarraco, south of Barcelona. There stood (and still stands) the lavishly decorated mausoleum of Constans, son of the emperor Constantine.[17] Through both Justina, her grandmother, and Gratian, her maternal uncle, Galla was related to the first Christian dynasty of Rome. Constans had been killed in 350 in Helena, a coastal Gallic town at the eastern edge of the Pyrenees. His corpse had been sent for burial on the imperial estate of Centcelles in an imposing mausoleum.[18]

15. *PL* 41, 805–808; E. Vanderlinden, "Revelatio Sancti Stephani," *REByz* 4 (1946), 178–217. See also S. Bradbury, *Severus of Minorca: Letter on the Conversion of the Jews* (Oxford 1996).

16. H. Sivan, "Between Gaza and Minorca: The Un/making of Minorities in Late Antiquity" (in press).

17. The attribute has been contested. For an overview of scholarly hypothesis, M. J. Johnson, *The Roman Imperial Mausoleum in Late Antiquity* (Cambridge 2009), 129–39.

18. Much is disputed about Centcelles, its mausoleum, the identity of the buried, the ownership of the estate, and the nature of the structure itself. I follow what seems to be a general consensus. Among numerous publications on the site, H. Schlunk et al., *Die Mosaikkuppel von Centcelles*, 2 vols. (Mainz 1988). For dissenting voices, see various contributors to J. Arce (ed.), *Centcelles: El monumento tardoromano: iconografía y arquitectura* (Rome 2002), with S. J. Keay's review, "The Late-Antique Complex of Centcelles (Tarragona)," *JRA* 17 (2004), 741–43. See also M. Sotomayor, "La iconografia di Centcelles: Enigmas sin resolver," *Pyrenae* 37 (2006), 143–73. I remain unconvinced by proposals assigning the mosaics to a private church of sorts owned by an ecclesiastical dignitary or to a local aristocrat commemorating his or her marriage. Of all the hypothesis, that of an imperial mausoleum, whether or not originally destined to house the corpse of Constans, remains the most acceptable. Cf. the lengthy journey of the corpse of the Spaniard Maternus Cynegius, whose widow arranged for the transfer from Constantinople back home to their estate, *Chron. Min.* I.244 (*Cons. Const.* s.a. 388). Whether this location can be identified as that of the palatial villa (or rural complex) of Carranque in the province of Carthaginensis (c. 40 km north of Toledo), remains a hotly debated question. See the various essays in D. Fernández-Galiano Ruiz, *Carranque: Centro de la Hispania Romana: Catálogo de la Exposición* (Madrid 2001); with the criticism of the hypothesis, J. Arce, "La villa romana de Carranque (Toledo, España): identificación y propietario," *Gerión* 21 (2003), 15–27 (available via the Web).

At Centcelles, Galla could admire the mosaics that covered the dome over Constans's tomb, their imagery aspiring to reassure the dead of his place among both the living and in heaven.[19] These depicted biblical and secular themes, be they the beautifully drawn figure of the *dominus*, owner of tomb and territory, the hunt, a favorite aristocratic pastime, or beloved biblical scenes like Daniel in the lion's den, the three Hebrews in the furnace, Jonah's cycle, Noah's ark, and Moses striking the rock. Even in the provinces, Galla would have realized, representational landscapes effectively conveyed the political and social universe of late antiquity. Perhaps most strikingly, Galla would have been impressed by the lavish use of gold on the mosaics at Centcelles.[20] Both color and technique Galla would later use to great effect in Ravenna.

For kin, like Galla, as for a casual yet privileged beholder, the Centcelles mausoleum drove home an ideology that balanced the dynastic creed, Nicene Christianity, with long-entrenched values of the nobility. She would have been familiar with the strategy from another mid-fourth-century imperial mausoleum, that of Constantina, daughter of Constantine, at Rome (S. Costanza).[21] Planted outside Rome's city walls, on the Via Nomentana, and in the inspiring and reassuring proximity of a church dedicated to the martyr Agnes, the imperial tomb rested atop a cemetery on the grounds of an imperial estate.[22] Its mosaic dome hovered above magnificent columns and capitals, all *spolia* (reused material) removed from older buildings in and outside the city walls. The surviving mosaics and those preserved only in Renaissance drawings created a palette of identity and participation, projecting a relationship of

19. K. M. D. Dunbabin, *Mosaics of the Greek and Roman World* (Cambridge 1999), 251–52; G. Mackie, *Early Christian Chapels in the West: Decoration, Functions, and Patronage* (Toronto 2003), 154–56.

20. D. James, *God and Gold in Late Antiquity* (Cambridge 1998), 58.

21. Mackie, *Early Christian Chapels*, 145–53. Apparently the mausoleum had been preceded by a baptistery; D. J. Stanely, "New Discoveries at Santa Costanza," *DOP* 48 (1994), 257–61. The ancient sources as well as the building's famed mosaics are discussed in H. Stern, "Les mosaïques de l'église de Sainte-Constance à Rome," *DOP* 12 (1958), 157–218. See now also H. Jones, "Agnes and Constantia: Domesticity and Cult Patronage in the Passion of Agnes," in *Religion, Dynasty, and Patronage in Early Christian Rome*, ed. K. Cooper and J. Hillner (Cambridge 2007), 115–39, esp. 116–17; J. J. Rasch and A. Arbeiter, *Das Mausoleum der Constantina in Rom* (Mainz am Rhein 2007); and Johnson, *Roman Imperial Mausoleum*, 139–56. Constantina was born c. 320 and married in 335 her cousin Hannibalianus, king of Armenia, who was killed in 337. She remarried in 351 another cousin, Gallus, and died in 354; Chausson, "Une soeur de Constantin," 154.

22. R. Krautheimer, *Rome: Profile of a City, 312–1308* (Princeton 1980), 25; A. Frutaz, *Il complesso monumentale di sant'Agnese et di Santa Costanza*, 2nd ed. (Rome 1969).

conformity between classicism and Christianity. There are tapestries of marine life; Cupids and Psyches, geometrical motifs, grapes harvested by *putti* (small cherublike figures), intricate vine designs, and a series of Old Testament scenes, perhaps paralleled with one from the New Testament. Figures like Cain and Abel, Elijah, Moses, Lot, and Noah were to provide a paradigm for the funeral mass, each interceding on behalf of the dead.[23]

Derivative yet innovative, the funerary art of the Constantinian dynasty derived its compositions from a wide array of iconographies and texts, superimposing one on another to create a new otherness. The dedicatory inscription of Saint Agnes (Sant' Agnese fuori le mura) joined the veneration of the martyr, whose remains had been laid to rest in the funerary basilica, to a new imperial discourse:

> I, Constantina, venerating God and dedicated to Christ,
> Having provided all the expenses with devoted mind
> At divine bidding and with the great help of Christ,
> Consecrated this *templum* of Agnes, victorious virgin,
> Because she has prevailed over the temples and all
>   earthly works,
> [here] where the loftiest roof gleams with gold.[24]

The first letters of the inscription, if read from top to bottom, form an acrostic proclaiming a bold equation "Constantina to/is God" (*Constantina deo*).[25] Galla's own patronage of saintly figures would be indebted to Constantina's infinitely metaphorical character of Christianized imageries. In 414/415, however, the presence of the dead Constans at Cencelles and of the living Galla in Barcelona staked a tenuous claim to dynastic continuity.

Barcelona: An Ephemeral Gothic Residence

Due to a spectacular effort to preserve late Roman Barcelona, the present-day tourist can literally walk along, or rather atop, the streets that Galla crossed when she and Athaulf settled there in 414/415. Like Narbonne,

---

23. Mackie, *Early Christian Chapels*, 150.

24. *ICUR* 8. 20752 (= *ILCV* 1768), lines 1–6, trans. J. Curran, *Pagan City and Christian Capital* (Oxford 2000), 128.

25. N. F. Denzey, *The Bone Gatherers: The Lost World of Early Christian Women* (Boston 2007), 252 n. 17.

the Goths' Gallic residence, Barcelona boasted walls, erected sometime in the fourth century, and punctuated by seventy-eight towers and four gates. To walk along the walls or to enter one of the numerous towers would amount to a virtual excursion into the history of late Roman urbanism. Layers superimposed upon layers unwittingly preserved the memory of the long-gone dead whose tombstones provided sound building materials. Narbonne's walls likewise constituted an artful patchwork of architectural history. Whoever commissioned and financed such engineering feats had to rely on an ingenious genealogy of stonemasonry.

At the turn of the fifth century, Barcelona (Colonia Iulia Augusta Faventia Paterna Barcino, to give it its full name) was a city in transition, and opportunistic enough to provide a capital to much-tried foreign invaders.[26] By 415 Barcelona had its fair share of pretenders to the throne. The city featured prominently during the (first) brief reign of the Spanish aristocrat Maximus. Elevated to the purple in 409, Maximus established his royal mint and possibly his chief residence in Barcelona between 409 and 411.[27] Upon his deposition, Maximus found refuge with the Vandals in southern Spain. The establishment of a Gothic court in Spain presided over by Athaulf, the scourge of the Vandals, reflected a triumph of localism over the language of imperial legitimacy.

Ever enterprising, already two decades before the appearance of Athaulf's Goths in Tarraconensis, pious citizens of Barcelona, led by Bishop Lampius, acclaimed, seemingly spontaneously, a distinguished foreigner, Pontius Meropius Paulinus (= Paulinus of Nola) as their priest.[28] A wealthy Aquitanian with considerable literary talent, Paulinus and his Spanish wife, Therasia, had been living on their Spanish estates in Tarraconensis and Carthaginensis since 389. To claim Paulinus as a church leader was a move calculated to force him to remain permanently in Barcelona, where he would be expected to disburse his

26. For the full name see the plaque dedicated to the *seviri Augustales* (college of priests) of the early second century; J. Beltrán de Heredia Bercero (ed.), *From Barcino to Barcinona: The Archaeological Remains of Plaça del Rei in Barcelona* (Barcelona 2001), no. 37, p. 129.

27. T. Marot, "Algunas consideraciones sobre la significacion de las emisiones del usurpador Maximo en Barcino," in *Congreso internacional La Hispania de Teodosio* (Salamanca 1997), II, 569–80.

28. Christmas 394; D. E. Trout, "The Dates of the Ordination of Paulinus of Bordeaux and of His Departure for Nola," *REAug* 37 (1991), 237–60; S. Mratschek, *Der Briefwechsel des Paulinus von Nola: Kommunikation und soziale Kontakte zwischen christilichen Intellektuellen* (Göttingen 2002), 59, 213, 227–35. Cf. the activities of Pacianus, Lampius's predecessor, against the Novatians in his see, Jerome, *Vir. Ill.* 106.

wealth and to employ his erudition and orthodoxy in pursuit of local Christian sectarians.[29]

Paulinus had held the office of governor of Italian Campania, a career leading to a steady climb through the ranks of the imperial administration. This was the path that his contemporary, the Spaniard Nummius Aemilianus Dexter, son of bishop Pacianus, Lampius's predecessor in the episcopal seat of Barcelona, had chosen to great advantage. Under Galla's father, Theodosius I, Dexter held several offices, culminating in the Italian prefecture in 395 C.E. (under Honorius).[30] At Barcelona, Galla could see the statue dedicated in his honor by the provincials of Asia whom Dexter had governed. This was the last statue to grace the old forum of Roman Barcelona, sealing a tradition of public homage to official benefactors born and bred in the city.[31]

With Dexter as the praetorian prefect of Italy, Lampius as the city's bishop, and Paulinus as its priest, the year 395, just two decades before Galla's arrival in Barcelona, must have been viewed by locals as the city's dawn of greatness. The city seemed poised to carry with vigor the Theodosian tradition of "dour Christianity," an uncompromising devotion to orthodoxy coupled with relentless pursuit of deviants.[32] However, episcopal and communal optimism in Barcelona in the wake of Paulinus's ordination had been miscalculated. Paulinus refused the proposed ordination. The arrangements made to extricate him from a lifetime commitment to Barcelona are unknown. But a later example may serve to shed light. In 415, Pinianus, one of Galla's Roman acquaintances, a young man of great wealth and excellent connections, was acclaimed presbyter by an enthusiastic crowd in African Hippo, where Augustine served as bishop.[33] Like Paulinus, Pinianus declined. The crowds kept pressing. They were inspired, according to Pinianus's

29. Cf. the orchestrated elections of Ambrose of Milan in 374, N. McLynn, *Ambrose of Milan: Church and Court in a Christian Capital* (Berkeley 1994), 42–52.

30. Matthews, *Western Aristocracies*, 111, 133; *PLRE I*, 251 (no. 3).

31. *CIL* 2.4512 = G. Fabre et al., *Inscriptions romaines de Catalogne IV: Barcino* (Paris 1997), 36 (*IRC*).

32. For the expression, P. Brown, "The Study of Elites in Late Antiquity," *Arethusa* 33 (2000), 333, although characterizing the military, rather than militant, form of Theodosian Christianity. See also N. McLynn, "Theodosius, Spain and the Nicene Faith," in *Congreso internacional La Hispania de Teodosio* (Salamanca 1997), I, 171–78. On Pyrenean peculiarities, J. Fontaine, "Société et culture chrétiennes sur l'aire circumpyrénéenne au siècle de Théodose," *Bulletin de littérature ecclésiastique de Toulouse* (1974), 241–82.

33. Augustine, *Ep.* 125.

mother-in-law (Ceionia Albina), not by his piety but by their own greed.[34] In the end Augustine extracted from Pinianus a vow that should he ever seek ordination of his own accord, the city of Hippo should be his residence and its people his congregation.[35] No such thing ever happened.

Paulinus and Therasia moved to Italian Campania, to settle in the town of Nola. In 410, during one of Alaric's raids, the Goths, now with Galla in train, captured Nola and Paulinus. Did Galla meet him in shared captivity?[36] If she did—no contemporary source bothered to record such a meeting—Paulinus could have imparted to her the prophetic verses that he had penned in 402: "If I were an unhappy prisoner of Gothic arms or among the harsh Alans, however many the chains weighing my neck the enemy would not bind my mind prisoner with my captive limbs."[37]

Whether the Barcelona cathedral had a share in the proceeds from the liquidation of Paulinus and Therasia's vast holdings in Gaul and Spain is unknown. It is not unlikely that they owned the urban space where construction of the city's major episcopal complex started precisely around the time that the couple left for Italy (Plaça del Rei).[38] Adjacent to the city walls, this residence-turned-ecclesiastical center was strategically located in a neighborhood that boasted industrial installations such as a winery, a factory to produce Barcelona's famed *garum* (fish sauce), and a *tinctoria* and a *fullonica* (dyeing establishments), all

34. Augustine, *Ep.* 126.
35. On this episode and on the problems raised by the scale and the impetuosity of the proposed redistribution of wealth on such a scale, A. Giardina, "Carità eversiva: le donazioni di Melania la Giovane e gli equilibri della società tardoromana," *Studi Storici* 1 (1988), 127–42; C. Lepelley, "Mélanie la Jeune, entre Rome, la Sicile, et l'Afrique: Les effets socialement pernicieux d'une forme extreme de l'ascétisme," *Kokalos* 43–44 (1997–1998), 15–32, esp. 25–26; K. Cooper, "Poverty, Obligation, and Inheritance: Roman Heiresses and the Varieties of Senatorial Christianity in Fifth Century Rome," in Cooper and Hillner, *Early Christian Rome*, 166–67.
36. On a possible Galla-Paulinus connection in 410, V. A. Sirago, *Galla Placidia e la trasformazione politica dell'Occidente* (Louvain 1961), 229, followed by Oost, *Galla Placidia*, 159, and by D. Trout, *Paulinus of Nola: Life, Letters, and Poems* (Berkeley 1999), 255. It is doubted, justly to my mind, by Mratschek, *Der Briefwechsel*, 516, 637. On the Goths at Nola, Augustine, *Civ. Dei* 1.10.2; *Cur. Mort.* 16.19. Whether Paulinus had been at that point already bishop is not entirely clear. Mratschek, *Der Briefwechsel*, 62. A connection between the two is verifiable for the year 419; see ch. 3.
37. Paulinus of Nola, *C.* 26, 22–25, Eng. trans. Walsh (ACW).
38. J. Beltrán de Heredia Bercero and C. Bonnet, "Nouveau regard sur le groupe épiscopal de Barcelone," *Rivista di Archeologia Cristiana* 80 (2004), 137–58; and Beltrán de Heredia Bercero, *From Barcino to Barcinona*, passim. On the donation of the domus, an act of a new kind of urban euergetism, Beltrán de Heredia Bercero, *From Barcino to Barcinona*, 40, 74.

eventually submerged under the episcopal palace, church, and necropolis.[39] Next to the new basilica a large baptistery was installed.[40] It would have been the place where Galla and Athaulf would have baptized their newly born son in 415.[41]

No ancient source refers to Galla's first pregnancy. Contemporary allusions point to pregnancies as periods of pain and fear. Birth pangs were unexpected and labor difficult and protracted. Women dreaded the birth of a malformed or crippled baby, or of a girl rather than a boy.[42] As soon as a child was born, Christian mothers would draw the sign of the cross, to "protect him with spiritual armor."[43] Names were accordingly chosen as harbingers of good luck for long life.[44] Galla's boy was named Theodosius, clearly after her father. It was also the name of the current emperor of the eastern empire, Galla's nephew. What hopes, aspirations, and expectations Galla and Athaulf had when they named the child were not recorded. Honorius had been childless, nor was he likely to marry a third time. Was Theodosius III the one destined to preside over a permanent home for the Goths under Attalus's imperial auspices, or was he the one to rule the western Roman Empire?

If Galla and Athaulf followed traditional Roman ceremonies upon the birth of their son, the first decision regarding the neonate would have been the father's. The baby was raised in paternal arms to signify his acceptance into the family. Nine days after the boy's birth the parents celebrated the naming of their son. This solemn occasion, the *dies lustricus*, occurring soon after the loss of the umbilical cord, severed the biological tie that bound the baby to his mother while marking his entry into society at large. On that day the baby donned a protective amulet (*bulla*) that he

39. Beltrán de Heredia Bercero, *From Barcino to Barcinona*, 100; the original Christian nucleaus (basilica, baptistery) and the domus/residence coexisted for a while until the remodeling of the fifth century. On the industrial spaces, Ibid., 58–71.

40. Ibid., 74.

41. Olympiodorus, fr. 26 (Blockley) does not allude to baptism. Oost, *Galla Placidia*, 134, suggests that the child had been baptized, in view of his later exhumation and reburial.

42. John Chrysostom, *Homily in Jo.* 34.3; in *Matt.* 18.5 and *de. Virg.* 57.4.66; B. Leyerle, "Appealing to Children," *JECS* 5 (1997), 246.

43. As Chrysostom recommended, *Hom. in I Cor.* 12.7; J. L. Maxwell, *Christianization and Communication in Late Antiquity: John Chrysostom and His Congregation in Antioch* (Cambridge 2006), 151–52.

44. Chrysostom, *Hom. in I Cor.* 12.7; Leyerle, "Appealing to Children," 248; and Maxwell, *Christianization and Communication*, 152, on the custom of lighting many lamps, naming each one of them, and selecting the name attached to the longest-burning lamp.

would carry throughout childhood. At birth, Theodosius III was swaddled, carefully and exactly, so as to control him as well as to mold his body to a desired shape. Such, at least, were the medical instructions left by Soranus.[45] These swaddling cloths were to be removed no later than two months after birth. Had Theodosius lived to his seventh year, which did not happen, he and his parents would have celebrated another rite of passage, his formal transition from childhood's training to formal education, a vital step preparing him to hold his place in society.[46]

Funerary Themes

Galla's boy died in infancy, his death deceiving the hopes that had been invested in him.[47] How long he lived and what he died of remains undisclosed. Most babies in antiquity had merely a fifty-fifty chance of surviving beyond their fifth birthday.[48] The joy that accompanied his emergence must have rivaled the grief attendant on his premature death. This was a bitter experience shared by mothers throughout the ages, a "catalogue of loss" eloquently described by John Chrysostom, priest at Antioch (386–398) and briefly bishop of Constantinople (398–404): "This mouth will never speak again. These eyes will never look again. These feet will never walk again. All these are destroyed and gone. He will never come home again."[49]So overwhelming was the sense of parental bereavement that funerary inscriptions recorded children entreating their grieving parents to cease to sorrow.[50]

---

45. Soranus, *Gyn.* 2.14–15, 2.42.

46. N. Norman, "Death and Burial of Roman Children: The Case of Yasmina Cemetery at Carthage: Part I, Setting the Stage," *Mortality* 7 (2002), 315–16.

47. Olympiodorus, fr. 26 (Blockley) on unfulfilled but unspecified wishes.

48. For statistics, K. Hopkins, "On the Probable Age Structure of the Roman Population," *Population Studies* 20 (1966), 245–64; B. Frier, "Roman Life Expectancy: Ulpian's Evidence," *HSCP* 86 (1982), 213–51; and B. Frier, "Roman Life Expectancy: The Pannonian Evidence," *Phoenix* 37 (1983), 328–44. See also K. A. Kamp, "Where Have All the Children Gone? The Archaeology of Childhood," *Journal of Archaeological Method and Theory* 8 (2001), 1–34; N. Norman, "Death and Burial of Roman Children: The Case of Yasmina Cemetery at Carthage: Part II, the Archaeological Evidence," *Mortality* 8 (2003), 36–47; and K. Bradley, "The Roman Child in Sickness and in Health," in *The Roman Family in the Empire*, ed. M. George (Oxford 2005), 67–92; and in general, B. Rawson, *Children and Childhood in Roman Italy* (Oxford 2003).

49. Chrysostom, *Hom. in II Cor.* 1.6; *Hom. in Matt.* 31.5; *de. Virg.* 56.1.6–15, 57.4.78–5.83; Leyerle, "Appealing to Children," 246–47, also for the expression.

50. M. King, "Commemoration of Infants on Roman Funerary Inscriptions," in *The Epigraphy of Death: Studies in the History and Society of Greece and Rome*, ed. G. J. Oliver (Liverpool 2000),

The small corpse of Theodosius III was placed in a silver coffin to be buried in a chapel outside Barcelona in 415.[51] Thirty-five years later it was brought to Rome for final internment in the family dynastic mausoleum at St. Peter's.[52] In shape the coffin would have resembled contemporary silver caskets, like the wedding chest named after the bride Projecta. Whether signifying weddings, harbingers of life, or funerals, the decoration of such items would have admirably served those crucial pointers of the human life cycle.[53] One such, bearing in all likelihood adaptable symbols like two angels holding a chrismon (a crosslike symbol formed of the first two letters of *Christ* in Greek), would have been deemed suitable to contain the body of a baby.[54] Projecta's wedding casket, an important component of her rich dowry, had been buried for safety during Alaric's sieges of Rome (408–410). Other caskets found their way to the Gothic camp in the course of the three-day sack of Rome in 410. Many were among the gifts that Athaulf presented to Galla at their wedding.

Had Galla commissioned an inscription commemorating the death of her son in Barcelona, its words could echo the poignancy reflected in a text inscribed on the tomb of a child by unnamed parents, also in Barcelona, where the epitaph was accompanied by a Chrism flanked by two doves holding an olive branch: "Here lies Magnus in peace, a child already numbered among the faithful. He lived three years."[55] It was believed that the precise enumeration of the infant's age would guarantee a safe passage from this world to the next:

---

132 (117–54). King sees in most such expressions conventions or stock themes. On Christian and pagan funerary inscriptions and their terminology, see the studies assembled in the third volume of C. Pietri, *Christiana Respublica*, 3 vols. (Paris-Rome 1997).

51. Olympiodorus, fr. 26 (Blockley). Speculations on the precise location of the burial continue among Spanish scholars, most recently J. Sales Carbonell, "Teodosi, fill d'Ataulf i Galla Placidia, mai va estar enterrat a Sant Cugat del Valles. Notes de topografia paleocristiana Barcelonesa (1)," *Gausac. Publicacio del grup d'estudis locals de Sant Cugat del Valles*, 24 (July 2004) 53–58, available via the Internet with an English abstract.

52. See ch. 6.

53. For provenance of the form and its long-term artistic repercussions, H. Sivan, "Funerary Monuments and Funerary Rites in Late Antique Aquitaine," *Oxford Journal of Archaeology* 5 (1986), 339–53.

54. Examples in R. R. Leader-Newby, *Silver and Society in Late Antiquity: Functions and Meanings of Silver Plate in the Fourth to the Seventh Centuries* (Aldershot 2004), 86–91.

55. Beltrán de Heredia Bercero (ed.), *From Barcino to Barcinona*, 31 and no. 306, p. 234 = *IRC* I, p. 200. "Hic requiescit Magnus puer fidelis in pace qui vixit anni III."

> Here rests Pascasia, the sweetest infant, who lived two years,
> three months, and ten days. She died on the third day of the
> calends of August, when Honorius was consul for the
> thirteenth time and Theodosius for the tenth.[56]

Yet maternal tragedy was measured mostly in loss and in silence. In Roman social and political practices, only men had the right of speech. On public occasions like funerals women could be seen, or rather heard, solely as professional mourners, lending incoherent cries to the general atmosphere of grief.

It is possible, however, to reconstruct the desperate struggle that the father would have put up to preserve the life of his son. We have several descriptions of such a scene from around the year 370, when the emperor Valens (365–387), an Arian like Athaulf, tried in vain to save the life of his sole son and heir, the boy Galates. One account, rather reminiscent of King David's reaction to the sickness and death of his first son by Bathsheba, is preserved in an oration honoring Bishop Basil of Caesarea (in Cappadocia), to whom Valens allegedly appealed to save his son:

> The emperor's son was sick and in physical pain. The father
> suffered with him (for what can fathers do?). From all sides he
> sought succor in this suffering, he selected the best physicians,
> he put faith in his prayer as never before and threw himself
> down on the ground. . . . But as no remedy could be found
> anywhere against the evil, he took refuge in the [orthodox-
> Nicene] faith of Basil. . . . Without hesitation or delay Basil was
> present and on his arrival the disease lessened and the father
> cherished greater hopes. And if he had not mixed salt water
> with fresh by believing in the heterodox [Arian] at the same
> time that he called for Basil, he probably would have received
> back into his arms a healthy and sound child.[57]

---

56. *CIL* XIII.2353 (422 c.e.), trans. in M. Carroll, *Spirits of the Dead: Roman Funerary Commemoration in Western Europe* (Oxford 2006), 274–75, and 276–77 for comments on recording the age of extremely young children in Christian inscriptions.

57. *Oratio funebris in laudem Basilii Magni* (= Greg Naz., *Homily* 43), 54, cited in K. Weitzmann, "Illustration for the Chronicles of Sozomenos, Theodoret and Malalas," *Byzantion* 16 (1942/1943), 119. Note that this scene is actually illustrated in the other account of the same episode, Socrates, *HE* 4.26, in which Domnica, Valens's wife, persuades her husband to call for Basil, but since Basil insists on the emperor's conversion from Arianism to the "right faith," Basil does not arrive and the child dies; Sozomen, *HE* 6.16; Theodoret, *HE* 4.16. See also P. Rousseau, *Basil of Caesarea* (Berkeley 1994), 351–53.

A single ancient source recorded the demise of Galla's firstborn. None commented on the mother's tears, or made verbal tribute to the dead child, or offered consolation to the parents. The limits of mourning remain undisclosed. In law as in literature, public expressions of maternal grief had to be kept within boundaries. Unbridled female emotions were not to disturb the masculine business of paying a fitting tribute to the dead. In late antiquity the juxtaposition of Christian commemoration with the civic discourse of mourning did little to arrest the process of neutralizing the mother. Funeral orations were ordinarily entrusted to the hands of skillful bishops, assessors and practitioners of the range of human emotions, and providers of consolation. Their virtuosity could invoke not only the stature of the dead but also, and more significantly, provide assurances for the living. The ideology of death, as expressed in surviving orations composed to honor the dead, recognized death as an incontestable component of society.[58] Maternal bereavement, however, or the emotions experienced by a woman upon the loss of a child, can only be formulated with hindsight, as expressions beyond canonical formulas. Feminine grief was rarely recorded.

Ceremonies surrounding the funeral itself would resemble, up to a point, those of an adult. The mother, or another family member, would close the dead child's eyes, while close relatives would call out his name.[59] This was the moment depicted on a child's sarcophagus from Rome.[60] At its center is the corpse of a young girl, tenderly laid to rest on soft cushions, her eyes shut, and her sandals and pet dog neatly arranged beneath the couch. Her grieving parents, veiled in mourning, are seated on each side of the couch, and flanking both are standing figures in attitudes of mourning, perhaps relatives, perhaps, but less likely, professional mourners. Her small corpse has been washed, anointed, and dressed, ready to receive last respects before burial. Along the road to the cemetery, a series of torches would light the way to dispel the pollution brought about by the child's death, or to lessen the child's terror. Following the burial the family would organize a

58. On changes in beliefs, practices, and attitudes associated with death in general, E. Rebillard, *In hora mortis: évolution de la pastorale chrétienne de la mort aux IV et V siecles dans l'Occident latin* (Rome 1994), passim.
59. Norman, "Death and Burial, Part I," 311–12.
60. Ibid., 313; J. Huskinson, *Roman Children's Sarcophagi: Their Decoration and Social Significance* (Oxford 1996), 13–15.

series of funerary meals both marking the tragedy of death and emphasizing the family's continuity.

We know the identity of the men who delivered the nuptial compositions for Galla's wedding with Athaulf in 414. We do not have a clue to the identity of those who delivered the funeral orations over their dead son in 415. It could have been the city's bishop, or the bishop of the Gothic camp. Two funerary sermons delivered in the early 390s by Ambrose, bishop of Milan, over the bodies of two emperors provide insights into tenets of Christian consolation.[61] One, delivered in 392, commemorated the death of Valentinian II, Galla's uncle, who died at eighteen of unknown causes, possibly suicide or murder. The other commemorated Theodosius's death in 395 at a ceremony that Galla attended, aged about five.[62]

Ambrose's imperial requiems banished maternity from the funerary realm. In *de obitu Valentiniani*, Ambrose made no reference to Justina, Valentinian's deceased mother and Ambrose's erstwhile bitter enemy. Neither Justina's distinguished ancestry nor her crucial role in ensuring her son's succession were mentioned, nor naturally her clash with Ambrose himself. Of Valentinian's living relatives, two out of his three sisters suddenly appear in the oration. These are Grata and Justa, whose inclusion is as striking as is the omission of Justina and Galla Placidia, Valentinian's third sister.[63] The surviving sisters' sole mission, according to Ambrose, was to spend the rest of their days in perpetual chaste mourning:[64]

> With your bitter laments do not tear away from you the
> brother implanted in your breast; do not turn him out with
> your lamentation and do not wake him from his rest. Let him
> remain in your hearts, let him live in your breasts, let him cling
> to your pious embraces as he used to do, let him press a
> brother's kiss on you. May he be ever present in your eyes, ever

---

61. S. G. MacCormack, *Art and Ceremony in Late Antiquity* (Berkeley 1981), 145–50, primarily on the Theodosian oration. Both have been newly translated with introduction and commentary in J. H. W. G. Liebeschuetz, *Ambrose of Milan: Political Letters and Speeches* (TTH 43) (Liverpool 2005), 358–99 (on Valentinian II) and 174–203 (on Theodosius). See also S. Lunn-Rockleffe, "Ambrose's Imperial Funeral Sermons," *JEH* 59 (2008), 1–17. On the stormy relations between Theodosius and Ambrose, McLynn, *Ambrose of Milan*, 291–360.

62. *De obit. Theod.* 34, refers to the presence of the emperor's children in Italy, probably meaning Honorius and Galla since Arcadius had remained throughout in Constantinople.

63. Perhaps Galla had not yet been born in 392.

64. *De obitu Val.* 36–51; with McLynn, *Ambrose of Milan*, 339.

in your kisses, ever in your conversations, ever in
your minds.[65]

Instead of a mother, the dead Valentinian is greeted upon arrival in
heaven by Gratian, his older half brother and Ambrose's protégé, who
had been killed a decade before.[66]

An inventive cleric entrusted with pronouncing the funerary sermon over Theodosius III in 415 could have conjured a celestial reunion
of distinguished blood relatives. Whether or not one was in attendance
is not known. Had there been such a one at Barcelona, he would have
depicted a touching scene of heavenly reunion between the soul of
Galla's child and Roman emperors, all deceased blood relatives. Perhaps
the funeral oration would have recruited even the child's Gothic ancestors,
headed by the indomitable Alaric.

If a Barcelona orator wished to emphasize the impeccable Christian credentials of the dead child and his surviving mother (Galla), he
could have resurrected Constantine himself. This is precisely what
Ambrose, bishop of Milan, had done when he engineered a fleeting
embrace between the souls of the deceased Theodosius I and Constantine, two wholly unrelated emperors. To bridge time and generative
cycles, Ambrose resorted to Helena, Constantine's mother, a dominant
figure in the family's Christian pantheon: "How fortunate was he [Con-
stantine] to have a mother like this. . . . How great was the woman . . .
[a] mother anxious for her son to whom rule of the Roman world
had fallen."[67]

The Ambrosian mother of Constantine, who in 395 had been conveniently dead for some six decades, emerges as a symbol of idealized
Christian motherhood. She not only produced a great son but, endowed
with divine instincts, she discovered the true cross in Jerusalem. Her
otherwise inexplicable appearance in a funerary sermon honoring Theodosius I must be accounted for as an effort to generalize and to glorify
the enduring stability of her orthodoxy. In Ambrosian terms, the capture of Galla, a tragedy to be averted, proclaimed the attachment of
mothers to their progeny and to orthodoxy. Had Galla's child lived,
an orator charged with his postmortem eulogy could easily claim that

---

65. McLynn, *Ambrose of Milan*, 41.

66. Ibid. On the relations between prince and prelate, T. D. Barnes, "Ambrose and Gratian," *AT* 7
(1999), 165–74.

67. *De obit. Theod.* 41 (Liebeschuetz).

Theodosius III, a distant scion of Constantine, would have been worthy of the imperial throne by virtue of his mother's exemplary piety. By the late fourth century, this was the prevailing opinion regarding Helena and Constantine, inaugurated by Ambrose and continued by Paulinus of Nola and Rufinus, two of Galla's earlier contemporaries.[68]

Still, of Ambrose's lengthy sermons not a single paragraph could have constituted a fitting tribute to Galla's grief over the death of her firstborn. A consolatory sermon delivered at Barcelona in 415 would have been better served by the moving tribute that Paulinus (of Nola), himself a bereaved parent, composed for friends (Pneumatius and Fidelis) who lost their child:

> He was previously a boy on earth, with famous parents and
> ancestral glory, but now he rightly dwells in heaven, for Christ
> the Lord adorned him with such a great blessing that he
> departed young in years and renewed by baptismal water.
> A double grace transported him to God, for he was doubly a
> child, both in span of age and through the water of the font.[69]

Paulinus recognized the asymmetries that governed the prolonged process of internal grieving in spite of the brevity of open tears: "Dutiful parents, I would not have you sin through copious weeping. Let not your love turn to blame. For it is a wicked love which laments a soul in blessedness, and a baneful affection which bewails one who takes joy in God."[70] More evocative than all the metaphors, images, admonitions, and biblical citations with which Paulinus peppered the consolation would have been the personal recollection of his own loss. His child, Celsus, died in Spain, like Galla's child, on the eighth day after his birth.[71] In poignant words addressed to the dead boy, Paulinus encapsulated the abiding pain that haunted parents:

> You are now a youthful dweller in the chaste land of the blest.
> You are your parents' grief but likewise their glory. You are the
> love, the longing, and the light of your family. Our pleasure in

---

68. Paulinus of Nola, *Ep.* 31.4, dated 403; Rufinus, *Hist. Eccl.* 1.7–8. On the "saintly" imagery of Helena and its influence on the shaping of the public image of Galla and other queens, F. E. Consolino, "La 'santa' regina da Elena a Galla Placidia nella tradizione dell'Occidente latino," in *Vicende e figure femminili in Grecia e a Roma*, ed. R. Raffaelli (Ancona 1995), 467–92.

69. Paulinus of Nola, *Carmen* 31, 1–6, trans. P. G. Walsh (ACW 40).

70. Ibid., 43–45.

71. Mratschek, *Der Briefwechsel*, 215 n. 31 on the date.

you was short but your own is long; yet the pleasure you bring can be long lived for us, too, if you remember us before the Lord. . . . It is certain that the kingdom of heaven belongs to children such as you were in age, purpose and father, like our own boy . . . who was summoned the moment he was bestowed. He was a child long desired but not awarded to us, since we were unworthy to rejoice in the devotion of a progeny. . . . We buried him alongside the martyrs with whom he shares the compact of the tomb, so that with the blood of the saints close by he may sprinkle our souls when they are in the fire after death.[72]

Few formal funerary sermons captured the mood of mourners as did the consolatory treatise that Gregory of Nyssa composed in 385 on the passing of Pulcheria, Galla's half sister and the young daughter of Theodosius I and Flaccilla, his first wife:

They filled the church and its forecourt, the square beyond, the alleyways, the tenements, and the cross-streets, the open spaces atop buildings—all one could see was a mass of humanity, as if the whole world had rushed to a single space in grief. And there one could view that sacred blossom brought forth on a golden bier. How dejected were the faces of all who gazed upon her! How their eyes flowed with tears! They struck their hands together and their keening too made known the pain that filled their heart.[73]

The girl, who had been seven or eight at death, was described in tender terms as a fragile being, as though destined to grace the earth for only a brief period of time, but whose sudden demise had the force of an earthquake:

Adorned with royal beauty the tender dove has just flown away on a bright wing. . . . [W]hether we call her a dove or a tender little flower who not yet had shone with full splendor . . . it was clear that we experienced a real tremor. . . . How is it possible to surmount the passions while remaining in nature and not

72. Paulinus of Nola, *C.* 31, 591–614 (Walsh trans.).

73. Gregory of Nyssa, *Oratio consolatoria in Pulcheriam*, 461–63 (Spira), Eng. trans. in K. G. Holum, *Theodosian Empresses Women and Imperial Dominion in Late Antiquity* (Berkeley 1989), 22.

be constrained by grief at this sight when death draws nigh not in old age but in the prime of life? Eyelids darken the eye's rays, ruddy complexion becomes pallid, the mouth is silenced and the blossoming flower of the lips is darkened, something difficult not only for the parents but for anyone who happens to behold this sight.[74]

Mothers, asserted the bishop, were creatures prone to grief yet also capable of rising to tragic heights, like the biblical Sarah contemplating the untimely death of her only son:

> What can I say about fragile female nature? If a woman is not instructed by a man concerning divine things, she does not acknowledge the hidden life as better than appearances and would not entrust the care of her son to a man. Indeed a mother's affection envelops her son and she embraced him with her arms at the time of death. . . . If evil is necessary, Sarah would not see Isaac slain. The sword would then pierce both.[75]

A few weeks after the death of Galla's firstborn Athaulf died, victim of assassination in Barcelona at the hand of a trusted servant. Orosius, a contemporary, claimed that the king's peaceful intentions vis-à-vis Rome, the fruit of his association with Galla, led to his death.[76] Contrary to Athaulf's symbiotic ideology, the Goths, it seems, sought war and not peace with Rome. Athaulf's leadership had become untenable.[77] Galla's position as a Gothic queen must have been seriously undermined with his unexpected and violent death. Olympiodorus, another contemporary, went so far as to conjure up a touching bedside scene. On his deathbed, he asserted, Athaulf enjoined his brother, an otherwise unknown figure, to hand Galla back to her brother in Italy to ensure Roman friendship.[78] Whether Athaulf further recommended Constantius as a future husband, just as another general, Boniface, was to do a few years later, is not stated.[79] Galla's detachment from the Goths indicated, as

74. Gregory of Nyssa, *Oratio* 462, 464 (Spira), Eng. trans. www.sage.edu/faculty/salomd/nyssa/flacilla.

75. Gregory of Nyssa, *Oratio* 468 (Spira), Eng. trans. C. McCambly (online).

76. Orosius 7.43.8–9.

77. Orosius 7.43.10.

78. Olympiodorus, fr. 26 (Blockley).

79. See ch. 4.

Oost surmised, a realization that married or single, Galla's presence in the Gothic camp had become a liability.[80]

Any generalization of Galla's state of mind following the two untimely deaths, of son and of husband, must remain beyond the reach of the historian. Contemporary consolations addressed to widows by theologians like Jerome consistently espoused perpetual widowhood, as though grief was irreparable. If Jerome had written from Bethlehem to Barcelona, a likely gesture of which, alas, there is no trace, his letter to Galla would have been saturated with the usual mixture of exhortation and admonition: "I have several times written letters to widows in which for their instruction I have sought out examples from scripture, weaving its varied flowers into a single garland of chastity."[81] He counseled widows to live in isolation from society, in the company of other widows or virgins.[82] Jerome could be harsh:

> Let your father grieve that you have in vain lost your virginity as the fruits of matrimony have not been yours. Where is the husband whom he gave to you? Even had he been lovable and good, death would still have snatched all away and his decease would have terminated the fleshly bond between you. Seize the opportunity and make virtue of necessity. . . . A widow who has ceased to have a husband to please . . . needs nothing more but perseverance only. She is mindful of past enjoyments, she knows what gave her pleasure and what she has not lost. By rigid fast and vigil she must quench the fiery darts of the devil.[83]

And he could be gentle, especially when addressing a bereaved mother who, like Galla, also lost a husband:

> I wish to check a mother's weeping and I groan myself. I make no secret of my feelings. This entire letter is written in tears. . . . My agony is as great as yours. Jesus knows it . . . the holy angels know it. . . . Yet why should that be hard to bear which we must one day ourselves endure? And why do we grieve for the dead? We are not born to live forever. Abraham, Moses, Isaiah,

80. Oost, *Galla Placidia*, 135.
81. Jerome, *Ep.* 123.1 (NPN trans.).
82. Jerome, *Ep.* 79.7.
83. Jerome, *Ep.* 54.6–7 (NPN trans.).

Peter, James and John, Paul the "chosen vessel" and even the Son of God Himself have all died. And are we vexed when a soul leaves its earthly tenement?[84]

That theologians like Jerome preferred to espouse the ideal of *univira*, a woman married once and never again, is understandable in view of his fervent preaching regarding sexual renunciation.[85] That Galla would have considered the state of *univira* seems equally likely. Female celibacy proved a potent combination of public piety and power. It allowed women vowed to virginity not only to bypass marriage but also to style themselves "brides of Christ," as Pulcheria did in Constantinople. By crossing the threshold of celibacy to adopt perpetual virginity, Pulcheria could exist, and thrive, without a masculine intermediary. By remaining in a state of widowhood, Galla could potentially play that same role that Pulcheria did as the power behind the throne. But she could also be consigned to a back room where widows were expected to pass the rest of their lives in the company of other widows, away from public eyes.

Athaulf's assassination catapulted his killer, Singeric, to the Gothic throne. He lasted a single week. In the course of his reign he executed Athaulf's children by his first wife and forced Galla to hike: "To spite Athaulf he ordered his queen, Placidia, to walk before his horse with the rest of the prisoners for a distance of twelve miles from the city."[86] Singeric's successor, Valia, achieved what both Alaric and Athaulf had failed to accomplish. He contracted a treaty with Honorius's government that allowed the Goths to settle on Roman territory in Gaul without fear of ejection.[87] Galla was traded for grain supplies, not, however, before the Goths eliminated many of the barbarians who had occupied the Spanish provinces since 409.[88] The new Gothic ruler treated Athaulf's widow honorably, a far cry from the treatment to which she had been subjected under Singeric.[89] It may be further surmised that Valia relinquished her with some relief, now that the Goths had been

84. Jerome, *Ep.* 39.2–3 (NPN trans.).
85. Brown, *Body and Society*, passim.
86. Olympiodorus, fr. 26 (Blockley).
87. The mechanisms of this settlement have been hotly discussed. Halsall, *Barbarian Migrations*, 422f. for summary of opinions.
88. Olympiodorus, fr. 26 and 30, the latter specifying Galla for grain, without the Gallic lands. Orosius 7.43.16–18 on Valia fighting on behalf of Rome.
89. Orosius 7.43.12.

granted a home of their own within the empire. Neither Goths nor Romans were as yet ready to advance mutual interests through marital alliances. But the marriage of Galla and Athaulf, unique in its setting and evolution, set a precedent. It demonstrated that mixed marriages of this sort need not entail an inevitable incorporation of the barbarian spouse into the fabric of the Roman state. The non-Roman was no longer expected to become Roman. Rather, the Roman partner could become a pawn in a dangerous game of political alliances.

Nothing is known of Galla's journey back to Italy. It could have been overland, reversing the direction she had taken in 412 with the Goths from Italy to Spain via the Gallic Mediterranean. It could have been by sea aboard a ship. That she was accompanied by a group of Goths loyal to Athaulf can be surmised from later references to her Gothic guards.[90] Nor do the sources disclose whether she took with her back to Italy the looted treasures of Rome that had once formed Athaulf's gift to his bride. Nor is it clear whether she took with her the silver coffin of Theodosius III. Around 430, in a Ravenna church honoring John the Evangelist, Galla had his name inscribed in a highly selected list of dead and living relatives.[91] Had he lived, Theodosius III could have become potential heir to both Roman and Gothic crowns. In death he became the honored if temporary denizen of the burial structure now known as the Mausoleum of Galla Placidia.[92]

90. Olympiodorus, fr. 38 (Blockley).

91. *ILS* 818. Mackie, *Early Christian Chapels*, 177 and 318 n. 123, following Oost, *Galla Placidia*, 274 n. 86. See ch. 6 for discussion.

92. This is the interesting hypothesis of G. Mackie, "The Mausoleum of Galla Placidia: A Possible Occupant," *Byzantion* 65 (1995), 396–404; and Mackie, *Early Christian Chapels*, 176–77. See also ch. 3.

CHAPTER THREE

The Making of an Empress
(417–425)

When Honorius was celebrating his eleventh consulship and Constantius
his second, they solemnized Placidia's marriage. Her frequent rejections of
Constantius had made him angry at her attendants. Finally, the emperor
Honorius, her brother, on the day on which he entered his consulship, took her by
the hand and, despite her protests, gave her over to Constantius, and the marriage
was solemnized in the most dazzling fashion.[1]

A Wedding in Ravenna

If Olympiodorus the Egyptian is to be believed, Galla's second wedding,
an affair no less resplendent than her first, was conceived as a combination of male mutual interests. Honorius, Galla's brother and the reigning
monarch of the western Roman Empire, deemed it prudent to reward his
most loyal military commander with the hand of his sister. Orosius, who
had waxed eloquence on Galla's union with Athaulf, concluded his history of the year 417 without even referring to her second marriage. Only
Jordanes, the sixth-century Gothic historian, lent the arrangement a
romantic hue. He featured Constantius as a knight in shining armor who
had been promised the hand of the princess if he set out to free her from
Gothic servitude and to return her to the arms of her loving brother.[2]
Jordanes failed to record Galla's own sentiments when she bade farewell
to Valia, the new Gothic king. Nor did Jordanes attempt to investigate
the first encounter between Galla and Constantius.

1. Olympiodorus, fr. 33 (Blockley). Cf. Sozomen, *HE* 9.16.2.
2. Jordanes, *Get.* 164–65.

Into the general gaiety that such weddings generally engendered, Olympiodorus introduced a jarring note. The historian claimed that Galla was an unwilling bride. The bridegroom, one assumes, had been overjoyed. After all, he had pursued the princess for half a decade and across three provinces. And while he had been engaged in fighting off barbarians and usurpers, not neglecting to consolidate his own position at court and in the army, she followed the conventional destiny of women, marriage and motherhood, albeit in unconventional and unpredictable surroundings.

Galla's apparent adamant refusal to marry could have gained theoretical support from imperial laws that continued to insist, at least in theory, on the need for a woman's consent to marriage. To be precise, while the laws condemned coercion, potential objections on the part of would-be brides were generally disregarded.[3] The contradiction was due to the tender age at which Roman girls were married off, too young to carry too much weight in familial considerations of suitable matches. By the age of twenty-five, however, women and men reached a legal age of maturity. At that point matrimonial decisions could be reached without parental or guardian approval. The fact that Honorius could coerce Galla into marriage suggests that as her older brother he was her legal guardian; it is also possible that in early 417 Galla had not yet reached her twenty-fifth birthday.[4] Ironically, the same Honorius had married a sister of his first wife in contravention of his and his predecessor's laws on incestuous marriage.[5] Whether Honorius further resorted to annulling her first marriage on the basis of a law that penalized marriages between Romans and barbarians is possible but remains highly conjectural.[6]

3. *CTh* 3.10.1, 3.6.1, 3.11.1 (coercion); *CJ* 5.4.20 of 409 on objections.

4. These considerations have not been taken into account in the debates regarding her date of birth (above). Yet they imply that she was born, at the latest, by December 393.

5. *CTh* 13.2.2 of 355 banned marriage between a man and his former wife's sister; *CTh* 3.12.3 of 396 reduced penalties for violation from death to financial fines; *CTh* 3.10.1 of 409 responded negatively to an attempt to obtain imperial dispensation to contract incestuous marriage. Honorius sent Thermantia, his second wife and sister of Maria, his first wife, back to her mother in 408 after the murder of Thermantia's father, *PLRE II*. She survived the slaughter of her mother in 410 (above) and lived in a nunnery apparently until her death in 415.

6. Maria's father, Stilicho, was half Vandal. *CTh* 3.14.1 (373) banned mixed marriages; H. Sivan, "Why Not Marry a Barbarian" (ch. 1 n. 38), 137–45. Note that the law does not invalidate such marriages, but rather forbids them. The death penalty was prescribed in cases in which such marriages harbored suspicion of criminal activity.

Reluctant brides in a late Roman context may, at first, evoke surprise. Historians of women in antiquity have habitually and correctly contextualized the lives of ancient women within the inexorable life cycle of daughter-wife-mother. Monolithic models of this sort render coherent passages and scenes that may not have been entirely homogenous. One revolutionizing element, Christianity, introduced a new interpretation of the institutions that dictated this ideal. When Matthew (10:34–36) positioned Jesus as disturber of familial norms, and Paul (1 Cor. 7:29, 34) advocated marital intimacy based on bonding with God, they created space to carve out disparities between the old pagan and the new Christian home.[7] Marriage between mortals came to characterize an arrangement for those incapable of living a life of a higher order. Rejecting marriage, an essentially masculine model, Christianity provided an alternative that allowed men, and women, to abandon the systematic quest, so typical of the nobility, for aggrandizement via matrimony. The new nobility, as defined by Matthew's and Paul's interpreters, numbered not only those born to position and power but also those committed to sexual renunciation.[8] As a singular mark of affiliation, marriage no longer affirmed female identity. Virginity acquired unparalleled dignity. It could be upheld, taught, or recaptured.

The horizons that stretched to accommodate and commemorate the new category of voluntary virginity are reflected in the pithy yet extravagant praise bestowed on a woman named Theodora:

> A gift of heaven, teacher of chastity, blessed by the Lord,
> "mother" and leader of Mygdonia and Gratissima, pious
> virgins and worthy offshoots of a holy root. Theodora, forever
> a virgin [aeiparthenos]. Her soul she offered to God, her sole
> ruler. Her body she left to the vigilance of her tomb.[9]

In the pre-Constantinian era of martyrs, the adoption of virginity invariably entailed the rejection of marriage. Spurned suitors and defied

7. G. Cloke, "Mater or Martyr: Christianity and the Alienation of Women within the Family in the Later Roman Empire," *Theology and Sexuality* 5 (1996), 37–57; Denzey, *Bone Gatherers*, 155–56.

8. Brown, *Body and Society*, passim.

9. U. E. Eisen, *Women Officeholders in Early Christianity: Epigraphical and Literary Studies*, trans. L. M. Maloney (Collegeville 2000), 97–99, found in Macedonia and dated to the fifth or sixth centuries C.E. Eisen regards the title "mother" as that of a spiritual mentor, but the phrasing suggests that the two other named women may have been her daughters and that Theodora earned rather than maintained a claim to perpetual virginity of the soul.

fathers fill the pages of narratives woven around young Christian women determined to preserve the integrity of their bodies at all cost.[10] When conventional martyrdom was no longer available, its radical fantasy became, with episcopal support, an ideal within reach. To achieve their aims, young girls resistant to the conventional reach of paternal authority had to adopt a polemical stand in public. Thus to achieve virginal autonomy in Ambrose's late-fourth-century congregation in Milan, a girl had to disrupt the Mass, rush to the altar, and insist on instant consecration.[11] As Ambrose described one such scene, it became clear that in this narrative the bishop displaced the image of the parental couple and specifically of the girl's recently deceased father. In the process of neutralizing the family, the bishop positioned himself as a marriage broker, facilitating the match between the girl and Jesus while asserting paternal rights to which he had no legal right.

The new model of virginal orthodoxy had a limited success beyond the erudite pages of theological discourse and of congregations presided over by powerful bishops.[12] While the theme of the reluctant bride continued to haunt biographies of outstandingly pious women, the value of marriage outweighed considerations of sexual renunciation. Even at the unprecedented scale of attempts to avoid marriage in late antiquity, the actual importance of marital matters ensured continuing collusion between the home and the church. Around 400, at Rome, the objection raised by the noble Melania the Younger, at fourteen, to marrying Pinianus, a boy hardly older than herself, emerged as an inevitable correlative to an inborn ascetic bent.[13] Overcome "by exceeding force" (*meta*

10. E. A. Castelli, *Martyrdom and Memory: Early Christian Culture Making* (New York 2004). Denzey, *Bone Gatherers*, 148–75. On Agnes, her rejection of marriage, and the ultimate conversion of her ardent suitor, Jones, "Agnes and Constantia" (ch. 2 n. 21), 136, who correctly concludes that the fight to marry off the would-be martyr reflects the importance of the marriage ideal.

11. Ambrose, *Concerning Virgins*, 1.12.63–65, paraphrased in Denzey, *Bone Gatherers*, 164.

12. Precisely the reason why such cases received so much contemporary coverage, Brown, *Body and Society*, passim, on the shrill voices of the devoted. The case of Demetrias, scion of the powerful clan of the Anicii, who undertook the veil of virginity between 410 and 413, demonstrates the publicity value, and rarity, of this phenomenon. Sivan, "On Hymen and Holiness in Late Antiquity" (ch. 1 n. 19), 81–93. See now also A. Kurdock, "Demetrias ancilla dei: Anicia Demetrias and the Problem of the Missing Patron," in Cooper and Hillner, *Early Christian Rome*, 190–224.

13. Melania would have been born c. 385; her biography was written by Gerontius, a close associate who, while extolling her piety, did not forebear from criticizing her extravagant acts of charity. Clark, *Melania*, passim; L. Coon, *Sacred Fictions: Holy Women and Hagiography in Late Antiquity* (Philadelphia 1997), 109–18, esp. 110 on the inner tension in the biography. On virginity and asceticism see, among many, J. W. Drijvers, "Virginity and Aceticism in Late Roman Western Elites," in *Sexual Asymmetry*, ed. J. Blok and P. Mason (Amsterdam 1988), 241–73.

pollen bias), namely family pressure, the reluctant bride turned after the wedding to confront her fresh spouse with an appeal to practice chastity. Husband and bride's family united in opposition to Melania's self-imposed sexual renunciation. The aristocratic necessity to propagate was further assisted by Melania's ecclesiastical counselors who, armed with appropriate scriptural references, reminded the young woman of her familial, and class, obligations.[14] She promptly produced two children, a girl and a boy. The latter, due to her incessant abuse of her body, arrived prematurely and died after being administered baptism. The girl, whom her parents had vowed to perpetual virginity, followed not much later. Struck by the double tragedy, the couple, having resolved to live without sex, had to reconfigure the traditional marital discourse. Vowed to chastity, doubts persisted regarding the legitimacy of their abstinence and legality of their subsequent actions.[15] The death of Melania's father effected a deathbed reconciliation that liberated the couple from familial but not from class constraints.

By 416, when the widowed Galla confronted an unyielding suitor aided by her own brother, Melania had become a cause célèbre. In the wake of the Gothic sieges of Rome (408–410), Melania and Pinianus had fled Italy for the safety of their African estates, where they continued to apply themselves to the disbursement of their vast income. Within seven years, a favored biblical figure, they accomplished an unheard-of feat of self-impoverishment.[16] They then embarked on a pilgrimage to Jerusalem via Alexandria (416 or 417), ultimately to settle in the Holy City.

Melania was Galla's slightly older contemporary. There is no indication that the two met, although such encounters in the exclusive circles of the Roman senatorial aristocracy were more than likely. Both young women were linked with Serena, the emperor Theodosius's niece and Galla's cousin, who had instituted herself as a mediator when Melania's brother-in-law tried to stem the couple's tides of charity. In 416 Galla could have appropriated for her own use Melania's mode of behavior. The families of both women had roots in Spain, Melania through her

14. 1 Cor. 7:16, 27; *Vita Melaniae* (*VM*) 4 (Gorce).

15. *VM* 7, the deathbed scene of Melania's father.

16. At what and at whose expense it is difficult to gauge. The couple's own vast household were prime victims, as indicated by the revolt of Pinianus's slaves in Rome (*VM* 10, Gorce), the necessity to involve Serena (*VM* 10, Gorce) and the intervention of Severus, Pinianus's brother, who promised to buy the slaves (*VM* 11, Gorce). Lepelley, "Mélanie la Jeune, entre Rome, la Sicilia, et l'Afrique" (ch. 2 n. 35), 15–32.

grandmother, Melania the Elder, and Galla through her father. Provenance and piety, a potent combination it would seem, failed to prevail upon Honorius, who himself boasted a double Spanish lineage, to allow his sister to follow her own inclination. Nor was Galla able to marshal support against the proposed marriage with Constantius by pointing to familial precedents—her own maternal aunts, condemned to perpetual virginity, and her nieces, who voluntarily had assumed the profession of vowed virginity in Constantinople.[17]

One other avenue of opposition was possible. To avoid the permanent threat of reproach, Galla could have rejected remarriage while insisting on remaining *univira*, a widow whose self-imposed single state proclaimed the superiority of the virtuous wife. The ideal, hardly a novelty, had been enthusiastically embraced and promoted in late antiquity.[18] Widowhood, if unencumbered by poverty, filled a void in the ecclesiastical and civic space:

> In memory of the well deserving Regina, mother, and widow
> who throughout her sixty years of widowhood was never a
> burden to the church. *Univira*, she had lived eighty years, five
> months, and twenty six days. Her daughter erected this tomb.[19]

Prized by theologians and courted by clerics, wealthy widows, if successful in avoiding remarriage, emerged as influential patrons in fourth-century Rome. Their homes provided hubs for intellectual activity as they presided over salons where erudite theologians devised strategies to promote virginity and to extol widowhood.[20] One would assume, therefore, that barring Constantius's ambition to marry into the imperial

17. See ch. 2 for Grata, Justa, Pulcheria, and her sisters.

18. See ch. 2. H. Funke, "*Univira*: Ein Beisiel heidnischer Gechichtsapologetik," *JAC* 8/9 (1965/1966), 183–88; B. Kotting, "Univira in Inschriften," in *Romanitas et Christianitas: Studia Iano Henrico Waszink*, ed. W. den Boer et al. (Amsterdam 1973), 195–206; and B. Kötting, *Die Bewertung der Wiederveheiratung (der zweiten Ehe) in der Antike und in der Frühen Kirche* (Opladen 1988).

19. *ILCV* I, 1581; Eisen, *Women Officeholders in Early Christianity*, 145, from the cemetery of S. Saturninus at Rome.

20. Such an unattached state (whether of widows or perpetual virgins) also posed a threat, since these women would have been especially susceptible to the lure of "heresy," as Augustine remarked. On the easily breachable frontiers of orthodoxy and heresy as drawn in the drawing rooms of these women, see the warnings regarding Pelagius that both Jerome (*Ep.* 130) and Augustine (*Ep.* 150, 188; *de bono viduitatis*) issued to various Anician women. P. Brown, "Pelagius and His Supporters: Aims and Environment," *JTS* 19 (1968), 93–114; P. Brown, "The Patrons of Pelagius: The Roman Aristocracy between East and West," *JTS* 21 (1970), 56–72; Kurdock, "Demetrias" (above n. 12), 203–12.

house and Honorius's need of his services, the presence of a pious widow would have been an asset at a court deprived of female presence.

Whether Galla would have become the kind of exemplary Christian widow, like the Roman noblewoman Paula, who had been an object of extravagant praise, will never be known. Few, of either sex, could rise to such an ideal since it demanded a radical change of life. According to Jerome, Paula's friend and admirer, only she among all mortals could achieve the kind of self-control over her body that he so greatly prized.

> Of all the ladies in Rome only one had power to subdue me, and that one was Paula. She mourned and fasted, she was squalid with dirt, her eyes were dim from weeping. For whole nights she would pray to the Lord for mercy, and often the rising sun found her still at her prayers. The psalms were her only songs, the Gospel her whole speech, continence her one indulgence, fasting the staple of her life. No other woman could give me pleasure but one whom I never saw eating food.[21]

Yet other testimonies, like a metrical inscription from the basilica of St. Agnes, the young woman whose rejection of marriage had led to her death, hint at a vogue that spread beyond the exclusive circles of the nobly born:

> In the course of a splendid life my chaste "Aphrodite" forged herself a road to heaven, where she now rejoices in Christ's halls. Rejecting things of the world, she constantly sought heavenly matters. Outstanding preserver of the law, exemplary teacher of the faith, she devoted her whole being at all seasons to holiness. For this reason she now commands the sweet smells of paradise where blades of grass bloom eternally. There she awaits God. There she will ascend to the highest realm. Abandoning all that is mortal, she left her body in the tomb. Here on earth her husband carved a space for it.[22]

21. Jerome, *Ep.* 45.3 (Eng. trans. NPN and LCL).
22. *ICUR* I 317; Eisen, *Women Officeholders in Early Christianity*, 93–94. Aphrodite was apparently a nickname for Theodora.

By modern calculations, Galla's second wedding, in January 417, exactly three years after her first, either coincided or followed shortly the celebration in honor of the eleventh consulship of her brother Honorius and the second consulship of Constantius (January 1). Had the day of the wedding coincided with the first, the nuptial festivities would have intensified the customary solemnities that accompanied the dawn of the consulships. A composition celebrating both events has not survived. We have a gap in the sequence of late ancient panegyrics between Claudian's poem on Honorius's sixth consulship in 404 and the verses delivered by the Spaniard scholar and soldier Merobaudes in honor of the consulship of Aetius (446 C.E.), his patron and the supreme commander of the western Roman army.[23] Had Galla's wedding day been settled on the twenty-first of the month it would have corresponded with the date of the deposition of St. Agnes who, in defiance of parental wishes, preferred to die a virgin and a martyr rather than to marry, an option that Galla was not likely to consider.

Unlike her first marriage, Galla's second drew scant notice. There was much less notoriety in marrying a Roman general of the same Nicene orthodox persuasion than in a wedding that had taken place in a Gothic camp in a Gallic province between the captive daughter of the most orthodox Roman emperor and a heretic barbarian chieftain. The wedding ceremony would have been solemnized with pomp due to the stature of the bride's family and the status of the bridegroom. This time around, a panegyrist could follow without restraint Claudian's lead of praising bridal ancestry, in the presence of the emperor himself, the bride's brother:

> If noble birth opens the first path to fame and all its causes are
> to be traced to ancestry, what blood more noble, what birth
> more gentle than that of royalty? Such majesty could not have
> flourished within the house of a mere commoner nor could
> glory so great have sprung from any simple home. You are
> famous for that your father [originally uncle] was an emperor,
> more famous by reason of the warlike deeds of your
> grandfather who carried the Roman eagles across the British
> channel and repulsed the armed bands of the Gaetulians.[24]

23. The latter, Aetius's third consulship, is the date attached by F. M. Clover, *Flavius Merobaudes* (Philadelphia 1971), 41.

24. Claudian, *Carmen* 30 (*Laus Serenae*), 34–41 (trans. M. Platnaeur, LCL).

Had the newlywed preferred to listen to a Christianized version of this profoundly pagan form of nuptial entertainment, the only model available was an epithalamium composed by Paulinus (of Nola). It eschewed the divinities that had presided for so long over lovers, extolling sobriety rather than gaiety, a theme hardly befitting an imperial wedding:

> Juno, Cupid, Venus, those symbols of lust must keep
>   their distance . . .
> There must be no mob dancing in decorated streets.
> None must strew the ground with leaves,
> Or the threshold with foliage.
> There must be no crazed procession through a city where
>   Christ dwells . . .
> There must be no trays lavishly laden with superfluous gifts,
> The bride must reject garments tricked with gold or
>   purple . . .[25]

Paulinus's advice regarding conduct, culminating in a call to live in chastity, could have pleased Galla but not her newlywed husband:

> Christ, instruct the newly married pair through your holy
>   bishop.
> Aid the pure hearts through these chaste hands,
> So that they may both agree on a compact of virginity.
> Or be the source of consecrated virgins.
> Of these prayers the first condition is preferable,
> That they keep their bodies innocent of the flesh.
> But if they consummate physical union,
> May the chaste offspring become a priestly race . . .[26]

A wedding of a princess with the chief commander of the Roman army in the west would have posed a welcome diversion from the discourse of dissension that had dominated court politics since the inception of Honorius's reign in 395. The emperor's second marriage (in 408) to a child bride, sister of his first wife and second daughter of Stilicho and Serena, probably generated anger rather than mirth. Stilicho's enemies at the imperial court would have been enraged at the continuing

---

25. Paulinus, *Carmen* 25, 9–40 (trans. Walsh).
26. Paulinus, *Carmen* 25, 231.

manipulation of the imperial marital bed by the bride's parents. Galla's residence up to 410 at Rome, rather than at the court, hinted at tension with Ravenna. The 417 festivities reinstated her as an integral member of the imperial dynasty. They underscored the singular bond uniting the Theodosian family, and they demonstrated the intimate interface between the court and capital. The presence of a Gothic retinue on the side of the bride would have sounded an ambiguous note. Perhaps she had them dressed in silk clothes, the same that they had worn at the wedding in Narbonne. Perhaps at the head of the Gothic group marched a man of royal Gothic and Suevic parentage whose son, Ricimer, was destined (in 457) to assume the supreme command of the Roman army and to marry a daughter of an emperor, just like Constantius.[27]

In the decade that followed the killing of Stilicho in 408, the western empire in general and Italy in particular had scant opportunity to indulge in joyful celebrations and public demonstrations of loyalty.[28] Victories over barbarians became rare and hardly worthy of recording. The last panegyric on Romans triumphing in battle over barbarians had been delivered in 402 by the redoubtable Claudian. But after 404 the court no longer boasted a poet of his stature and ability to celebrate the doubtful results of indecisive clashes. Still, the death of Galla's first husband at the hand of a Gothic rival was commemorated with great cheerfulness in faraway Constantinople:

> In the same year [415 C.E.] in the month Gorpiaeus on the 8th day before Kalends of October [September 24], a Friday, it was announced that the barbarian Athaulf had been killed in the northern regions by the lord Honorius. And lamps were lit, and on the following day chariot racing was held so that a processional entry was also made.[29]

27. Olympiodorus, fr. 38 (Blockley) on Galla's barbarian retinue. On the possible membership of Ricimer's family in that body, P. MacGeorge, *Late Roman Warlords* (Oxford 2002), 182. Ricimer's mother was a daughter of Wallia, who may have been a brother of Athaulf, Olympiodorus, fr. 26; MacGeorge, *Late Roman Warlords*, 178. On Ricimer's spectacular career, Ibid., 165ff. See also A. Gillett, "The Birth of Ricimer," *Historia* 44 (1995), 380–84, dating Ricimer's birth to c. 418.

28. On the significance of such occasions (imperial anniversaries, birthdays, and victories) within the context of the city of Rome in late antiquity, M. Humphries, "From Emperor to Pope? Ceremonial, Space, and Authority at Rome from Constantine to Gregory the Great," in Cooper and Hillner, *Early Christian Rome*, 33–34, noting correctly the physical absence of emperors from Rome throughout the fourth and fifth centuries.

29. *Chron. Pasc.* s.a. 415, Eng. trans. M. Whitby and M. Whitby, *Chronicon Pascale 284–628* (Liverpool 1989) (TTH 7), 64.

Contests with usurpers, in other words civil wars, although celebrated, hardly provided promising material for effusive verbal praises. The last panegyric celebrating a victory of Romans over Romans had been delivered by the Gaul Pacatus in Rome in 389 following Theodosius's victory over Magnus Maximus, a fellow Spaniard.[30] To another would-be panegyrist of the same event, Paulinus of Nola, the theme of victory of one orthodox emperor over another orthodox emperor in a civil war appeared fraught with difficulties.[31] Still, public executions of usurpers provided entertainment during feasts of imperial anniversaries. On Honorius's thirtieth (*tricennalia*) in 422, five years after Galla's second wedding, Maximus, another Spanish usurper who had been raised twice to the throne, once in 409–411 and again in 420, was executed during public games held in Ravenna on the occasion.[32] To mark the revival of the city of Rome after years of Gothic siege, sack, and low morale, the emperor Honorius graced the city with a rare imperial presence in 416.[33]

> The emperor himself [Honorius] visited the city [Rome] and by gesture and word indicated his approval of the city's revival [from the Gothic sieges and sack]. Ascending the tribunal he ordered Attalus to ascend the first step of the tribunal. . . . [H]e cut off two of the fingers of his right hand, namely the thumb and the forefinger, and then exiled him.[34]

The ceremony of imperial *adventus,* the first in over a decade, clearly gained gaiety with the slicing of Attalus's fingers after he had been made

30. Nixon and Saylor Rodgers, *In Praise of Later Roman Emperors,* 437–519 (introduction and English translation), 647–74 (Latin text of Mynor's edition).

31. H. Sivan, "The Last (Prose) Gallic Panegyric: Paulinus of Nola and Theodosius I," *Studies in Latin Literature and Roman History* 7 (1994), 577–594; Mratschek, *Der Briefwechsel,* 83–89.

32. *Chron. Gall.* 452 s.a. 422; *Marc. Comes* s.a. 422; Jordanes, *Rom.* 326, with *PLRE II,* 745 (Maximus 7) who is indeed to be identified with *PLRE II,* 744, Maximus 4. T. Marot, "Algunas consideraciones" (ch. 2 n. 27), 569–80.

33. From 408 till his death in 423, Honorius was in Ravenna with the exception of two brief visits to Rome in August 414 and May 416, Gillett, "Rome, Ravenna" (ch. 1 n. 17), 138.

34. Olympiodorus, fr. 26.2 (Blockley). The year was probably 416. *PLRE II,* 181, opts for 415 or 416 or 417; the last is unlikely. On the march through Rome along Honorius's carriage, Prosper, *Chron. C.* 1263 (*CM* I, 468). Humphries, "From Emperor to Pope?," 32–33, on the occasion as an opportunity to reassert the legitimacy of the imperial authority over the city of Rome and, I might add, to demonstrate publicly the concern of the court for the fortunes, or rather the misfortunes, of the former imperial capital. Ibid., 37, on governmental financing of restoration projects at the Forum and the Colosseum.

to walk in front of the imperial carriage.[35] It was an odd twist of fate for a man who had been the prefect of Rome before Alaric had bestowed the purple on him. Galla's presence was not attested.

Echoes of the May 416 celebration reverberated all the way to Constantinople, where the mutilation of Attalus was translated into another victory celebration:

> A theatrical spectacle was performed in the presence of Ursus, Prefect of the City [of Constantinople], to celebrate the victory against Attalus the usurper, in the month Daisius, on the 4th day before Kalends of July [28 June], a Wednesday. And chariot racing was also held for the same victory in the month Panemus, on Nones of July [7 July].[36]

There were multiple reasons for general rejoicing in January 417—an imperial consulship, the wedding of one of the two consuls, and hopes for a brighter future based on a new treaty between the Roman government and the new Gothic king. With the customary twist of facts, it would have been possible to present the agreement as a Roman triumph. Such an exhibition would have trumpeted the emperor's military might as well as his orthodox credentials. In 404, when Honorius paraded through the streets of Rome celebrating Stilicho's victory over Alaric (in 402), the victorious procession deliberately diverged from the traditional course of imperial triumphal marches:

> The emperor arrives. Let us see to whom he will rush, where he would choose to kneel. Will it be the temple of the emperor [Hadrian] or the memorial of the fisherman [Peter]? Laying down his crown, the emperor beat his breast where the body of the fisherman lies.[37]

---

35. The ceremonial procession had been labeled an *adventus* with triumphal elements, conducted like a pilgrimage; P. Liverani, "Victors and Pilgrims in Late Antiquity and the Early Middle Ages," *Fragmenta* 1 (2007), 83–102, esp. p. 95.

36. *Chron. Pasc.* s.a. 416 (Eng. trans. M. Whitby and M. Whitby).

37. Augustine, *Sermo cum pagani ingrederentur*, in F. Dolbeau, "Nouveaux sermons e saint Augustin pour la conversion des païens et des donatistes," *REAug* 37 (1991), 76 (section 26, lines 527–29) = *Vingt-six sermons au peuple d'Afrique* (Paris 1996), 266 (using *currerit* rather than *curavit*), with Liverani, "Victors and Pilgrims," 83. The *adventus* that Augustine mentioned has been dated to either 404 (Dolbeau), following the 402 victory over Alaric at Pollentia, or 407, following the 406 victory over Radagaisus at Fiesole. Honorius is attested at Rome in both years; Gillett, "Rome, Ravenna," 138.

Product of complex strategy, the alliance between Galla and Constantius presented a portrait of a marriage marked by unbounded potential. The interests of the state were well served by linking the emperor with the supreme commander of the army through marital ties in addition to the loyalty that all soldiers owed to their emperor. As Galla's husband, Constantius could aspire to secure what Stilicho had failed to obtain, a share of the throne itself. As a married woman, Galla could preside over the court that for decades had only female figureheads.

The dramatic turn of events that culminated in 417 with Galla's second wedding and Constantius's second consulship also yielded artistic enterprises. One such is a fragmentary ivory leaf that disappeared from Berlin during the Second World War.[38] A female figure, identified as a muse, perhaps Erato, muse of erotic poetry, perhaps Kalliope, muse of epic poetry, dominates the composition. The muse is flanked by two considerably smaller figures, a nude male, probably a cupid, and a portrait bust with bare shoulders, perhaps a specific (dead?) individual, perhaps an ideal or heroicized male. A fragmentary inscription refers to the honorary title *patricius*, apparently further hinting at an unusual combination of a second consulship combined with the patriciate. In 417 Constantius bore both titles.[39] Perhaps, then, the inscription, the muse, the cupid, and the hero were designed to depict a bridegroom as a winner in the contest of love and of war.

Learning the Roman Ropes: Disputed Papal Elections and the Ravenna Court

Pious optimism in the wake of the wedding, however, appeared somewhat misplaced. Less than two years after Galla and Constantius were married, the Ravenna court found itself embroiled in sorting out the internal affairs of the church of Rome (i.e., the papacy). We are

38. R. Delbrueck, *Die Consulardiptychen und verwandte Denkmäaler: Studien zur spätantiken Kunstgechichte* (Berlin 1929), no. 36; W. F. Volbach, *Elfenbeinarbeiten der Spätantike und des frühen Mittelalters*, 3rd ed. (Mainz 1976), no. 34; K. J. Shelton, "The Consular Muse of Flavius Constantius," *Art Bulletin* 65 (1983), 7–23.

39. On the patriciate and consulships, T. D. Barnes, "Patricii under Valentinian III," *Phoenix* 19 (1975), 155–70. Note, however, that among other contenders to the double honor of patriciate and second consulship were Flavius Merobaudes (cos. 377, 383; with Barnes, Ibid., 162), Petronius Maximus (cos. 433, 443), and Aetius (cos. 432, 437, 446).

exceptionally well informed about the complex and uneven progress of the papal schism at Rome in 419–420 through a series of imperial letters preserved in a sixth-century collection now known as the *Collectio Avellana*.[40] Two of the letters have been attributed to Galla's hand. These have the incomparable advantage of displaying the manner in which she made a place for herself at the court she had just joined, reflecting an understanding of the intricacies of contemporary ecclesiastical politics.

It all started with the unexpected death of Pope Zosimus in 418. Elections ordinarily followed. This time around two contestants appeared, Eulalius and Boniface, each claiming to have been duly elected as successor. The church failing to resolve differences, the matter was then referred to the Praefectus Urbi, the highest civil authority at Rome, and ultimately to the emperor himself. In the muddled version of the prolonged affair as preserved in the *Book of Pontiffs* (*Liber Pontificalis*), a sixth-century compilation of papal biographies, Galla featured as chief mediator between Rome and Ravenna:

> Boniface and Eulalius were ordained in rivalry on the same day. . . . On hearing this the empress [Galla] Placidia, with her son the emperor Valentinian,[41] then residing in Ravenna, reported the matter to the emperor Honorius in residence in Milan.[42] The two emperors sent a warrant ordering that both men [Eulalius and Boniface] should leave the city. . . . At Easter, however, Eulalius, relying on the fact that he had been ordained in the Constantinian basilica [the Lateran], dared to reenter the city to perform baptisms and to celebrate Easter there, while Boniface celebrated the Easter baptism at the basilica of the martyr Agnes. When the emperors heard of this they . . . ejected Eulalius . . . and sent a warrant recalling Boniface into Rome, appointing him as bishop [pope].[43]

As supporters and opponents of the two candidates stood ready to wage war over the most elevated office in the Catholic Church,

---

40. These were edited by O. Günther, *Epistulae imperatorum pontificum aliorum Avellana que dicitur collectio* (*CSEL* 35) (Vienna 1895). On the collection and its original anti-Damasus bias, K. Blair-Dixon, "Memory and Authority in Sixth-Century Rome: The *Liber Pontificalis* and the *Collectio Avellana*," in Cooper and Hillner, *Early Christian Rome*, 59–76.

41. Just then born, in 419; emperor only from 425.

42. Ravenna, rather.

43. *Liber Pontificalis*, 44 Eng. trans. R. Davis, *The Book of Pontiffs* (Liverpool 2000), 34–35.

Symmachus, the city's prefect, informed the Ravenna court of the danger to urban order.[44]

Far from correcting the inherent instability of the electoral system, the ultimate civic authority in Rome, its prefect, could at best become a passive, if not helpless, spectator of religious passions at a distance. Honorius decreed in Eulalius's favor. Partisans of Boniface accused the prefect of partiality in his report to the emperor.[45] Honorius ordered both Eulalius and Boniface to appear at the court where resolution was to be reached by an assembly of bishops that the emperor gathered in Ravenna. The dignitaries failed to build consensus. As Easter was approaching, Honorius empowered the bishop of Spoleto to conduct services at Rome, simultaneously banishing the two papal contenders from the city.[46] As a last-ditch effort the court resolved to summon yet another ecclesiastical synod, neither at Rome nor in Ravenna but in Spoleto, as though distance from the tumult at Rome and the intrigues at court could guarantee a satisfactory solution.

That papal elections could spill into the streets and culminate in bloodshed had been evident from the tumult that had accompanied the disputed rise of Damasus to the papal throne in 364, an affair that marred the dawn of the reign of Valentinian I, Galla's grandfather.[47] The compiler of the *Collectio Avellana* who recorded the 418–419 disruptions bore little love for the fourth-century pope whose manipulative and violent tactics were neither forgotten nor forgiven.[48] In 419 the court could ill afford a repetition of the 366 fiasco that the *Collectio Avellana* registered with gusto:

> Damasus sent in the gladiators, the charioteers, the
> gravediggers, and all the clergy armed to the teeth with swords
> and clubs to besiege the basilica. They joined battle in
> earnest. . . . From all sides the Damasans broke into the basilica
> [later St. Maria Maggiore] and killed a hundred and sixty

---

44. *Collectio Avellana* (*CA*) 14, recaptured in *CA* 15; the latter translated in P. R. Coleman-Norton, *Roman State and Christian Church* (London 1966), II, no. 352.

45. *CA* 17 (presbyters pro Boniface); *CA* 18 (Honorius's response) (Eng. trans. Coleman-Norton), II, no. 353; *CA* 19 (Symmachus's reply).

46. *CA* 21–24 (Eng. trans. Coleman-Norton), II, no. 355–58.

47. N. McLynn, "Christian Controversy and Violence in the Fourth Century," *Kodai* 3 (1992), 15–44, esp. 16–19.

48. *CSEL* 35.1–4 (ed. Gunther). An English translation is available via the Internet at www.fourthcentury.com/index.php/avellana. *Amm.* 27.3.11–13 on the 364 elections.

people, women as well as men. They wounded several more, many of whom were to die later.[49]

To ensure the success of the projected synod, Honorius widened the net of invitees to include eminent bishops from North Africa as well as the most famous of all Italian bishops, Paulinus of Nola. Honorius's invitation to the African bishops emphasized the need for wide participation. Galla's two letters, one addressed to Aurelius of Carthage, the senior provincial bishop, the other to seven other African bishops, including Augustine of Hippo and Alypius of Thagaste, echoed Honorius's approach:

> We would have wished for another cause to see you and to benefit from your august presence. But since unbridled ambition had ushered a battle over the papacy wholly incommensurate with the holy mode of life of such an office, a gathering of bishops, smaller in size than that the number that synodal customs decree, deferred a decision regarding this matter to a larger assembly of the most learned men of whom your sanctity is the foremost. Nor should the rewards of purity and merit be revealed through anyone other than such men, once the faults that the sacred precept of the divine faith are eschewed. Although the letters of the emperor, my blood brother, would have sufficed, I have adjoined my own request for the prompt arrival of your sanctity. I am asking you, holy master and venerable father, that you would grant this double benefit, namely your benediction that we so desire and your much needed opinion, and laying aside all matters deign to exert your effort over confirming the bishop that none would contest.[50]

In her letter to the seven African bishops, Galla reiterated her disappointment over the failure of the Ravenna synod to resolve the contested elections in spite of their number, which she must have deemed sufficient. She concluded her invitation with words that betray her conviction of her own powers of persuasion:

---

49. *CA* 1 (*CSEL* 35.3), Eng. trans. in K. Blair-Dixon (above n. 31), 59.
50. *CA* 27 to Aurelius. Coleman-Norton's translation is as opaque as the original, which I have simplified for the sake of clarity.

Although the sacred authority of the emperor, my blood
brother, calling upon you to Italy to attend a synod must not
be neglected, we deem it vital to add letters of our own serenity
in which I pray thee to grant the greatly desired appearance of
your beneficial presence without delay, a request that you
likewise would consider pleasing to the Almighty. For the sake
of a distinguished bishop and the merits of a holy life you
understand that the reward of the judgement that you will
proffer regarding this vexed matter are in the hands of God.[51]

Enlisting the entire African episcopal contingent reflected the court's
shrewdness as well as an acknowledgment of the indispensable experience that these bishops had acquired in handling fragile situations
that threatened the imperial vision of unity.[52] Imperial laws on heresy,
be they on Donatism, Pelagianism, or Manichaeism, had become an
ideological cornerstone in the African way of dealing with dissenters.
Nor did Galla disclose in her letter her own preference for either Eulalius or Boniface.[53]

Referring to herself as the emperor's "blood sister" (*domni germani
mei Augusti principis*), Galla deployed this peculiar mode of self-
reference to equate two people whose harmonious relations were far
from assured. At the dawn of the fifth century women belonging to the
imperial family, wives, daughters, and sisters of emperors, carved a
niche that consolidated their place inside civic and religious spaces.
Already around 400 Eudoxia, wife of the eastern emperor and Galla's
half brother, Arcadius (395–402), did not hesitate to pick a quarrel with
the redoubtable bishop of Constantinople, John Chrysostom, to the detriment of the latter.[54] Nor did she hesitate to promote the interests of a
remote episcopal see, like that of Palestinian Gaza, where her intervention and donation led to the undermining of the pagan infrastructure in
the city and to the construction of a large church.[55] At the court of

51. *CA* 28, once again simplifying for sake of clarity.
52. P. Brown, "Religious Coercion in the Later Roman Empire: The Case of North Africa,"
History 48 (2007), 295.
53. Oost, *Galla Placidia*, 158, claims that Galla and Constantius favored the cause of Eulalius, presumably following Honorius's initial lead, but Galla's own letters do not provide a clue
either way.
54. Holum, *Theodosian Empresses*, 69–78.
55. Sivan, *Palestine in Late Antiquity*, passim, esp. 328–47.

Eudoxia's son, Theodosius II, his wife (Eudocia) and his sister (Pulcheria) were to emulate each other as patronesses of the ecclesiastical establishment. Often bitter rivals, the two imperious women provided complementary poles of piety and enterprise, sharing the public stage in conflict and in complicity. Galla's wedging into ecclesiastical elections at Rome matched the trail that the princesses of the Constantinopolitan court had blazed by virtue of either their power of procreation or their commitment to sexual renunciation. Even after her 417 marriage with Constantius, Galla's standing at the court largely depended on her "blood brother," as she styled Honorius. According to Olympiodorus, Honorius held his newly recovered sister in great affection that he demonstrated constantly and publicly.[56]

By far the most interesting document issuing from Galla's chancellery in spring 419 was a letter to Paulinus, bishop of Nola (in Campania), in which she invited the aged cleric to attend the forthcoming synod at Spoleto:

> To the holy and venerable bishop Paulinus. It had been widely
> held among us that no resolution could be reached by the
> bishops who had arrived at the synod [in Ravenna] since when
> your beatitude had not been able to undertake the hazards of a
> journey [from Nola to Ravenna] so injurious to your health.
> Through the absence of your holiness vices that one would not
> wish for have been rejoicing while immoderate and inveterate
> ambition [sc. Eulalius], long desiring to fight against the
> blessed man of holy life [sc. Boniface] and the very goodness
> of the apostolic institution [sc. the papacy], now trust that
> walls [sc. the Lateran basilica], too, can be taken by violence.
> Surely an entanglement worthy of unraveling only through the
> blessed life of your sublimity! We announce therefore that the
> judgement [of the synod] is to be postponed so that the divine
> directives that you follow and fulfil may be pronounced by
> your blessed mouth. There is no other producer of such
> precepts besides you who is especially esteemed as a disciple of
> the apostle himself. Therefore, holy master and venerable
> father, just servant of God, having put aside the divine labor
> [of your office] indulge us with your service by granting us the

56. Olympiodorus, fr. 38 (Blockley).

boon of your visit, if so it is to be called, so that when everything has been set aside, have the kindness to come without delay to preside over the synod [at Spoleto], at a time when the air is soothingly balmy, fulfilling our desire and bestowing your blessing.[57]

Since rejecting his election as presbyter in Bacelona (in 394/395), Paulinus had become a venerable figure in Italy, patron of a powerful saint, and exemplary host.[58] Among his correspondents were the outstanding theologians of the day, including Augustine, Jerome, Rufinus, and Sulpicius Severus. Galla's invitation was couched in terms that Paulinus would have found difficult to refuse. She praised the mild climate of Spoleto and its relative proximity to Nola. Ravenna's air had been notoriously noxious, its marshes hardly salubrious. The letter gave no hint of previous acquaintance or shared experience, neither deemed relevant to the subject at hand. Nor did it disclose her own preferences, other than designating the rival papal parties in general terms of vices versus virtues.[59] To assign so prominent a role to a bishop in his seventies who had thus far refrained from embroilment in papal affairs was an ingenuous way of avoiding the admission of failure. By making Paulinus the chief arbiter, the transmitter of divine ordinances, Galla could announce that the court deferred its judgment in the matter to the ultimate authority, God.

Galla's letters to the bishops showed her grasp of the importance of the linkage of the religious and political discourses. They established the court as unified and as a unifying element. By echoing and adding to Honorius's orders, the letters symbolized the united front of the imperial siblings. By insisting on wide-ranging representation from both

57. CA 25, cf. the German translation in Mratschek, *Der Briefwechsel*, 643, with her indispensable notes on pp. 644–66, and the opaque translation of Coleman-Norton, II, no. 359.

58. S. Mratschek, "*Multis enim notissima est sanctitas loci*: Paulinus and the Gradual Rise of Nola as a Center of Christian Hospitality," *JECS* 9 (2001), 511–53; and Mratschek, *Der Briefwechsel*, passim, on Paulinus's wide-ranging correspondence and the multiple functioning of Nola's cult of Felix. See also D. Trout, "*Amicitia, auctoritas*, and Self-fashioning Texts: Paulinus of Nola and Sulpicius Severus," *Studia Patristica* 28 (1993), 123–29; and D. Trout, *Paulinus of Nola: Life, Letters, and Poems* (Berkeley 1999).

59. CA 25 (CSEL 35.70: *vitia gratulantur*). Mratschek, *Der Briefwechsel*, 512–17, on the letter in general. According to H. Chantraine, "Das Schisma 418/419 und das Eingreifen der kaiserlichen Gewalt in die römische Bishofwahl," in *Alte Geschichte und Wissenschaftsgeschiche: Festschrift K. Christ*, ed. P. Kneissl and V. Losemann (Darmstadt 1988), 87f., the two camps, vice versus virtue, represented Boniface, whom Galla supported, and Eulalius, his rival, whom she opposed. Oost, *Galla Placidia*, 158, 167, believes the opposite.

Italy and Africa, the court acted as a promoter of ecclesiastical unity. In the fluctuating landscape of papal politics it was critical to present the court through masculine ceremony endorsed by feminine piety. Moreover, as a former resident of Rome, Galla would have been fully aware of the constant fermentation that characterized papal, imperial, and senatorial relations in the city.

In the context of the struggle between two papal factions, the inability of the local civic authorities, the aversion of the court to interfere, the inconclusiveness of synods held in the shade of the palace at Ravenna, and the ultimate unilateral decision of the emperor without episcopal endorsement illuminated the need to forge a balance between Rome and Ravenna. To ensure coexistence rather than competitiveness would become the underpinning of Galla's papal politics. The contested papal elections of 418/419 further established Galla's new husband, Constantius, as a model of political prudence. In the sole missive that he signed during the feverish correspondence that had accompanied the affair, he instructed the prefect of Rome, in response to the latter's two lengthy reports regarding Eulalius's disregard of the imperial injunction to stay out of Rome, to follow Honorius's instructions to the letter.[60] His own will or opinion, if he had any, were withheld.[61] Notwithstanding their lack of originality, the letters issued by Galla and by Constantius, by virtue of repetition and insistence, constructed the couple as an indivisible unity complementing the authority of the emperor.

Scenes from the Court

Had a panegyric addressed to Galla survived, it would in all likelihood have resembled the sole surviving example of an oration addressed to an empress in late antiquity, Julian's speech to Eusebia, wife (or rather one of the wives) of the emperor Constantius II (Julian's uncle).[62] The speech

---

60. *CA* 29 and 32 (Symmachus's reports); *CA* 30 (Constantius's response). Eng. trans. of the latter in Coleman-Norton, II, no. 363.

61. In the same year (418 or 419) Constantius reiterated the imperial order to expel Pelagius and his chief supporters from Rome, *PL* 45.1750; 48, 404–7. Eng. trans. in Coleman-Norton, II. no. 373 (who wrongly dates it to 421). Oost, *Galla Placidia*, 150 n. 42, on the date. Brown, "Pelagius and His Supporters," on the impact of the movement on the social landscape of Roman Christianity.

62. Eng. trans. in *The Works of the Emperor Julian*, Loeb I, 285–93. On Eusebia, see the incomparable entry in . . . *Wikipedia*.

contains the conventional themes of birth, ancestry and connections, upbringing, her suitability as an imperial consort, and, above all, the conventional wifely virtues, here amplified by her husband's eminent position. Eusebia is expected to exert a mitigating influence (temperance, justice, wisdom) over her husband—the woman's soft touch, so to speak. It seems that, important as she clearly was, she had no existence outside the marriage:

> She has become [soon after their wedding] the partner of her husband's counsels, and though the emperor is by nature merciful, good and wise, she encourages him to follow yet more becomingly his natural bent, and even turns justice to mercy. . . . She never urged her husband to inflict injury of any kind, nor punishment or chastisement even on a single household, much less on a city or a kingdom.[63]

A panegyric composed in Galla's honor as an imperial consort would likewise have dwelled on such virtues. No handbook of rhetoric offered guidelines on how to address an empress whose rank outshone that of her husband who, in turn, was not the sole emperor of the western Roman Empire.

We know little of the brief, yet apparently tumultuous, marriage of Galla with Constantius. An insight is provided by two curious incidents, each dealing with miracles and miracle makers. One involved a man named Asclepius, steward of the estates that she and Constantius owned in Sicily:

> R[h]egium is the metropolis of Bruttium. Alaric wished to cross from there to Sicily but was prevented. The reason was that a statue endowed with magic powers was standing there and it thwarted the crossing. This statue was consecrated by the ancients to ward off the fires of Etna and to prevent the barbarians from crossing by sea. In one foot there was a perpetual flame, in the other a never ending spring. When it was destroyed, Sicily later suffered harm from both Etna's fires and the barbarians. It was Asclepius, who had been appointed steward of the Sicilian estates of Constantius and [Galla] Placidia, who overthrew the statue.[64]

63. Loeb trans. I, 305–9. See also Tougher (below, ch. 4 n. 14) on the speech.
64. Olympiodorus, fr. 16 (Blockley).

The island had its fair share of apparitions where ghosts of enemy cavalry would be seen charging, especially at high noon.[65] That Galla, and Constantius, would order or condone the demolition of a venerable statue a decade after it had apparently so effectively put a stop to Alaric's attempt to cross over to Sicily (in 410) and thence to Africa reflects a determination to fight local traditions touched by magic. Attitudes toward pagan monuments, like Rhegium's statue, varied considerably, from preservation and veneration as art objects to defacement, dismemberment, and destruction.[66] The destruction of the Sicilian statue, as Olympiodorus maintained, was an act of spectacular and unnecessary brutality. It was hardly unique. The destruction of the Sarapeum in Alexandria (c. 390) and of the Marneion in Gaza (c. 400), two temples whose divinities had presided over the welfare of the inhabitants for centuries, provided a precedent.[67] Moreover, the miraculous powers invested in the Sicilian statue deflated imperial claims of earthly victories over barbarians. By ridding Sicily of the fiery and watery monument that had saved the island from the Goths, Galla had the opportunity at the dawn of her second marriage to dissociate herself from her Gothic past.

Olympiodorus, the historian who reported the affair of the Sicilian statue, also recorded another episode in which statues were destroyed by an imperial order, this time before, rather than after, performing due miracles. When the court was informed of the discovery of a treasure of silver statues in Thrace, the emperor (whom Olympiodorus identified as Constantius III) ordered their removal.[68] Subsequent excavations revealed three silver statues carved to represent barbarians, each facing northward toward barbarian lands. Local traditions had sanctified both locality and statues in the belief that they provided much-needed protection. The forced removal of the statues, claimed Olympiodorus, left

65. Damascius, *Philosophical History* 50 (ed. and trans. P. Athanassiadi).

66. H. Saradi-Mendelovici, "Christian Attitudes toward Pagan Monuments in Late Antiquity and Their Legacy in Later Byzantine Centuries," *DOP* 44 (1990), 47–61, esp. 59.

67. J. Hahn, "The Conversion of Cult Statues: The Destruction of the Serapeum and the Transformation of Alexandria into the 'Christ-Loving' City," in *From Temple to Church: Destruction and Renewal of Local Cultic Topography in Late Antiquity*, ed. J. Hahn et al. (Leiden 2008), 335–65, on the former; Sivan, *Palestine in Late Antiquity*, passim, on the latter.

68. Olympiodorus, fr. 27 (Blockley). On this episode, as well as on the Rhegium statue, G. Marasco, "La magia e la guerra," *Millennium: Jahrbuch zu Kultur und Geschichte des ersten Jahrtausends n. Chr.= Yearbook on the Culture and History of the First Millennium CE* 1 (2004), 99–103.

Thrace open to Gothic, Hunnic, and Sarmatian invasions, just as the destruction of the Sicilian statue denuded Sicily of defense.[69]

Acts of deliberately violating pagan monuments had already been associated with another female member of the Theodosian house, namely Serena, Theodosius's niece and adopted daughter, in whose execution in 409 Galla apparently had been complicit. In 394, on the occasion of an imperial visit of Theodosius I to the city after his victory over the usurper Eugenius, Serena entered the temple of the goddess Cybele at Rome and unceremoniously removed precious ornaments from the neck of the goddess's statue, placing them on her own neck.[70] The humiliation of the Great Mother had been designed to counteract the fanfare with which Nicomachus Flavianus, Eugenius's chief senatorial supporter, had celebrated the goddess's festival in the very same year at the very same place.[71] Nor did Serena's gesture pass without protest and punishment, according to Zosimus. Years later (in 409) she had to submit her own neck to the executioner.

As protector of Christian and imperial values, Galla turned from the destruction of inanimate objects to the execution of humans who, like the Sicilian and the Thracian statues, bore an unsanctioned message of salvation:

> A certain Libanius, an Asian by race, came to Ravenna during the reign of Honorius and Constantius. Libanius was a consummate magician, able to achieve results even against barbarians without resorting to weapons, which was precisely what he promised to do. He was granted permission to make the attempt. But when his promise and his high repute came to

69. Marasco, "La magia e la guerra," 102, dates the Thracian episode to 421 but notes that Thrace apparently belonged then to the east rather than the west. The reference to Constantius is explained on grounds of Olympiodorus's organization of his work. The omission of both Honorius, the senior emperor, and of Theodosius II remain inexplicable. Perhaps the similarity between the Rhegium and the Thrace incidents led Olympiodorus deliberately to associate both with Constantius and with Galla, whose name was omitted in the extracting of the Thrace story by Photius. P. Heather and J. F. Matthews, *Goths and Romans 332–489* (Oxford 1991), 262, assign the Thracian episode to 427 and link it with the resettlement of the Pannonian Goths in Thrace. I am less convinced by the constant reference to Galla's religious zeal as an explanation (Marasco, "La magia e la guerra," 99; Sirago, Galla Placidia e la trasformazione, 205; Oost, *Galla Placidia*, 102, 144; Caffin, *Galla Placidia*, 175) as an explanation of the reactions to either the Rhegium or the Thracian statues.

70. Zosimus, 5.38.2–5.

71. Matthews, *Western Aristocracies*, 242, on Flavianus and Cybele in 394, dating the solemnities to March. The connection with Serena's defiance of the same goddess has not been hitherto made. On Flavianus's eventual rehabilitation under Galla's auspices, see ch. 4.

the ears of the empress [Galla] Placidia, the magician was put
to death. For [Galla] Placidia threatened Constantius that she
would break up their marriage if Libanius, a wizard and an
unbeliever, remained amongst the living.[72]

How, precisely, Libanius intended to win wars over barbarians is not
disclosed. Would he have used a spell, like those pronounced to rid the
sick of illness, while likening barbarians to the maladies that attack various parts of the human body?

Go away, no matter whether you originated today or earlier:
this disease, this illness, this pain, this swelling, this redness,
this goiter, these tonsils, this abscess, this tumor, these glands
and the little glands I call forth, I lead forth, I speak forth,
through this spell, from these limbs and bones [depart?].[73]

Would he have demonstrated his control over nature, inciting the elements to strike the barbarians? According to Iamblichus (c. 250–325),
it was precisely "power through sympathy" and "sympathy through
power" that moved the gods to act through the magus (magician):[74]

The theurgist, by virtue of mysterious signs, controls the power
of nature. Not as a mere human being or as one possessing a
human soul, but as one of a higher rank of gods, he gives
orders that are not appropriate to the condition of man. He
does not really expect to perform all these amazing things. But
by using such words he shows what kind of power he has and
how great he is, and that because of his knowledge of these
mysterious symbols he is obviously in touch with the gods.[75]

What appeared objectionable in Galla's circles was not the promise
of victories but Libanius's unauthorized form of divination. The rise of
the so-called holy man in late antiquity was made possible by dazzling
miracles.[76] If performed in the name of Christ, the mantle of legitimacy

---

72. Olympiodorus, fr. 36 (Blockley).
73. *De medicamentis* 15.11, Eng. trans. G. Luck, *Arcana Mundi* (Baltimore 1985), 73.
74. Luck, *Arcana*, 4.
75. Iamblichus, *Mys.* 6.6., Eng. trans. Luck, *Arcana*, 22–23.
76. P. Brown, "Sorcery, Demons and the Rise of Christianity: From Late Antiquity into the
Middle Ages," in *Witchcraft Confessions and Accusations: Association of Social Anthropologists
Monographs* 9 (1970), 56–72; P. Brown, "The Rise and Function of the Holy Man in Late Antiquity,"
JRS 61 (1971), 80–101.

would descend upon both magician and magic.[77] Gaza's first holy man, Hilarion, appeared in the mid-fourth century on the Gazan racing stage as a saintly supporter of a charioteer who proclaimed his victory in the races as a proof of Jesus' superiority over the Gazan "enemies of God," namely pagans.[78] In Spanish Tarragona, a monk named Fronto charged local noble families and clergy with sorcery and heresy.[79] The accusation alienated even the governor, who sent a servant to "stop Fronto from barking." That same day the servant died of a stroke, an event that some interpreted as a murder, others as a miracle. The line between the two must have run rather thinly.

At Ravenna, Libanius apparently won over both Honorius and Constantius. If he appeared in 421, as seems likely, his timing was rather poor.[80] Precisely then, the emperor least needed supernatural support: the Goths had been defeated and peacefully settled in Aquitania (the southwestern Gallic region); northern Gaul that seemed all but lost in 416 apparently returned to the Roman fold; the barbarians who had invaded Spain in 409 had been defeated; and there were even prospects of restoring Britain to the imperial fold.[81]

Neither Honorius nor Constantius apparently attempted to save their alleged savior from Galla's wrath. The legal process against Libanius, if such was instituted, could have relied on an imperial law of 389 that empowered individuals to expose magicians:

> If anyone should hear of a person who is contaminated with
> the pollution of magic, or if he should apprehend or seize such
> a person, he shall drag him out immediately before the public

---

77. On magic in late antiquity, see the review of D. Frankfurter in *BMCR* 2005.05.32. On criminalizing magic and magicians as religious deviants, see J. C. Rives, "Magic, Religion, and Law: The Case of the *Lex Cornelia de sicariis et veneficiis*," in *Religion and Law in Classical and Christian Rome*, ed. C. Ando and J. Rüpke (Stuttgart 2006), 47–67; on legislation banning magic, C. Pharr, "The Interdiction of Magic in Roman Law," *TAPA* 63 (1932), 269–95.

78. Jerome, *VH* 2 (c. 350); Sivan, *Palestine in Late Antiquity*, passim.

79. Augustine, *Ep.* 11* (Divjak), dated to 419.

80. On this episode, Marasco, "La magia e la guerra," 117, who maintains that the court accepted Libanius at a moment of extreme danger from barbarians without, however, further specification.

81. Halsall, *Barbarian Migrations*, 224–34, on the supremacy of Constantius, although his assumption of the 418 Visigothic settlement as a temporary solution is not borne out (p. 232) unless the arrangement had been conceived along the lines of traditional *hospitalitas*, H. Sivan, "On Foederati, Hospitalitas and the Settlement of the Visigoths in AD 418," *American Journal of Philology* 108 (1987), 759–772. On Constantius's career see, in great detail, W. Lütkenhaus, *Constantius III: Studien zu seiner Tätigkeit und Stellung im Westreich 411–21* (Bonn 1998).

and shall show the enemy of the common safety to the eyes of the courts.[82]

Libanius's grim end was likewise anchored in precedents and legal provisions. Magic was often equated with treason—in Antioch, when notable intellectuals and local dignitaries were accused of treason, the allegedly guilty were subjected to torture and execution, while the books that allegedly contained their magical arts were burned in public.[83] Libanius's past successes would have been his downfall. As in the case of successful charioteers, "when victory cannot be attributed to the quality of the horses, it is inevitably attributed to magical cheating."[84] If the whole affair was accurately reported, Galla seized both popular prejudice and legal precedents to bring about Libanius's death.

She apparently also threatened Constantius with divorce. If reported correctly, in this case Galla could resort to a law of Constantine that granted women unilateral divorce if husbands were guilty of murder, of preparing poisons, or of disturbing the peace of the dead.[85] Rescinded by Julian (c. 360), this law was revived in March 421 by Galla's own brother and husband. It allowed women to divorce their husbands even on grounds of character defects and trivial faults, but penalized such displays of marital dissatisfaction with loss of dowry and with forbidding second marriage.[86] If the husband was guilty of serious criminal acts, such as adultery and the promotion of paganism (the latter including divination and magical arts), she could keep her dowry and remarry after five years.

Whatever unanimity or discord Galla and Constantius would have shared in matters of orthodoxy, the marriage was marred by what the historian Olympiodorus regarded as Galla's negative influence over a person who, prior to his marriage, had been a "cheerful and affable man."[87]

---

82. *CTh* 9.16.11 = *CJ* 9.19.9 (Eng. trans. Pharr).

83. *Amm.* 29.1–2 (370). On burning of bodies and books, J. Herrin, "Book Burning as Purification," in *Transformations of Late Antiquity: Essays for Peter Brown*, ed. P. Rousseau and M. Papoutsakis (Farnham 2009), 205–22.

84. Cassiodorus, *Var.* 3.51.2 (Eng. trans. Barnish). On the association of magical practices and charioteers, P. Lee-Stecum, "Dangerous Reputations: Charioteers and Magic in Fourth Century Rome," *G&R* 53 (2006), 224–34.

85. *CTh* 3.16.1 (331 C.E.); J. Evans Grubbs, *Law and Family in Late Antiquity: The Emperor Constantine's Marriage Legislation* (Oxford 1995), 228–29.

86. *CTh* 3.16.2; Evans Grubbs, *Law and Family*, 234.

87. Olympiodorus, fr. 23 (Blockley), on Constantius's bonhomie at parties versus his gloominess in public.

Constantius had been free of greed until he married Placidia. When he was joined to her, he fell into lust for money. After his death Ravenna was inundated from all sides with suits over his misappropriation of possessions. But Honorius' unresponsiveness and the close relationship of Placidia to him rendered both the complaints and the power of justice ineffectual.[88]

The extent of the couple's holdings is unknown. The affair of the Sicilian statue implied that they had estates on the island.[89] Compared with the vast geographical spread of senatorial properties, the land owned by the couple, if only in Italy and Sicily, would have been rather modest.[90]

By 419, following the birth of a son, Valentinian, two concerns, or rather ambitions, would have been uppermost in Galla's mind. One was the formal recognition of her son as the "noblest child," a crucial step on the way to the imperial throne. The other would have been her own elevation to the rank of Augusta, a title reserved for emperors and one rarely bestowed on female members of the imperial family. It denoted a status that no other member of Roman society, besides the emperor, possessed or could aspire to. On February 8, 421, Honorius elevated his brother-in-law as coemperor and Augustus, "rather unwillingly" and after much nagging on Galla's part.[91] The appointment followed Constantius's third consulship in that year. It was followed by another ceremony, the joint proclamation of Galla as Augusta by brother and husband. Galla's relatives at the court in Constantinople did not rejoice.[92]

Whatever reasons propelled Constantius to the purple, the man himself had second thoughts regarding the whole affair, since he apparently regretted the constraints of court ceremonials and greatly missed

88. Olympiodorus, fr. 37 (Blockley).

89. The Sicilian patrimony may have formed the basis of the holdings of the Ravennate church, recorded by Agnellus 31 and 111, Oost, *Galla Placidia*, 267; with W. Schild, *Galla Placidia* (Halle 1897), 65. See now A. Fasoli, "Il patrimonio della chiesa Ravennate," in *Storia di Ravenna*, ed. A. Carile (Venice 1991), 2.1.389–400.

90. A. H. M. Jones, *The Later Roman Empire*, 2 vols. (Norman Okla. 1964), 782, on patterns of senatorial landholding.

91. Olympiodorus, fr. 33 (Blockley).

92. Philostorgius, *HE* 12.12 (Eng. trans. P. R. Amidon). Olympiodorus, 43.1 (Blockley) on the "restoration" of the title to Galla in late 424 as part of the preparations to return her and her children to the west. R. S. Bagnall et al., *Consuls of the Later Roman Empire* (Atlanta 1987), 420, maintain that the consulship was recognized by the eastern court although the dissemination of his name was late.

the parties that he used to enjoy.[93] Many of the men who obtained the purple in the fourth century had come, like Constantius, from camp to court. Some may have missed the camaraderie of their fellow soldiers; others perhaps relished the exceptionally cumbersome court rituals. Constantius's reign lasted a few months, as he had dreamed, and he died in the midst of preparing an expedition against his new relatives in the east.[94]

Galla's reaction to the loss of her second husband is not recorded. Her literary talent probably did not extend to touching tributes like the one that the noble Paulina composed in honor of her husband, the Roman aristocrat Praetextatus:

> Because of you [Praetextatus], everyone proclaims me holy, everyone proclaims me blessed, because you yourself have spread my goodness throughout the world. Though unknown I am known to all. For with you as my husband, how could I fail to please? The mothers of Romulus' city seek me as a model and regard their offspring as beautiful if it resembles yours. . . . Robbed of all of this I, your grief stricken wife, am wasting away. Happy would I have been had the gods granted that my husband had outlived me.[95]

Nor can one envisage the convivial Constantius addressing Galla with the touching words that Praetextatus addressed to Paulina:

> Paulina, partner of my heart, nurse of modesty, bond of chastity, pure love and loyalty produced in heaven, to whom I have entrusted the deep hidden secrets of my heart, gift of the gods who bind our marriage couch with friendly and modest ties. By the devotion of a mother, the gratitude of a wife, the bond of a sister, the modesty of a daughter, and by all the loyalty friends show we are united by the custom of age, the pact of consecration, by the yoke of the marriage vow and

93. Olympiodorus, fr. 33 (Blockley).

94. The timing may have been propitious since the east was locked in battle with both Persia and the Huns, neither bringing a decisive victory although the former was celebrated on coins and in literary accounts, including a poem by the talented empress Eudocia; Holum, *Theodosian Empresses*, 122, 129; T. Urbainczyk, *Socrates of Constantinople: Historian of Church and State* (Ann Arbor 1997), 32–33.

95. *CIL* 6.1779 = *ILS* 1259 (Rome, late fourth century), Eng. trans. in B. Croke and J. Harries, *Religious Conflict in Fourth Century Rome* (Sydney 1982), 106–8.

of perfect harmony, helpmate of your husband, loving, adoring, devoted.[96]

More than likely, Galla and Honorius would have erected a tombstone that described the deceased *cursus honorum*, namely all the offices that he had held, culminating in his elevation to the imperial throne.

The removal of the court's most effective mainspring prompted a paradox:

> The affection of Honorius towards his sister [Galla] grew so great after the death of her husband that their immoderate pleasure in each other and their constant kissing on the mouth caused many people to entertain shameful suspicions about them.[97]

An attempt to read this ambiguous relationship as an expression of womanly wiles sealed Galla's fate at the court. Several of her closest attendants (Spadusa, Elpidia, and Leontius) hatched a plan that entailed public brawls between Galla's Gothic retinue and unnamed parties. How and why this domestic dissension spilled into the streets of Ravenna and who stood to benefit from sowing strife between the royal siblings is to be sought in the web of intrigues that customarily vibrated through the imperial courts. It must have been obvious that Galla's status hinged on the will and whim of her brother, especially after Constantius's demise. Someone had instigated allegations of unlawful seizure of property by Constantius. These allegations failed to tarnish the reputation of the dead emperor, nor were previous owners able to regain lost assets, but the events pointed to Galla's vulnerability.[98] Galla's enemies turned to incite friction among the groups that roamed the narrow alleys of Ravenna. Regardless of outcome, such clashes would have highlighted Galla's inability to control her own retinue.

Soiled by allegations of sexual misconduct (with her own blood brother, to use her favorite expression when describing Honorius), Galla fell from favor. She lost the much-coveted title of Augusta, thus effectively reverting to the status of an ordinary citizen.[99] Contemporary

---

96. Ibid.

97. Olympiodorus, fr. 38 (Blockley).

98. Olympiodorus, fr. 37 (Blockley); Oost, *Galla Placidia*, 171, regards this as the opening move by Placidia's enemies in the power struggle after Constantius's death.

99. Olympiodorus, fr. 43 states that Theodosius II gave Placidia back her title, implying that she had lost it at some point. If this is accurate, the most likely point was her exile in 423.

chroniclers were ignorant of the specific reason that led to her expulsion, or voluntary removal, from the court.[100] It was effective enough to engineer considerable distance between Galla and Ravenna. A move to Rome in 423 may have followed. But shortly thereafter, Galla and her children fled to Constantinople. The hasty move was probably connected with the elevation of John to the imperial throne after Honorius's sudden death in 423. Perhaps she fled John to avoid a repetition of the harsh treatment to which she had been subjected in 415 at the hand of Athaulf's killer and successor. The journey by sea to Constantinople proved exceptionally difficult. Upon return to Italy, Galla dedicated a church in honor of John the Evangelist, to whose help she ascribed timely succor:

> When she was going through the precarious dangers of the
> sea, with a storm having arisen, the keel tossed by waves,
> thinking she would be drowned in the deep, she vowed to
> build a church for the apostle [John]. And she was freed from
> the fury of the sea. Within the apse of this church over the
> heads of the emperors and empresses, it reads thus: "Confirm,
> God, that which you have accomplished for us, from your
> temple in Jerusalem, kings offer you gifts." And above it reads:
> "To the holy and most blessed apostle John the Evangelist,
> *Galla Placidia Augusta*, with her son *Placidus Valentinianus
> Augustus* and her daughter *Iusta Grata Honoria Augusta* fulfill
> the vow of liberation from the dangers of the sea."[101]

In spite of the tenuous connection of John the Evangelist with saving from the sea, Galla's choice appears deliberate. John had been associated with Theodosius's victory over the usurper Eugenius in 394.[102] Galla's

---

100. Prosper s.a. 423 refers to the expulsion to the east (*pulsa ad orientem cum filiis*). In the sixth century Cassiodorus (*Chron.*) claimed that she had been suspected of collusion with the enemy (*ob suspicionem invitatorum hostium*). The latter may have been an embellishment recalling not Galla's but her daughter's "invitation" to Attila the Hun.

101. Agnellus, *LPR* 42, Agnellus of Ravenna, *The Book of Pontiffs of the Church of Ravenna*, trans. D. M. Deliyannis (Washington, DC 2004), 151 and below ch. 4. J. B. Bury, "Justa Grata Honoria," *JRS* 9 (1919), 1–13, prefers to assign the storm and the vow to Galla's return with the eastern Roman infantry under Ardaburius aboard ships in 425. Perhaps trouble arose on both the outbound and the return journeys. That the return required a divine messenger to extricate Ardaburius from his sailing troubles in 425 was reported by Socrates, *HE* 7.23.

102. Theodoret, *HE* 5.24.

main and continuous claim to a public role in a government invariably conceived as entirely male rested on her dynastic connections and the legitimacy of her lineage.

A number of the major players in the months following Constantius's death, Galla's disgrace, and Honorius's death (421–423), can be identified. All were military men. They included Asterius, who emerged in 420 as *comes Hispaniarum* (in charge of the troops stationed in Spain) and was ennobled with the title of *patricius* some time between 420 and 422; Castinus, who became *comes domesticorum* (commander of the *protectores*, the troops that accompanied the emperor) in 420/421, and who inherited Constantius's supreme command of the army (*magister utriusque militiae*, chief of staff and commander of infantry and cavalry), in 422–425 and consul in 424, under John); and Bonifatius, the man destined to become his archrival, who had risen to fame during Athaulf's siege of Marseilles in 413, to become a military tribune in 417 in Africa and *comes* (commander of the troops) stationed in the province in 423/424–425.[103] The fourth of the soldiery quartet was Felix, who was to succeed Castinus as *magister utriusque militiae* in 425 (under Galla and Valentinian III), a man whose beginnings remain obscure.[104] Felix's wife bore the name Spadusa. She could have been the Padusia named as Galla's confidante who coconspired to deprive her patroness of her court privileges.[105]

Castinus elected to support John, chief notary, who seized the throne at Rome in 423. Both miscalculated the extent of the opposition.[106] They had to contend with Galla's sole supporter in the west, Bonifatius, *comes Africae* (governor and commander of the troops stationed there), who controlled the granaries that fed the citizens of Rome.[107] In Constantinople, Theodosius II refused to recognize John's

---

103 .*PLRE II* (Asterius 4); *PLRE II* (Castinus 2); *PLRE II* (Bonifatius 3). Castinus owed his 424 consulship to John rather than to Theodosius, pace *CLRE* s.a. 424 and contra O. Seeck, *Regesten der Kaiser und Päpste für die Jahre 311 bis 476 n.C.* (Stuttgart 1919), 349, and his followers. Whether Castinus also contributed to Galla's disgrace and exile, as claimed by G. Zecchini, *Aezio, l'ultima difesa dell'Occidente romano* (Rome 1983), 127–32, no. 25, is possible but difficult to prove. On Galla's return in 425 Castinus was indeed exiled, allegedly finding refuge in Africa with Bonifatius.

104. *PLRE II* (Felix 14).

105. Oost, *Galla Placidia*, 170.

106. *PLRE II*, 595 (Ioannes 5).

107. *PLRE II*, 238, suggests that Bonifatius may have been appointed *comes Africae* by Theodosius II, a likely but unprovable proposition. His loyalty to Galla may have stemmed from an appointment by her brother rather than her nephew.

regime, preferring eventually to support Galla's son.[108] In 425 mother, son (Valentinian), and sister (Honoria), accompanied by contingents of the eastern army, were sent back to Italy after Theodosius II conferred on Valentinian the title of Augustus, effectively making him Honorius's heir and emperor of the western Roman Empire. That Galla had a significant say in the matter should not be doubted.[109] By late 425 Valentinian III, age six, was installed in Ravenna as emperor.[110] Chief among the men who smoothed the transition between John and Valentinian III was Candidianus, the namesake of the man who had engineered the Narbonese wedding of Galla and Athaulf in 414.[111] Celebrations followed:

> [Galla] Placidia and her son the Caesar entered Ravenna. Helion, the master of the offices and patrician, went to Rome and, when all had assembled there, he placed the robe of the emperor upon Valentinian who was in his seventh year. At this point the History ends.[112]

On this seemingly happy note ended the records that the historian Olympiodorus gathered. John lost his head, having first his hand cut off in the northern Italian city of Aquileia, perhaps in the very presence of Galla and Valentinian.[113] Aetius, another of John's supporters, decided to change sides and was subsequently engaged to fight wars on behalf of Galla and Valentinian. The throne of Valentinian I and Theodosius I once again rested on the head of a direct if rather puerile descendant. Galla, once again an Augusta, seemed poised to hold the reins of empire.

108. Theodosius II had coins minted in her name as a mark of recognition of her status already in 424. She is named Aelia Placidia Augusta with no reference to Galla. The reverse shows Victory and a large cross; P. Grierson and M. Mays, *Catalogue of Late Roman Coins in the Dumbarton Oaks Collection* (Washington, DC 1992), 230–31.

109. Galla has been accredited with the initiative of Theodosius II to send an army to seize the city of Salona on the Dalmatian coast in 424/425 after Honorius's death to prevent it from falling into John's hands. Her sojourn there on the way back to Italy has been linked with the city's defensive improvements; J. J. Wilkes, "A Pannonian Refugee of Quality at Salona," *Phoenix* 26 (1972), 388–89 [377–93].

110. He had been raised to the rank of Caesar at Thessalonike on October 23, 424, and precisely a year later at Rome.

111. *PLRE II* Candidianus 2 and Candidianus 3. Could the two be one and the same man? The possibility should not be dismissed as the editors of *PLRE* suggest.

112. Olympiodorus, fr. 43.1 (Blockley). I agree with Seeck, *Regesten* 350, contra *CLRE* s.a. 426 that Valentinian III was proclaimed Augustus in Rome and not in Ravenna (on October 23).

113. Olympiodorus, fr. 43.2 (Blockley). This is the last time that the city features in history before its destruction by Attila in 452 and its transfer to Grado; C. Sotinel, *Identité civique et Christianisme: Aquilée du IIIe au Vie siècle* (Rome 2005), passim.

The moment of Valentinian's investiture was commemorated in a beautiful intaglio, now at the Hermitage, created by an artist who signed his name as Romulus.[114] The picture contains five figures. At its center stands a boy atop a platform, with a chrismon (a Chi-Rho) conspicuously above his head. Flanking him are two men: one, wearing a diadem, is shown in the act of placing a tunic (chlamys) on the boy; the other, slightly smaller than his counterpart, is crowning the boy with a wreath. Two winged figures further flank the two males, each holding a laurel wreath above their heads. The moment thus captured is not entirely clear. It may have related to the naming of Valentinian, Galla's son, as *nobilissimus puer* (the most noble boy of all) in 421 by Honorius and Constantius III. More likely, this unparalleled object of art represented Valentinian's double coronation—his 424 elevation in Thessalonike to the rank of Caesar by Theodosius II, and the 425 proclamation as Augustus in Rome by Helion, Theodosius's ambassador. Galla's absence from the all-male representation seems pointed.

Yet the citizens of the African town of Lambaesis recorded the moment of elevation in a beautifully phrased inscription that features Galla as her son's guardian. Depicted as mother of a Christianized Jupiter, she is a worthy member of an imperial trio:

> Rising as the brightest star of this earthly realm,
> Valentinian, under the guardianship of the illustrious
>   Placidia,
> Consecrating the rule of arms, puts aside his thunderbolts;
> Theodosius, reveling in peace, pursues his learned craft.[115]

A triumphant return of the mother notwithstanding her omission from the coronation intaglio. Gold coins (*solidi*) minted in Galla's name in

114. The following relies on MacCormack, *Art and Ceremony in Late Antiquity*, 229 and plate 43 with its ample caption.

115. "Fulgida conscendens terraeni sidera regni / [imperiu]m dedicans armorum fulmina condit / [Placidiae] gra[ndis t]utela Valentinianus: / pace fruens doctam exercet Theodosius artem." *CIL* 8.8481 = *ILS* 802 (Lambaesis, North Africa), text and translation in C. W. Hedrick, *History and Silence: Purge and Rehabilitation of Memory in Late Antiquity* (Austin 2000), 203. Translation here is based on both Hedrick and C. Kelly, "Empire Building," in *Interpreting Late Antiquity*, ed. P. Brown et al. (Cambridge Mass. 2001), 175; note also Kelly's different rendering of the third verse as "Devoted to the clash of arms, he preserved the empire." According to Kelly, the inscription had been set up in Sitifis (Mauretania, modern Sétif in Algeria) in 425 following Valentinian III's elevation to coemperorship, with C. Lepelley, *Les cités de l'Afrique romaine au Bas-Empire* (Paris 1979–1981), 2:497–503.

Aquileia and Rome in 424/425 proclaimed Galla's newly acquired status as the imperial mother par excellence. Their obverse bears her portrait bust surrounded by the legend "DN Galla Placidia PF Aug" (*domina nostra, pia felix, augusta*; our lady, GP, pious and fortunate, *augusta*). She is bedecked and bejeweled, her crown bestowed not by humans but by the very hand of God. On her shoulder a chrismon is conspicuously displayed.[116] The obverse displays a winged victory holding another chrismon. Such repetition seems pointed. On both intaglio and coins mother and son proclaim their religious affiliation. Both are shown legitimized by a higher authority. Yet Valentinian's rank, as depicted on the intaglio, is indebted to human sources of authority; Galla's status is derived directly from the ultimate source of all, God.

In spite of the "marvelous good fortune" that one historian accredited Galla with in 425, the territory of Valentinian III was hardly a coveted heirloom.[117] The Visigoths had marched beyond their Aquitanian territories to menace Arles, capital of the Gauls; the Vandals were still in Spain, as were the Suevi, while the northern frontiers were in constant danger of further barbarian invasions. The loyalty of either civil administrators or of generals was far from assured, easily withering under the weight of accusations of conspiracies.

116. Grierson and Mays, *Catalogue of Late Roman Coins*, 230–31, noting similarities and differences between these and the coins minted in Pulcheria's name in the early 420s, the apparent source of inspiration of Galla's issues.

117. Prosper, s.a. 425: "Placidia Augusta et Valentinianus Caesar mira felicitate Iohannesm tyrannum opprimunt et regnum victores recipiunt."

CHAPTER FOUR

Restoration and Rehabilitation
(425–431)

*Rejoice with us, senators, in the excellent work of our reign, recollect
with us and lend your approval to the restoration of the senator's memory and
dignity to you and to our country.*[1]

*Galla Placidia Augusta discharged the vow made to the holy
and most blessed apostle John the Evangelist when freed
from the danger of the sea.*[2]

Amnesty and Senatorial Politics

On October 23, 425, Valentinian was proclaimed Augustus at Rome.[3]
That Rome, the old imperial capital, and not Ravenna, Honorius's
favored residence, or Milan, capital of the western empire in the late
fourth century, was the stage for the confirmation of Valentinian III as
the new ruler of the western provinces hints at a confluence of nostalgia
and necessity. Galla had spent her adolescence in the city. In 423 when
she had to leave Ravenna under duress, she headed to Rome before
turning east to Constantinople. In 425 Galla and her children returned
to Rome with pomp and ceremony. Their progress throughout the

1. "Gaudete ergo patres conscripti, optimo imperii nostri opere, ut nobiscum recognoscitis et redditam vobis et patriae senatoris eius memoriam et dignitatem probate," *CIL* 6.1783 (Rome, 431), reproduced in Hedrick, *History and Silence*, 3–5 (text and trans.); 247–58 (notes).
2. "Sancto et beatissimo apostolo Ioanni Evangelistae Galla Placidia Augusta . . . liberationis periculum maris votum solvit," *CIL* 11.276 = *ILS* 818 = *ILCV* 20 (Ravenna), reproduced in Rebenich, "Gratian" (ch. 1 n. 13), 372.
3. See ch. 3 n. 111 on the location.

streets of the ecstatic city would have echoed the fanfare of the famed *adventus* of the emperor Constantius II in 357.[4] Then, as perhaps in 425, mother and son would have been borne "in a golden chariot, shimmering in the glitter of various kinds of precious stones." Rome's gaping citizenry, decked in its festive best, would have accompanied the stately parade with shouts of approval and sonorous hymns. By one account, so much gold on display would have stunned and amazed onlookers, even to the point of instilling terror.[5] These "choreographed ceremonies," or arrested moment of majestic return, associated legitimacy with ritual.[6] Soon the mosaics of Ravenna, likewise gleaming with gold, would represent the idyllic and the heroic, and the aspirations of the Valentinian-Theodosian dynasty to float in an eternal present.

The presence at Rome of the new child emperor, his mother, and contingents of the eastern Roman army was calculated to project a message of monopoly. Helion, the officer who conducted the investiture ceremonies, was an appointee of Theodosius II.[7] So was the new chief attorney (*quaestor sacri palatii*), a legal expert named Antiochus who held the quaestorship in 425–426.[8] A year before the Roman ceremony, another formality had taken place at Thessalonike where Theodosius II appointed Valentinian Caesar. The city was an imperial residence (of the eastern emperors) and metropolitan of the Illyric prefecture, a much-contested territory. Illyricum had belonged to the west under Valentinian I but was ceded to Theodosius I and the eastern government in 379. In 387 Thessalonike offered asylum to Valentinian's widow, Justina, and her children (Valentinian II and Galla, Galla Placidia's mother). In that city, Justina launched a tearful and eloquent appeal to Theodosius to reinstate her son as emperor, a petition that she reinforced with the presentation of her lovely daughter to the seasoned and widowed soldier.[9] The crowning of the young Valentinian III in 424 in a

---

4. Ammianus Marcellinus 16.10.4–10. Although Eusebia, Constantius's wife, accompanied him to Rome in 357, it is unclear whether she participated in the *adventus*.

5. Eusebius, *In Praise of Constantine* 5.6, with C. Kelly, "Empire Building," 173. In general on the use of gold, Janes, *God and Gold*, passim.

6. Kelly, "Empire Building," 172, for the expression.

7. *PLRE II*, 533 (Helion 1)—he was *magister officiorum* in the east between 414 and 427 and rewarded with the patriciate between 424 and 425. He may have been one of Galla's supporters at the court of Theodosius II.

8. T. Honoré, *Law in the Crisis of Empire* (Oxford 1998), 112, for Antiochus the younger; ibid, 256, for the older Antiochus as the western quaestor.

9. See ch. 1.

city that his maternal grandfather and namesake had once controlled was a reminder of historical irreversibility.

From Thessalonike, five laws were issued in the names of both Valentinian and Theodosius II. These dealt with heretics, clerics, and the pope.[10] Galla's imprint seemed evident in a small yet significant detail— one of the laws referred to the bishop of Rome as "pope" (*papa*), a term that Galla had used in her correspondence on the disputed papal elections of 418/419.[11] In the vast corpus of laws that bore the name of Theodosius (II), this was the only time that the Roman bishop was designated by this term.

At Rome the senate would have accompanied the rituals of Valentinian's accession with a carefully orchestrated reception, noisily accompanied by multiple acclamations.[12] To judge by another ceremonial presentation (of a book rather than an imperial family) to the same august senate at Rome (in 438), the senators would have heaped hundreds of good wishes on the ruling emperors, Theodosius II and Valentinian III, not neglecting to confer their blessing on the men who held chief positions in the western government.[13] Whether in 425 any senatorial acclamations included Galla is unknown. We can, however, reconstruct a fleeting image of Galla's Roman visit in 425 with the help of the emperor Julian (361–363). In a panegyric honoring the empress Eusebia, wife of his uncle the emperor Constantius II, Julian alluded to her solo visit to Rome in 354:

> I could very properly have given an account of this visit,
> describing how the people and the senate welcomed her with
> rejoicing, how they set out to meet her with enthusiasm, how
> they received her as is their custom to receive an empress.
> I could have reckoned up the amount of the expenditure, how

10. Sirmondian Constitution 6; *CTh* 16.5.62–3, 16.2.46, 16.5.64, 16.2.47, issued between July 9 and October 8, 425; Honoré, *Law*, 248–49.

11. *CTh* 16.5.62, with Honoré, *Law*, 249; see also ch. 3.

12. C. Roueché, "Acclamations in the Later Roman Empire: New Evidence from Aphrodisias," *JRS* 74 (1984), 181–99; H. U. Wiemer, "Akklamationen im spätrömischen Reich: Zur Typologie und Funktion eines Kommunikationsrituals," *Archiv für Kulturgeschichte* 86 (2004), 27–73. On acclamations at ecclesiastical synods and in public assemblies, see also R. MacMullen, *Voting about God in Early Church Councils* (New Haven 2006), 12–23.

13. F. Millar, *A Greek Roman Empire: Power and Belief under Theodosius II* (Berkeley 2006); Matthews, *Laying Down the Law*, 46–47. Of the 748 acclamations recorded in 438, 453 were addressed to Theodosius II in remote Constantinople and to Valentinian at Rome in front of the senators. See also below.

generous and splendid it was, how costly were the preparations, and how large were the sums she distributed to the presidents of the tribes and the centurions of the people.[14]

Yet the unqualified audible devotion that the senate would have displayed in 425 toward the reinstatement of the Theodosian dynasty in the west would have been tempered by recent recollections of senatorial collaboration with a usurper. In 423, during the vacuum created by Honorius's sudden death, a man named John had been proclaimed emperor at Rome with the support of the Roman senate, the Ravenna court, and the army.[15] John's reputed moderation and sense of justice would have won him senatorial admirers. His reputation was based on the fact that he neither gave ear to slanderers, nor set his hand to rob men of money, precisely the kind of abuse associated with Galla and Constantius during the latter's rule in 421.[16] John's relations with specific senators went unrecorded. In 425 Anicius Acilius Glabrio Faustus, member of a wealthy and well-established senatorial clan, was prefect of the city of Rome, an appointment conferred either by John (deemed usurper) or by Galla Placidia. If authorized by the former, such a connection failed to hurt Faustus's career.[17]

Equally meager is the information regarding the activities of the senate between 425 and 437, the dates usually associated with Galla's regency and Valentinian's minority. Yet, in one case at least, it is possible to glean her policies vis-à-vis eminent members of this influential body. A lengthy letter dated to 431 and inscribed for posterity in the Roman forum of Trajan was addressed by the two reigning emperors, Valentinian (age twelve) and Theodosius II (then about thirty years old), to the senate.[18] The occasion commemorated was the rehabilitation of a Roman

---

14. Julian, *Oration to Eusebia* (*Or.* 3, 343–44, Loeb trans.); see S. Tougher, "In Praise of an Empress: Julina's Speech of Thanks to Eusebia," in *The Propaganda of Power: The Role of Panegyric in Late Antiquity*, ed. M. Whitby (Leiden 1998), 105–23.

15. Socrates, *HE* 7.23, claims that Theodosius II concealed Honorius's death while keeping an eye on the west, presumably deliberating the succession. I would agree with Millar, *Greek Roman Empire*, 55, that Theodosius II never intended to reunite the empire in spite of advocating its legal unity.

16. Procopius, *BV* 3.3.7 (on John); see ch. 3 on Galla and Constantius.

17. Note also the establishment of a family's "hall of fame" in the forum that the Anicii Acilii had established at Rome; R. E. A. Palmer, *Studies of the Northern Campus Martius in Ancient Rome* (Transactions of the American Philosophical Society 80) (Philadelphia 1990), 48–50, esp. 50 for the expression.

18. Hedrick, *History and Silence*, passim, for lengthy analysis of the inscription.

nobleman, Virius Nichomachus Flavianus. Flavianus, the text asserts, had fallen from imperial grace because of the "jealousy of scoundrels" and "underhanded insinuations."[19] The sinister if somewhat vague verbal hand of fate that felled Flavianus overshadowed a complicated plot. Back in the early 390s Flavianus switched sides, abandoning Theodosius I (Galla's father) to support a usurper (Eugenius) by whom he had done well, reaching the highest of all civil honors, the consulate, in 394. When Eugenius was defeated by Theodosius I in 394, Flavianus committed suicide. By 431 Flavianus had been in his grave for over thirty-five years, condemned to "oblivion" (*damnatio memoriae*) for taking the wrong side in a civil war.

Galla's precise contribution to these rehabilitative proceedings remains conjectural yet not without foundation. The younger Nichomachus Flavianus, son of the disgraced consul of 394, suddenly reemerged in 431, after more than two decades of apparent inactivity, to assume the position of the praetorian prefect of Italy and Africa.[20] His most notable achievement during his 431 prefecture was to spearhead a familial endeavor to rehabilitate the grand old man, his father, an activity not ordinarily associated with the duties and responsibilities of an imperial praetorian prefect. Sometime between 400 and 408, when Galla resided in Rome, the younger Flavianus had dedicated a statue to the emperor Arcadius.[21] The monument had been erected in the heart of Rome, far from Arcadius's eastern domain. Perhaps the younger Flavianus hoped to prompt the eastern emperor to rehabilitate his father. In vain, as it turned out.

In the imperial letter of 431, the name of Arcadius's son preceded that of Galla's son. The order was perfunctory since Theodosius II was

19. *CIL* 6.1786 lines 18 and 21, with ibid., 2–3; the reasons recall those associated with Galla's fall from imperial grace in 423.

20. *PLRE I*, he was last heard of in 408 as *praefectus urbis Romae* (the supreme civil authority in the city). In 414 he was sent to Africa as member of a grievance committee charged with collecting complaints, *CTh* 7.4.33. The temporal coincidence between the prefecture of the younger Flavianus and Aetius's appointment as supreme military commander in 431 led E. Stein, *Histoire du Bas Empire*, trans. J. Palanque (Paris 1959), I, 340, to adduce collaboration between Aetius and the senatorial aristocracy in that year, a hypothesis refuted by refuted by B. L. Twyman, "Aetius and the Aristocracy," *Historia* 19 (1970), 480–503.

21. *AE* 1934.147, text reproduced in Hedrick, *History and Silence*, 26, with emendations. The date is either between 400 and 408, during Arcadius's lifetime, or earlier, in 399–400, ibid., 29. Cf. the erection of a statue in honor of the *comes* Theodosius, Arcadius's grandfather and the father of Theodosius I in 384, Symmachus, *Rel.* 9; with D. Vera, "Le statue del senato di Roma in onore di Flavio Teodosio e l'equilibrio dei potere imperiali in età Teodosiana," *Athenaeum* 57 (1979), 381–403. Unlike Arcadius, the career of the *comes* had indeed been based in the west.

the senior emperor. Nor would he have the slightest interest in senatorial politics at Rome or in rehabilitating dead Roman senators.[22]
Moreover, in 431 Theodosius was fully occupied with the ecclesiastical
controversies that led that very year to the summoning of an ecumenical
council at Ephesos.[23] The junior emperor, Valentinian III, was too young
to play politics. The most likely source of the gracious imperial assent to
the rehabilitating enterprise remains Galla herself.[24]

An imperial ban on memory meant a disruption of senatorial
lineage since commemorations of the dead, so crucial for the prestige of
living, were disallowed by law. Flavianus had been put under the ban by
Theodosius I, the founder of the dynasty that continued to rule both
parts of the empire. His rehabilitation entailed the reversal of Theodosius's injunction. Yet in the imperial letter of 431 the two dead men, Flavianus and Theodosius I, were cast as close associates whose friendship
and mutual respect had succumbed to malice and insinuation. Flavianus's most notable achievement, according to this letter, had nothing to
do with his spectacular if tarnished administrative career. Rather, the
senator's claim to eternal fame and ultimate imperial pardon was a literary feat, the composition of a work of history (*annales*), of which Theodosius I himself desired to be honored as its dedicatee.[25] A 431 audience
who knew little history would have wondered why Theodosius's sons
had been remiss in rehabilitating their father's favorite writer.

The letter's plan of rehabilitation reflected an inverted world in
which men passed nearly seamlessly from oblivion to the heart of the
forum. It was a world in which intellectual pursuits represented a form

22. Hedrick, *History and Silence*, 223, noting, however, an indirect link between the letter's
reference to scribal practices and Theodosius's hobby of copying and correcting manuscripts.
I wonder whether the matter of Flavianus's rehabilitation would have been discussed in Constantinople prior to the dispatch of Galla back to the west.

23. S. Wessel, "The Ecclesiastical Policy of Theodosius II," *Annuarium Historiae Conciliarum*
33 (2001), 285–308. But he did find time to send military contingents to Africa in 431 to help to stem
the Vandalic invasion, below.

24. As Oost, *Galla Placidia*, 231, already argued. I agree albeit for different reasons.

25. The loss of the *annales* has not prevented a welter of scholarly hypotheses, Hedrick, *History
and Silence*, 145–47, for a brief review of the speculations. The debates around the lost annals are
reminiscent of the intense speculations that have surrounded another lost work, the contemporary
ecclesiastical history of Gelasius of Caesarea; P. Van Nuffelen, "Gélase de Césarée, un compilateur
du cinquième siècle," *Byz.Z* 95 (2002), 621–39. Whether or not Flavianus was the author of the notorious *Historia Augusta*, as has been recently suggested, is another question; S. Ratti, "Nicomacque
Flavien sr. et l'Histoire Auguste: la découverte de nouveaux liens," *REL* 85 (2007), 204–19.

of safe archaism or "anachronism."[26] Yet the Roman reveling in pursuit of the past, like Flavianus's *Annals*, masked what the Christian regime could constitute as imprudence if not impiety. The elder Flavianus had been a pagan and an instrumental figure in the so-called pagan revival of the later fourth century.[27] In 431, the year of his public rehabilitation, Flavianus was resuscitated as a literary character in the *Saturnalia*, a fictitious banquet convened by Macrobius's pen to indulge in discourse on the varieties of (pagan) religion. The *Saturnalia* assembled its senatorial crew in 384, placing it in the comfort of the imposing home of the noble Praetextatus, one of Flavianus's closest associates.[28] The Rome it conjured was a pre-Alaric Rome, a relatively tranquil haven under the rule of Valentinian II, Galla's uncle. It was a Rome hovering between the old and the new faiths, paganism and Christianity, a perfect backdrop for intellectual excursions into Rome's pre-Christian past.[29] Macrobius himself, like the 384 guests, was probably a believer in the old gods.[30] The *Saturnalia*'s intricately braided worlds of the Republic, the late fourth century and early 430s, re-created a civil world in subtle apposition and opposition to the dominance of Christianity at the court and in the army.

26. For the latter, Matthews, *Western Aristocracies*, 370–71.

27. I am not sure that I subscribe to the banishing of such a term, in spite of its "secularization," to use the current term; A. Cameron, "Vergil Illustrated between Pagans and Christians," *JRA* 17 (2004), 510. See now R. Lizzi Testa, "*Augures et pontifices*: Public Sacral Law in Late Antique Rome (Fourth–Fifth Centuries AD)," in *The Power of Religion in Late Antiquity*, ed. A. Cain and N. Lenski (Farnham 2009), 251–78, on occasions that allowed pagans to express their religious identity in public. On Flavianus as the butt of the controversial and anonymous *Carmen contra paganos*, A. Coskun, "Virius Nicomachus Flavianus, der Praefectus und Consul des *Carmen contra paganos*," *Vigiliae Christianae* 58 (2004), 152–78.

28. On Praetextatus as butt of antipagan polemics, L. Cracco-Roggini, "Il paganesimo romano tra religione et politica (383–394 d.C.): per una reinterpretazione del *carmen contra paganos*," *Memorie dell' Accademia Nazionale dei Lincei, Classe di scienze morali, storiche e filologiche*, ser. 8 vol. 23 (1979), 3–143.

29. I am combining Matthews's views (*Western Aristocracies*, 372) with Cameron's, "The Date and Identity of Macrobius," *JRS* 56 (1966), 25–38. See also Hedrick, *History and Silence*, 79–85. On the Christianization of the city, C. Pietri, *Roma Christiana: Recherches sur l'Église de Rome, son organisation, sa politique, son idéologie de Miltiade à Sixte III (311–440)* (Rome 1976); on the Christianization of the Roman senatorial aristocracy, M. R. Salzman, *The Making of a Christian Aristocracy: Social and Religious Change in the Western Roman Empire* (Cambridge Mass. 2002).

30. And member of the senate who held the prefecture of Rome just before the younger Flavianus, *PLRE II*, 1102 (Macrobius Ambrosius Theodosius) (Theodosius 20 and 8). His precise religious affiliation remains a matter of scholarly discord. I tend to favor the pagan.

Women were altogether absent from the Saturnalian party. Such occasions were not staged for the display of female wit and learning. Yet a princess did appear, not a contemporary lady who would have disrupted the gentle tenor of the all-male assembly, nor a participant in the erudite conversation. Rather, Macrobius revived the memory of Julia, notorious daughter of Augustus, the first emperor of Rome. By 431 c.e. both father and daughter had been in their graves for nearly four centuries. The vast temporal distance between princess and banqueters ensured that her inclusion was merely a form of antiquarianism. Julia was ripe to become a butt of polite laughter.

To enliven discussions regarding the Roman calendar and religious festivals, Avienus, the most elusive of all the Saturnalian narrators,[31] introduced a jocular diversion. His idea was to incur laughter with a retelling of jokes ascribed to venerable men (*ioci venerum ac nobilium virorum*), among whom Augustus held a place of honor. The Augustan jokes involving Julia received a peculiar introduction, as though Avienus's interlocutors would have failed to appreciate her wit without the guidance of a brief biography:[32]

> She was in her thirty-eighth year, a time of life verging on old age, even if sound of mind. But she was abusing both paternal indulgence and her luck. Noted for love of literature and surpassing erudition, both easy to acquire in such a household, and besides endowed with gentle and humane spirit, all of which garnered her great favor, those who knew her vices marveled at such discrepancy.[33]

Examples of Julia's wit included the following:

> When Julia listened to a serious minded friend trying to persuade her to do better by composing herself in light of her father's frugality, she said: He forgets that he is an emperor; I remember that I am an emperor's daughter. (*Sat.* 2.5.8)

---

31. Unlike the other Saturnalians, Avienus's historicity is disputed; J. Long, "Julia-Jokes at Macrobius's Saturnalia: Subversive Decorum in Late Antique Reception of Augustan Political Humor," *International Journal of the Classical Tradition* 6 (2000), 341.

32. *Sat.* 2.1.8. Cf. Sallust's famed description of Sempronia, who collaborated with Catiline.

33. *Sat.* 2.5.2; my translation is based on Long, "Julia-Jokes," 347–48; and A. Richlin, "Julia's Jokes, Galla Placidia, and the Roman Use of Women as Political Icons," in *Stereotypes of Women in Power*, ed. B. Garlick et al. (Westport, Conn. 1992), 70.

Whether intended as comic relief or calculated to shock "even broad minded Christians,"[34] Julia's humor was ready to counter an inflexible code of morality with pertinent exceptions.[35]

Behind the ghosts of both the disgraced and long-dead princess and the men gathered to celebrate the pagan feast of the Saturnalia in 384 lived an author under a regime headed by a woman, Galla, whose age in 431 corresponded precisely with that of the jocose Julia and whose Roman past was as shady as Julia's.[36] In 431 members of the Roman senate would have remembered Galla's collusion with the senatorial decision to execute her cousin in 408/409, nor forgotten her disappearance from Italy in the company of meandering Goths in 410, her elevation to the rank of Augusta a decade later, and her exile from the court in 423 due to accusations of immorality. The audience of the *Saturnalia* and its Julia jokes would have witnessed the untidiness of history. Julia died in exile. Galla returned to Rome in triumph, transformed into a model mother.[37]

A retelling of Julia's history, focusing on Julia's troubled relationship with her father, lent itself to a discourse of paradoxes. The jokes betrayed an aristocratic commitment to a well-monitored past; Julia's humor pointed to moments of disorder and overindulgence. The new, post-425 Galla presented a bewildering new front—a chaste widow, a devoted mother, and a politician ready, once again, to collaborate with the senate of Rome, this time on a mission of filial piety rather than of familial persecution. Amnesty was in the air. The gesture suited to perfection the self-congratulatory mode of the Roman senatorial aristocracy of Macrobius's *Saturnalia*. In 431 such a mood matched that of Galla's court. She had little to lose from a display of imperial magnanimity and much to gain. A project of rehabilitating a grand old pagan author, a venerable

34. As Richlin, "Julia's Jokes," 83, argues using, however, a broad chronological spectrum that goes well beyond the chronology of the *Saturnalia* itself, thus endowing Macrobius with both puns and prophecy, the latter attribute seems unlikely. Moreover, even the notable figures of late ancient asceticism, like Paula and the two Melanias, emphatically did not possess the "ability to control their bearing of children" (ibid., 83). Each had to produce, or attempt to produce, an heir prior to familial approval of sexual renunciation. Perhaps the perils of raising daughters, rather than Honoria's behavior in the late 440s, had been the aim of the *Saturnalia*'s Julia's souvenirs.

35. Long, "Julia-Jokes," 351.

36. The age calculations relating to Galla (see ch. 1) can be augmented by this detail, which implies that if she was thirty-eight in 431 she would have been born in 393.

37. A metamorphosis enshrined even in law—one of Galla's first laws, issued already in January 426 (*CTh* 5.1.7) guaranteed the right of mothers to inherit their son's estate.

senator and once favorite of her father Theodosius I, proclaimed both her power and parentage. As an erstwhile citizen of the city of Rome she was well aware of the advantage of alliances with influential and wealthy senatorial clans.

It must be emphasized that in favoring the senatorial aristocracy, regardless or perhaps because of their religious affiliation, whether Christian or pagan, Galla's policy of amnesty presented no novelty. In the wake of his 388 victory over Magnus Maximus, who had ruled most of the west after killing the emperor Gratian in 383, Galla's father appointed several pagan senators to key positions in the western administration. Among these, the elder Flavianus was appointed quaestor (member of the imperial consistory) and later praetorian prefect (chief civil official) of Italy, Africa, and Illyricum, while Symmachus (also a pagan), who had composed a panegyric honoring Maximus, was not only pardoned but also received the signal honor of the consulship in 391.[38] The fact that in 393, under the usurper Eugenius, Symmachus held the public games celebrating his son's appointment as quaestor, and the elder Flavianus celebrated a consulship bestowed by the same usurper pointed less to senatorial readiness to switch sides as to the necessity to reach a modus vivendi with the emperor nearest to Rome. Men like Flavianus and Symmachus were experienced administrators and useful to any regime. A similar pattern of alternate rise and fall can be traced in other instances, of which Manlius Theodorus, a correspondent of Symmachus and a Christian, was not atypical. Theodorus held the Gallic praetorian prefecture under Gratian (c. 380), then retired to his estate only to reemerge years later as Honorius's praetorian prefect of Italy in 397 and consul in 399.[39] Regardless of religious affiliation, the Roman senatorial aristocracy, with its exalted lineage and fabulous wealth, was vital for a political reconstruction organized around a child emperor and a court in Ravenna.

Galla, like Theodosius, entrusted key positions to key senatorial figures. Flavius Anicius Auchenius Bassus was appointed to manage the imperial treasury in late 425. In 431 he was honored with the consulship.[40] Bassus even had a hand in setting up an epitaph to mark the tomb

38. R. M. Errington, "The Praetorian Prefectures of Virius Nicomachus Flavianus," *Historia* 41 (1992), 439–61.

39. *PLRE I* (Theodorus 27); Matthews, *Western Aristocracies*, 262–63.

40. *PLRE II*, 220 (Bassus 8), and below ch. 6.

of Monica, Augustine's mother, in Ostia (Rome's port town), where she had died in 387.[41] Men like Bassus, with impeccable lineage and vaunted Christian piety, were to become Galla's mainstay in a political universe dominated by military men.

Maneuvering the Military

John's brief reign (423–425) engendered another mutation and reconciliation. Flavius Aetius, an ambitious young soldier whom John had sent in 425 to obtain Hunnic help against the army that Theodosius II dispatched with Galla and Valentinian, returned to Italy only to find his patron presumed dead.[42] Notwithstanding, the two armies, barbarian mercenaries and Roman soldiers of the imperial army, joined battle.[43] The indecisiveness of the outcome engineered an agreement that relieved Aetius of standing trial for potential treason, as well as rewarding him with a title (*comes*) and with the supreme military command over the Gallic prefecture (*magister utriusque militiae per Gallias*). The amicable arrangement was sealed with a generous subsidy provided in all likelihood from Galla's treasury: "[Aetius's] barbarians were persuaded to lay aside their anger and their arms with the assistance of gold, and having given hostages and accepted pledges, they retired to their own lands."[44]

Bribing barbarians to lay down their arms had been a much-tried tactic of the eastern court. In the west, Honorius's government had consistently refused to bow to a similar mode of extortion, as did the Roman senate, an approach that resulted in Alaric's three sieges and ultimate sack of Rome (408–410). Having lived with barbarians for six years and in Constantinople for two may have taught Galla the values of both a timely bribe and a timely war.

---

41. Rossi, *ICUR II*, 252; with Matthews, *Western Aristocracies*, 367, although the Bassus of the inscription could have been the consul of either 408 or 431.

42. *PLRE II*, 21f. (Aetius 7) provides pointers for his career.

43. At this point the denomination of either "Roman" or "barbarian" when it came to designating members of opposing sides began to blur. The ethnic composition of the so-called Roman army was exceptionally diverse and, more to the point, its loyalty to a reigning emperor depended on the loyalty of its commander to the same imperial establishment. Aetius's Huns serve as a useful reminder of how easy it was to wield large groups of mercenaries on multiple sides, be they helping usurpers, fighting for legitimately seated emperors, or turning against the same group by using others.

44. Philostorgius, *HE* 12.14 (Eng. trans. Amidon); Prosper, *Chron.* s.a. 425.

In 425 the presence in Italy of two generals, Ardabur and Aspar, both appointed by Theodosius II to head the campaign against John, ensured the application of Theodosian policies in the west. Perhaps at that point Aspar was even offered the western throne. The proposal apparently originated in senatorial circles leery of a court about to be presided over by a child emperor and a female regent, as well as of an army barely recovered from civil war. Aspar refused, asserting that never before had a man of barbarian extraction assumed the imperial throne.[45] He was to reappear in 431 in the west, in Africa, sent there by Theodosius II to help Boniface against the invading Vandals. On the latter occasion Aspar remained in Africa three years, assuming the consulate in 434, an honor apparently, and exceptionally, conferred by Galla.[46]

In the charged atmosphere following John's fall, Galla had to generate competing yet complementary discourses to retain her newly acquired and rather precarious position. The subsequent murderous rivalry between Galla's two top generals, Aetius and Boniface, each so outstanding as to lay claim to the bizarre title "last of the Romans,"[47] reveals the difficulties entailed in managing an empire where the tranquil pursuit of studies (the happy lot of the eastern Roman emperor) remained a remote dream.

The situation in Galla's early regency (425–431) reflected paradoxes of femininity: she had the theoretical right, through son and nephew, both legitimate living emperors, to appoint men at will. In reality, she had to place herself under the authority of generals who commanded her own army. In hindsight, as narrated by Procopius from the vantage point of the reconquered west in the sixth century, the web of intrigues that entailed the realignment of court and the top military brass seemed, paradoxically, to ensure the continuation of the Valentinian-Theodosian dynasty:

45. *Acta syn. habit. Rome* V, MGH AA XII, 425: "aliquando Aspari a senatu dicebatur ut ipse fieret imperator; qui tale refertur dedisse responsum: Timeo ne per me consuetudo in regno nascatur" (it was rumored that the senator proposed to Aspar that he himself become emperor. Such, however, was the response he gave: I fear lest through my personal precedence a custom should arise [of making generals kings by senatorial will?]). Cited in *PLRE II*, 168, with reference to the year 467, but 425 appears more likely.

46. *Consuls of the Later Roman Empire* s.a. 434. R. C. Blockley, *East Roman Foreign Policy: Formation and Conduct from Diocletian to Anastasius* (Leeds 1992), 60. The two consuls of the year were both in the west, contrary to the practice of one eastern, one western consul, each appointed by their respective emperor.

47. The title was awarded by Procopius in his *BV* 3.14, for no apparent reason other than his somewhat deluded judgment of their character.

There were two Roman generals, Aetius and Boniface, especially valiant men and in experience of many wars inferior to none of that time. . . . One, Boniface, was appointed by [Galla] Placidia general of all Libya [*comes Africae*]. This was not in accord with Aetius' wishes who, however, concealed his displeasure for their hostility had not yet come to light. . . . But when Boniface had departed [to return to Africa], Aetius slandered him to [Galla] Placidia, saying that he was setting up a tyranny to rob her and the emperor of all Libya. He added that it would be easy for her to find out the truth—should she summon Boniface to Rome, he would never come. . . . She acted accordingly. Aetius, anticipating her, secretly wrote to Boniface, alerting him that the mother of the emperor [= Galla] was plotting against him wishing to put him out of the way.[48]

Such was the beginning, barely two years after Galla returned to Italy, of a story strewn with fatalities.[49] Boniface, who had apparently been a staunch supporter of Galla throughout the early 420s, did rebel (in 426/427). Procopius presented Galla as gullible enough to lend credence to Aetius's accusations against Boniface. Perhaps she was. Boniface may have made other enemies at the court. To reinforce his troops in view of the impending campaign, Boniface recruited Vandal auxiliaries, a move that led to the mass migration of the entire Vandalic confederacy from Spain to Africa in 429.[50]

In Rome the friends of Boniface, remembering the character of the man and considering how strange his action was, were greatly astonished to think that Boniface was setting up a tyranny, and some of them at the order of [Galla] Placidia

48. Procopius, *BV* 3.14–19, Eng. trans. Dewing (Loeb), reproduced with modification in R. W. Mathisen, "Sigisvult the Patrician, Maximinus the Arian, and Political Stratagems in the Western Roman Empire c. 425–40," *Early Medieval Europe* 8 (1999), 175.

49. Such indeed is also the impression gleaned from the illustrations accompanying the Ravenna annals for the years 423–429 reflecting assassinations and earthquakes; B. Bischoff and W. Koehler, "Eine illustrierte Ausgabe der spätantiken Ravennater Annalen," in *Medieval Studies in Honor of Kingsley Porter*, ed. W. Koehler et al. (Cambridge, Mass. 1939), 128–33.

50. Mathisen, "Sigisvult," 189–91, for a convincing refutation of the accusation formulated by Procopius (*BV* 3.25) and followed by numerous modern scholars that designed Boniface as the traitor who lured the Vandals with a promise of surrendering the African provinces to them, naturally without imperial authorization.

went to Carthage. There they met Boniface, and saw the letter of Aetius, and after hearing the whole story they returned to Rome as quickly as they could and reported to Placidia how Boniface stood in relation to her. And though the woman was dumbfounded, she did nothing unpleasant to Aetius . . . but she disclosed to the friends of Boniface the advice Aetius had given and . . . entreated them to persuade him, if they could, to return to his fatherland and not to permit the empire of the Romans to lie under the hand of barbarians.[51]

Double dealings and belated revelations proved too late to save Africa from the Vandals but not to repair cordial relations between Galla and Boniface.[52] She rewarded him (in 432) with the top command of the western armies (*magister utriusque militiae*), in which capacity he fought, near Rimini, not against Rome's enemies but against Aetius, his chief rival, winning the battle but losing his life.[53]

Several aspects of this convoluted chain of events in Galla's early regency deserve attention. When Galla dispatched Sigisvult in 427 to Africa to deal with Boniface, the former arrived with a formidable theologian in his entourage.[54] Instead of rejoining armies on the battle-field, this Arian clergyman, Maximinus, engaged in erudite debates with no lesser mind than Augustine, bishop of Hippo.[55] Maximinus's mission to Africa may have been calculated to win Boniface over—or rather to enlist the services of his wife, Pelagia.[56] The rebellious general had married a Gothic princess. The possibility that Galla and Pelagia

---

51. Procopius, *BV* 3. 27–29 (Loeb trans.). Oost, *Galla Placidia*, 221 n. 46, prefers Prosper's version, in which the rivals are Felix (rather than Aetius) and Boniface. He may well be correct, although for the purpose of my presentation the precise identity of the contenders is significantly less crucial than their mode of operation and its outcome.

52. Already in 431 Bishop Capreolus of Carthage was unable to attend the council at Ephesos. His letter of apology refers to the Vandal occupation and to the general situation in North Africa as factors that inhibit even the summoning of a regional synod, let alone the sending of an embassy to Ephesos. Capreolus's letter is preserved in the acts of the council of Ephesos (*Gesta* 61, *ACO* 1.1.2), with T. Graumann, "Reading the First Council of Ephesos (431)," in *Chalcedon in Context*, ed. R. Price and M. Whitby (Liverpool 2009), 34.

53. *PLRE II*, 237–40, for succinct summary of a vexed chronology. And Mathisen, "Sigisvult," for sorting out the difficulties.

54. Mathisen, "Sigisvult," 176–77, on possible prior acquaintance between Galla and the Gothic (?) Sigisvult.

55. Augustine, *Collatio, PL* 42.707–42; with Mathisen, "Sigisvult," 178.

56. *PLRE II* (Pelagia 1).

had known each other need not be discounted. Little is known of Pelagia. She was of royal blood, married two Roman generals, and converted to Catholicism.[57] Boniface's presence in Gaul is attested in 413 at Marseilles, precisely when Athaulf, Galla, and the Goths were also there.[58] Had Pelagia, like Galla before her, been joined as hostage, traded over to the Roman camp only to be wooed by its commander? The marriage of Galla and Athaulf provided a precedent, as did those of other military men.[59]

Galla's gamble on Pelagia through Maximinus paid off. Maximinus's public appearances in African theological debates had the desired effect. Boniface, Sigisvult, and Galla's court were once again reconciled. Bloodshed was avoided. The glory of that war, as Augustine remarked, was precisely the avoidance of human bloodshed and the establishment of peace by peaceful means.[60] Pelagia's history underlines the feminine thread that bestowed legitimacy on participants in the savage rivalry over the supreme and sole command of the Roman army in the early fifth century.[61] Upon her marriage with Boniface, Pelagia apparently converted from Arianism to a Nicene form of Christianity, although her newly acquired dogmatic identity did not prevent her calling upon an Arian priest to baptize her daughter by Boniface. Nor did she refrain from urging her husband to adopt a policy of toleration toward Christian schismatics in Africa, much to Augustine's chagrin.[62] On his deathbed Boniface, mortally wounded by Aetius, whose army he had just vanquished, commended Pelagia to marry Aetius, his own deadly rival.[63] Odd advice from a man who upon the death of his first wife

57. Nor is her chronology known prior to Augustine's references to her faith in *Ep.* 220.4 in the late 420s when she was married to Boniface. All other sources relate to her marriage with Aetius.

58. Olympiodorus, fr. 21 (late 413).

59. A. Demandt, "The Osmosis of Late Roman and Germanic Aristocracies," in *Das Reich und die Barbaren*, ed. E. Chrysos and A. Schwarcz (Vienna 1989), 75–89; R. Soraci, *Ricerche sui conubia tra Romani e Germani nei secoli IV–VI* (Catania 1974).

60. Augustine, *Ep.* 229.

61. Her later history is especially interesting, if she is to be identified with an unnamed wife of Aetius whose hostility to Majorian in the late 440s failed to bar his road to the throne, Sidonius, *Pan.* 5.130–304; with MacGeorge, *Late Roman Warlords*, 183, also on her possible blood connection with Ricimer.

62. Augustine, *Ep.* 220.

63. Marcelinus Comes, s.a. 432. Oost, *Galla Placidia*, 235, on Pelagia's substantial "dowry" consisting of Boniface's wealth and his personal troops.

reputedly contemplated withdrawal into a monastery, yet kept mistresses even after his second marriage (to Pelagia).[64]

By 430 Aetius had managed to rid himself of another potential contender for the position of sole commander of the army. That year, Felix, who had been the chief commander of the entire western army between 425 and 430, *patricius* and consul in 428, was killed by rioting soldiers. Aetius had accused him of conspiracy against the throne. This time there is no reference to Galla's involvement. The rioting and Felix's murder took place in Ravenna, on the steps of the Basilica Ursiana, not far from the imperial palace.[65] The precise affiliation of the soldiers was never disclosed. The order to start a brawl could have been issued by Aetius. The basilica had just been completed by Ravenna's bishop, Ursus, who "lined its walls with most precious stones and arranged diverse figures in multicolored mosaics over the vault of the entire sanctuary."[66] Yet no sight or sound presented a gorier contrast with the sanctuary's serenity than the cries of the slain priest who attempted, in vain, to aid Padusia, Felix's wife, whom the rioters also killed. Stenches and sounds would have reverberated to the palace itself. They would have provided a demonstration of the fragility of imperial power at the very heart of the capital.

Padusia's story, like that of her husband Felix, illustrates the vagaries of power and patronage. She had been Galla's confidante at the court during the early 420s. Yet she apparently had something to do with Galla's removal from the court in 423.[67] Galla, then, would have had several scores to settle with both Felix and Padusia. Felix had been accused of plotting the murder of Patroclus, bishop of Arles, who had

64. Not to mention shunning Augustine's advice to practice chastity, give alms, pray, and fast, while engaging in minimal warfare; Augustine, *Ep.* 220; with R. Tomlin, "Christianity and the Late Roman Army," in *Constantine: History, Historiography and Legend*, ed. S. N. S. Lieu and D. Montserrat (London 1998), 39–40.

65. Below for the possibility that Agnellus's report of an emperor killed in the Ravenna riots may have confused Valentinian I with Felix. Was the latter accused of aspiring to the throne? Also, was Felix involved in the killing of a man named Pirrus at Rome, recorded by the Ravenna annals in 428, the year of his consulate? Bischoff and Koehler, "Eine illustrierte Ausgabe" (above n. 49), 128.

66. Agnellus, *LPR* 23 (Eng. trans. Deliyannis, slightly modified). The chronology of the bishops of Ravenna in late antiquity is exceptionally muddled. Cf. Oost, *Galla Placidia*, 273, for John I as bishop between 396 and after 431, vs. Deliyannis, Ibid., 307, on Ursus I as bishop during the same period and John I as bishop between 477 and 494.

67. See ch. 3.

been an appointee of Constantius, Galla's second husband.[68] Back in 412, Patroclus's appointment to the chief Gallic see, seat of the prefect of the Gauls, generated considerable resentment among the Gallic clergy.[69] In spite of such unsavory beginnings, Patroclus acquired considerable power, mostly at the expense of neighboring bishops, and often with the assistance or tacit approval of the bishop of Rome. He even benefited from John's brief rule (423–425), securing further concessions for his see.[70] In 426, barely a year into Galla's restoration, Felix instigated the assassination of the bishop in Arles. The general, however, had not been invested with a command that extended to Gaul. Rather, the man officially in charge of military affairs in Gaul was Aetius.[71] Galla proved incapable of stopping this form of infringement, nor able (or willing?) to prevent the killing of a prelate who had been favored by her late husband.

A series of tragic distortions guided the confused alliances that confounded even contemporary historians. Galla's function as the de facto ruler of the western provinces presupposed power. But it is precisely her role as the emperor's mother that limited her influence. In an empire constantly under siege by barbarians breaching external and internal frontiers, and perpetually threatened with provincial revolts and pretenders to the throne, military men became a key factor in the stability of the regime. The loyalty of such men as Boniface, Felix, and Aetius to the legitimate ruler, however, could never be taken for granted. Nor did these generals hesitate to command the kind of devotion that citizens were expected to cultivate vis-à-vis the imperial family alone. When he viewed a military parade headed by Boniface, Augustine observed how the ceremonial appearance of such seasoned soldiers at the head of their armed followers evoked admiration as well as fear.[72]

68. Prosper, *Chron.* 1292, s.a. 426; with Mathisen, *Ecclesiastical Factionalism and Religious Controversy in Fifth-Century Gaul* (Washington, DC 1989), 73, and passim on Patroclus, his ambitions, and his connections with the court of Honorius and Galla.

69. Prosper, *Chron.* 1247 s.a. 412, cited and translated in R. W. Mathisen, *Ecclesiastical Factionalism*, 35–36.

70. Sirmondian Constitution 6 (July 425); with Mathisen, *Ecclesiastical Factionalism*, 72.

71. Hence perhaps the secrecy that Prosper s.a. 426 reported, with Mathisen, *Ecclesiastical Factionalism*, 73.

72. *PL* 33.1095–98, spurious correspondence between St. Augustine and Boniface, c. 450, Eng. trans. in J. J. O'Donnell, *Augustine: A New Biography* (New York 2005), 170.

Patronage and Piety: The Making of Matriarchy

Staged spectacles and carefully orchestrated ceremonies projected confidence of men, generals and emperors, convinced of their proper place and status. Their public gestures implied an exclusive relationship between the realm controlled, at that point in Roman history, by God, and the terrestrial sphere ruled by the emperor. The difficulties of generating a language that would convey the unique status of imperial women like Galla must not be underestimated. In the mid-fourth century Julian presented the empress Eusebia as a perfect partner of her husband, the emperor Constantius II.[73] At that point, all three, emperor, empress, and royal panegyrist, were Christians.

Imperial Christianity, ever solicitous to demonstrate its religious commitment to Constantine's adopted creed, added precious relics to the imperial public paraphernalia. Mediating between the powers on earth and in heaven, relics also acted as a bridge over gender disparity. They enabled empresses to hold an important position in public. An *adventus* ceremony that featured relics instead of an emperor or a general would allow the empress to take center stage in the stately procession. It would also provide an opportunity to display the sumptuous clothes of rank. Such an occasion would further become a showcase of imperial female piety, proclaiming the princess's attachment to the right form of the faith.

In early fifth-century Constantinople, with a court boasting princesses vowed to perpetual virginity, the path to power led through sexual renunciation. Pulcheria, Galla's niece and sister of Theodosius II, a woman younger than Galla by some five years, tenaciously and wisely resisted pressures to marry. She was rewarded with the coveted rank of Augusta, crowned, as her coins proclaimed, by the hand of God.[74] This was the first time that a princess gained such prominence without producing an heir to the throne.[75] The novelty of Pulcheria's position resided in opposing marriage plus maternity with voluntary celibacy, rendering imperial female virginity a viable alternative to becoming a childbearing empress.

---

73. Julian, *Oration to Eusebia*, III, above.
74. Holum, *Theodosian Empresses*, 94–97, with the brief yet excellent summary of G. Greatrex online (*De Imperatoribus Romanis*, www.roman-emperors.org).
75. Holum, *Theodosian Empresses*, 32, on Fausta's image, which explicitly associates her rank with childbearing.

Pulcheria would have provided a useful model for Galla on several scores. Between 414 and 419 her coins showed her bejeweled bust with a hand of God holding a crown over it (obverse), and a seated Victory holding a Chi-Rho on a shield (reverse).[76] This was the very type minted at Ravenna on the occasion of Galla's elevation to the rank of Augusta in 421.[77] But Galla added a Chi-Rho to her shoulder ornament, a singularity that would continue to differentiate her coinage from the monotonous repertory that governed the coinage of all the Theodosian empresses. In 424, during Galla's Constantinopolitan period, the mint of Constantinople issued three series, honoring Pulcheria, Eudocia (Theodosius's wife), and Galla, respectively.[78] All three women were designated by the *nomen* Aelia, an appellation that neither Galla nor Eudocia bore. Name and imagery harked back to Aelia Flaccilla, first wife of Theodosius I and grandmother of Theodosius II and of Pulcheria.[79] The reverse displayed a standard figure—a Victory holding a long cross, as though the Christianization of that venerable goddess would ensure the empire's eternal triumph.[80]

An avid collector of saintly relics, Pulcheria used occasions such as the deposition of relics to advertise simultaneously her piety and her avowed virginity. We possess a visual testimony of these tendencies in the shape of a carved ivory tablet that features the arrival at the capital of the arm of St. Stephen, all the way from the Holy Land.[81] Decked in

76. Grierson and Mays, *Catalogue of Late Roman Coins*, no. 436.

77. Ibid., nos. 817 and 818. The seated Victory already appeared on coins minted in Flaccilla's and Eudoxia's names, Holum, *Theodosian Empresses*, figs. 6 and 7.

78. Galla had her own residence in the city; Agathias, *Greek Anthology*, 16.41, with A. McLanan, *Representations of Early Byzantine Empresses: Image and Empire* (New York 2002), 19. It is unclear whether Galla's Constantinopolitan palace had been assigned to her from infancy or built during her exile there. It was still associated with her name in the sixth century.

79. Holum, *Theodosian Empresses*, 22, for Aelia as "a title of female distinction and dynastic exclusiveness," with reference to Claudian, *Laus Serenae*, 50–56. Cf. the *nomen* Flavius so widely adopted by the men of the Theodosian dynasty; A. Cameron, "Flavius: A Nicety of Protocol," *Latomus* 47 (1988), 26–33. On Flaccilla's coinage, Holum, *Theodosian Empresses*, 34 and figure 6.

80. Grierson and Mays, *Catalogue of Late Roman Coins*, no. 437 (Pulcheria, roughly dated to sometime between 420 and 430), nos. 454 and 455 (Eudocia, roughly dated to sometime between 423 and 429), and no. 824 (Galla, 424–25). M. McCormick, *Eternal Victory: Triumphal Rulership in Late Antiquity, Byzantium and the Early Medieval West* (Cambridge 1986), passim, on the myth of eternal triumph.

81. The following description is based on the Trier ivory. For its association with Pulcheria and the year 421, K. Holum and G. Vikan, "The Trier Ivory, Adventus Ceremonial, and the Relics of St. Stephen," *DOP* 33 (1979), 115–33; for an overview of the controversy regarding the ivory's protagonists and date, McLanan, *Representations*, 25. On the discovery of Stephen in Palestine in 415, Sivan, *Palestine in Late Antiquity*, passim.

richly embroidered garments, Pulcheria is seen tightly embracing a huge cross. She is facing the relics, which are carried in an especially commissioned casket, carefully and conspicuously held by a bishop seated atop a chariot. A set of privileged spectators witness with patent admiration how the empress graciously accepts a folded scroll containing a narrative of the relics' discovery. She, the only woman on view, stands next to a building about to be completely roofed, confident of her place as patron and donor. The *martyrium* that housed the relics was built on Pulcheria's own estate and financed at her expense. Like Helena, Constantine's mother, and like Eudocia, her own sister-in-law, Pulcheria also staked a claim to the Holy Land by leaving her stamp on the Jerusalem skyline.[82] She endowed the holy city with a golden cross, a donation commemorated with a special issue of gold coins (*solidi*) that depicted the Augusta as an equal of the male Augusti.[83]

To use, as Pulcheria did, her avowed virginity as a determinant of distinction was an avenue not quite open to Galla. Nor was the mode of operation adopted by Eudocia, wife of Theodosius II since 421, a useful precedent. Eudocia reverted to the module of maternity and procreation to exert power and patronage. Ultimately, both she and Pulcheria depended on the will and whim of the emperor, husband and brother, and his courtiers. A widow, and a mother of a reigning emperor, Galla had to forge a new balance between maternity and the responsibilities of her position.

An examination of Galla's collective representation points to a peculiar conflation. Her coinage reflected strategies that her eastern contemporary counterparts, Pulcheria and Eudocia, had adopted. With neither fertility nor virginity as paramount parameters, Galla could cultivate a space where she could construct a new personality of a queenly regent. At hand was also a close if controversial model, that of Justina, her maternal grandmother. Like Galla, the twice-widowed Justina, mother of a boy emperor (Valentinian II), used her guardian status to cross a fundamental threshold between two separate domains, that of the emperor and that of the emperor's womenfolk.

Similarities between Justina and Galla are striking, even startling. Each had to safeguard the interests of a son who was too young to rule by himself. During her son's adolescence (383–388), Justina had to tread

82. L. Brubaker, "Memories of Helena: Patterns in Imperial Female Matronage in the Fourth and Fifth Centuries," in *Women, Men and Eunuchs*, ed. L. James (New York 1997), 52–75.

83. Holum, *Theodosian Empresses*, 109; J. P. C. Kent, *The Divided Empire and the Fall of the Western Parts 395–491* (The Roman Imperial Coinage 10) (London 1994), 75, pl. 8, no. 218–21.

carefully and deftly among competing paradigms of power—a usurper (Magnus Maximus) who occupied half of the provinces; senators whose ambitions dictated collaboration based on immediate rewards; ambitious generals ready to use imperial soldiers against the emperor; and bishops keen on carrying the banner of orthodoxy to extremes. Both women kept Gothic guardsmen to ensure their personal safety. That these Goths were Arian, followers of doctrines deemed heretical in 325, was potentially a problem. When Justina and Valentinian II moved to Milan (c. 380), then capital of the western Roman Empire, they lived in close and explosive proximity to Ambrose, the city's outspoken Catholic bishop. The history of the subsequent clash between Justina and Ambrose, known primarily through the bishop's reports, highlighted ruptures between political functions and dogmatic heroics.[84]

Justina's espousal of an Arian (or homoian) form of Christianity was in itself hardly novel. Both Helena, Constantine's mother, and Eusebia, Arian herself and wife of Constantius II, Constantine's heir, lent support to followers of Arius.[85] Justina extended her patronage to competent Arian bishops, like Auxentius, who headed a Milanese coalition of homoian Romans and Goths. Galla empowered Maximus, the Arian bishop, with negotiating an African settlement. When Justina, in perfect compliance with an imperial law, requested Ambrose to allocate one church in Milan for use by Arians, she probably did not anticipate a strike, with the bishop defiantly occupying the church as though under siege. Justina apparently had underestimated the bishop's popularity and his network of fervent Catholics, opponents of both Arianism and barbarians. The war between the widow and the cleric spilt into texts that cast Justina as "that woman who wherever she proceeded dragged with her a gang of all her [Arian] followers," a veritable latter-day Jezebel.[86] Her centrality in the affair suggests that the creed espoused by widowed empresses in control of a court ruled by a boy emperor was instrumental in shaping the public face of the regime.

A capital city, whether Milan or Ravenna (after 402), would have posed a constant threat of competition between imperial and episcopal

84. Matthews, *Western Aristocracies*, 188–90, for pithy summary; McLynn, *Ambrose of Milan*, 158–208; Liebeschuetz, *Ambrose of Milan*, 124–173.

85. Holum, *Theodosian Empresses*, 24, on Helena favoring Arianism. Sozomen, *HE* 3.1, on Eusebia's adoption of Arianism.

86. Ambrose, *Ep.* 76 (20).12 and 18: "quocumque femina ista processerit secum suos omnes coetus vehit." Cf. Augustine's *rabies femina*, *Conf.* 9.7.15. McLynn, *Ambrose of Milan*, 171.

spheres. The consistency of antagonistic discourse carved by the much-publicized clashes between the empress mother and Ambrose of Milan cast Justina primarily as a "heretic," a charged term in late antiquity. At the core of the conflict between court and cleric in the mid-380s was control over the young emperor's heart. Blood or faith? Maternal rights or a bishop's claim "to be the emperor's sole interlocutor before God"?[87] Ambrose expected Justina to pose as a widow seeking solace and guidance after the murder of her stepson Gratian in 383. In his world she was to pose as a woman who knew her place and was ready to place her young child in the bishop's steady arms.[88] Or perhaps he relished an empress who would descend at once from her lofty throne to meet him and to offer her head to his hands, asking for his blessing.[89] Ambrose hardly anticipated a Justina capable, just like him, of wielding her popularity as an effective weapon. Her followers raised din and clamor in the churches where Ambrose preached.[90]

Ambrose felt trapped. He cast himself as a victim of feminine machination headed by a queen and aided and abetted by a group of hysterical, heretical women:

> When Ambrose had gone to Sirmium to ordain Anemius as
> bishop, there was an attempt to drive him out of the church by
> the powerful queen Justina and a multitude who had gathered
> around her so that they could proceed, in the same church but
> with the heretics in charge instead of Ambrose, with the
> ordination of an Arian. Ambrose, taking no notice of the
> disturbances created by a woman, had taken his place at the
> tribunal when one of the Arian consecrated virgins . . .
> grabbed his clothing, wanting to drag him to the women's
> section so that he could be beaten by them and driven out of
> the church.[91]

In the end Justina had to yield. Without trying to universalize a single case, proximity of capital and court could breed discord, the locale

---

87. McLynn, *Ambrose of Milan*, 179, for the citation.

88. Ambrose, *de ob. Val.* 28. See also K. Cooper, "Insinuations of Womanly Influence: An Aspect of the Christianization of the Roman Aristocracy," *JRS* 82 (1992), 150–64.

89. As Leontius, bishop of Tripoli, demanded of the empress Eusebia, in vain it seems, Philostorgius, *HE* 7.6a (Amidon trans.).

90. Rufinus, *HE* 2.15, with McLynn, *Ambrose of Milan*, 179.

91. Paulinus, *V. Amb.* 11.2, trans. in McLynn, *Ambrose of Milan*, 92.

exacerbating and sharpening the stakes. Galla could ill afford to be prey to forceful feminization of all types of behavior that are expressed by an essentially masculine model. In the opening years of the fifth century, Eudoxia, wife of Arcadius (Galla's half brother) and mother of Theodosius II, challenged John Chrysostom, bishop of Constantinople. At stake were decisions that touched the domain of his episcopal colleagues, as well as the rights of widows to dispose of their property at will.[92] Like Ambrose, Chrysostom employed biblical rhetoric to recast Eudoxia as both a Jezebel intent on unlawful acquisitions and as a Salome (Herodias) desiring the heads of saintly men.[93] Unlike Justina and Eusebia, Eudoxia knew how not to stray from her normal role in public, or so it seemed when

> in a church called The Apostles placed her son Theodosius, who now so happily reigns but was then quite an infant, before John's knees and adjuring him repeatedly by the young prince her son, with difficulty prevailed upon him to be reconciled.[94]

This gesture of reconciliation and homage echoed a similar policy that her father-in-law, Theodosius I, had adopted when he accorded to Meletius, a troublesome yet influential bishop, a special welcome in full view of the scores of bishops who had been summoned (in 381) to attend a church council in Constantinople. As soon as Meletius entered the imperial palace

> [h]e [Theodosius], leaving aside all the other [bishops], ran to the great Meletius and, like a child who loves his father and has for a long time enjoyed the sight of him, he threw his arms around him and kissed his eyes, lips, breast, head and the right hand that had given him the crown.[95]

In spite of these touching public ceremonies, Eudoxia successfully engineered John's exile. Perhaps one of her winning arguments was John's own preaching on the overarching value of asceticism, virginity, and sexual renunciation. Such an alternative to marital bliss and procreation would have denied dynasty continuity.

---

92. Holum, *Theodosian Empresses*, 69–78.
93. *Hom. ante exil.*, PG LII 431, with Holum, *Theodosian Empresses*, 75; Palladius, *Dial.* 8, with Holum, *Theodosian Empresses*, 72 and 74 n. 105. Socrates 6.18.1–5; Sozomen 8.20.1–3.
94. Socrates, *HE* 6.11 (Eng. trans. NPN).
95. Theodoret, *HE* 5.7.

West and East, Milan and Constantinople, produced two patterns of tension between imperial and episcopal courts. From the start Galla was careful to advertise her orthodox credentials. Reaching Rome in 425, she and Valentinian paid a visit to the church of Santa Croce in Gerusalemme.[96] The excursion would not have escaped the attention of the senators who had espoused John's cause nor that of Rome's ecclesiastical authorities. At the church an inscription loudly proclaimed the close relations between the court and its orthodox creed: "May the kings of the earth and all peoples, leaders and all judges of earth praise the name of the Lord. Valentinian, Placidia and Honoria, Augusti, have paid their vow to the Holy Church Hierusalem."[97] Santa Croce in Gerusalemme had been the palace church of the empress dowager Helena, mother of Constantine, who had endowed it with a relic of the True Cross.[98] The narrative that linked Helena with the discovery of the True Cross had been concocted by Ambrose, in 395, when he delivered the funeral oration over the corpse of Theodosius I, Galla's father.

The brief residence of the imperial family at Rome in late 425 served to reconnect Galla with the church, the aristocracy, and her own faith. When at Rome she could pray at the oratory of Felicitas that Pope Boniface (418–422), the man whose election to the papacy she countenanced, had built for his own burial.[99] The structure, lavishly endowed with gifts from the grateful pope, had been a refuge in time of distress and doubt during Alaric's sieges. Post-410 Rome had ample room for restoration and improvement. Renovations were spearheaded by the church and by pious individuals. Galla may have been present at the ceremony that laid

---

96. The moment was later commemorated on an ivory casket (known variously as the Pola or Samagher), where the two are accompanied by a person identified as Helion; M. Guarducci, *La capsella eburnea di Samagher: Un cimelio di arte paleocristiana nella storia del tardo impero* (Trieste 1978), 106–120. For another interpretation, emphasizing the similarity between the front scene depicted on the casket, interpreted as the Lateran baptistery erected by Sixtus III between 432 and 440, and the Lateran façade shown on the ivory diptych commemorating the consulship of Felix in 428, T. Buddensieg, "Le coffre en ivoire de Pola, Saint-Pierre et le Lateran," *Cahiers archéologiques* 10 (1959), 157–200 (with relatively good reproductions as well). Another side of the same Pola casket depicted an adult Valentinian, his wife Eudoxia, and their daughter Eudocia. On imaging the latter, see also Merobaudes, *Carmen* 1, in ch. 5. The casket is also the earliest dated (439) depiction of the tomb of Christ in the church of the Holy Sepulchre in Jerusalem, scarcely a century after its construction; G. P. S. Freeman-Grenville, "Review of S. Gibson and J. E. Taylor, *Beneath the Church of the Holy Sepulchre, Jerusalem. The Archaeology and Early History of Traditional Golgotha*," *Journal of the Royal Asiatic Society* 6 (1996), 94.

97. *ILS* 817 = *ICUR* II.11, p. 435 n. 107 = *ILCV* 1775 (Eng. trans. Oost), 270.

98. Krautheimer, *Rome*, 24; Brubaker, "Memories of Helena," 52–75.

99. Mackie, *Early Christian Chapels*, 257.

the foundations for Santa Sabina, a basilica considered "the most graceful and splendid Early Christian church to survive in Rome."[100] One mosaic panel at S. Sabina depicted three somberly dressed matrons, each representing a different faith, Christianity, Judaism, and paganism, a proximity that belied the irreducible distance between them. The theme conformed to actuality. As Galla vowed at the church of the Holy Cross in Rome, she was to remain faithful to her promise to uphold dynasty and dogma.

100. Krautheimer, *Rome*, 45.

CHAPTER FIVE

A Bride, a Book, and a Pope
(437–438)

A Body of Laws and a Bride from the East

Harmony [*Concordia*] of the table portrayed hovers
   over the doors,
As does the sacred pair of the imperial house
Where festive guests carry on eternal banquets
and the royal couches are resplendent with purple coverlets.
Sparkling at the center of the ceiling is the emperor himself,
With his wife, like the bright stars of heavens on high.
He is the much revered salvation of the land.
In front of our protector a recent exile weeps over sudden
   loss of power.
Victory has restored the world to the one to whom nature has
   given it,
And an illustrious court has furnished a bride from afar.
Here when [you behold] his sacred mother seeking the kisses of
   her placid son
You would think that you see the Castalian god with his mother;
When [you see] his sister standing by you would think that
The shining moon glitters with her brother's light . . .
Look, a young child only recently come into the world
Already carries the mystic rites in her young heart
Attesting God's presence within her by her cries.[1]

---

1. Merobaudes, *Carmen* 1, ed. and trans. F. M. Clover, *Flavius Merobaudes: A Translation and Historical Commentary* (Philadelphia 1971), 11 (English, slightly modified), 60 (Latin), 16–27 (commentary).

By 437, when Valentinian III, Galla's son, attained his majority, Galla had been the dominant figure at the court for a dozen years. Turning eighteen, Valentinian was fit to rule alone, in theory as well as in practice. The moment of transition was also marked by a wedding. In late 436, Rufius Antonius Agrypnius Volusianus, an eminent member of the Roman senatorial aristocracy,[2] sailed to Constantinople to conduct marital negotiations on behalf of the Ravenna court. The bride-to-be was Licinia Eudoxia, daughter of Theodosius II and Eudocia, granddaughter of Arcadius, Galla's half brother. Valentinian and Licinia had been betrothed as children, just before Galla returned to the west in 425.[3] Between restoration and marriage, the domain that Galla and Valentinian received had diminished dramatically. Britain was all but lost; Vandals occupied good portions of Roman North Africa; Goths had been in control of the Gallic southwest (Aquitania) for two decades; and Sueves controlled the Spanish northwest.[4] Valentinian's credentials as potential husband of the daughter of the most powerful monarch of the Mediterranean were perhaps no longer quite obvious.

Notwithstanding, Volusianus successfully negotiated a marital settlement before his sudden death in January 437, still in Constantinople. Valentinian left Ravenna in July 437. The wedding had been scheduled to take place in Thessalonike, a city that marked the frontier between the eastern and western parts of the Roman Empire. It was also the city where Valentinian had been hailed Caesar back in 424, in Galla's presence.[5] The venue was then changed to Constantinople, apparently at the request of the well-brought-up young man, and out of consideration for his future in-laws. This is at least what Socrates, the church historian, claimed somewhat coyly. There would have been a more weighty reason to switch locations. Thessalonike was the chief city in Illyricum, a region that had become a bone of contention between the eastern and western governments. By the late 430s much, if not the whole, of Illyricum belonged to the Eastern Roman Empire. Yet the pope at Rome continued to assert his supremacy over the see of Thessalonike, and indeed over the entire diocese, a state of affairs that neither Theodosius II nor the patriarch of Constantinople

2. See his intricate family tree in Chausson, "Une soeur de Constantin: Anastasia," 142; and Chausson, *Stemmata aurea*, passim.

3. *Marc. Com.* s.a. 424.

4. These developments are covered in practically every book that touches on the history of the west in the fifth century. See Halsall, *Barbarian Migrations*, passim, for an overview, esp. p. 248 on the significance of the decade between 434 and 442.

5. Socrates, *HE* 7.44.

endorsed.[6] Neither emperor nor cleric would have regarded Thessalonike as neutral wedding territory. For both, the location embodied concession to papal aspirations. The wedding was moved to the bride's own city, within a stone's throw of her parents' palace.[7]

That it was a lavish affair need not be doubted, in spite of the absence of eyewitness accounts. If we had any, these would have resembled the wedding panegyric of 307 C.E. that an unnamed man had addressed to both groom (Constantine) and father-in-law (Maximian). Then, as in 437, the oration celebrated simultaneously two ostensibly unrelated events. In 307 these were the elevation of the bridegroom to the rank of Augustus and his marriage with the latter's daughter (Fausta). The subject was not so much the nuptials itself as the promising marital alliance between two powerful men, an emperor (the Augustus Maximian, with a daughter, Fausta) and a Caesar (Constantine, currently unmarried) about to become an Augustus and a relative:

> What event in human affairs could be more conducive to renown and glory, or more certain to provide security, than that there be added to your pristine harmony and your unbroken loyalty this pledge, too, venerable for its most intimate union of the highest names, inasmuch as an emperor has given a daughter in marriage to an emperor? . . . For what more precious thing could you give, or you receive, since with this marriage alliance of yours, Maximian, your youth has been renewed for you through your son-in-law, while you, Constantine, have been enhanced by the name of Emperor through your father-in-law?[8]

The bride made a fleeting appearance, but not at the wedding itself. Rather, her engagement at a tender age to Constantine, at least a decade before the wedding itself, was recalled not by the power of memory but through a brief *ekphrasis*, an artful description of a work of art:

> There is no doubt that he [Maximian] who had chosen you [Constantine] of his own accord long ago to be his son-in-law,

6. T. Jalland, *The Life and Times of St Leo the Great* (London 1941), 175–204, esp. 202–3.

7. I am less certain than Oost, *Galla Placidia*, 244, that the marriage symbolized the union of the two parts of the empire. Had this been the case, Theodosius's ministers would not have elected Marcian in 450.

8. *Pan. Lat.* VII (VI) 1.4, 2.1, Eng. trans. and commentary Nixon and Saylor Rodgers, *In Praise of Late Roman Emperors*, 191–92.

even before you could have sought this [marriage], was erecting for you at an early date that sacred pinnacle of divine power. For this, I hear, is what that *picture in the palace at Aquileia, placed in full view of the dinner guests*, demonstrates. In it a young girl already adorable for her divine beauty, but as yet unequal to her burden, holds up and offers to you, then still a lad, Constantine, a helmet gleaming with gold and jewels, and conspicuous with its plumes of a beautiful bird, in order that her betrothal present might enhance your beauty, a result which scarcely any ornaments of clothing can produce.[9]

No imaginative operation was required of a panegyrist in 437, if asked to perform a similar feat. Like his counterpart 130 years before, he could have lavished compliments on the two male protagonists, the senior emperor Theodosius and his junior imperial colleague, Valentinian, already a blood relative (Galla was Theodosius's aunt) and about to tie the family knot even tighter. And once again like the early orator, the panegyrist could dispense with an address to either bride or mothers-in-law. While the presence of Eudocia, Theodosius's wife, at the Constantinopolitan wedding of her daughter can be taken for granted, that of Galla is far from certain.

A few years after the 437 wedding, one of the attendees, a young Spanish soldier who had accompanied Valentinian to Constantinople, embarked on an *ekphrasis* of a palatial dinner banquet, a literary feat reminiscent of that devoted to the picture in the Aquileian palace.[10] At the center of the composition that may have embellished the formal reception room at Valentinian's Ravenna palace was a majestic rendering of the reigning couple of the Eastern Roman Empire, Theodosius II and Eudocia.[11] In front of them was Valentinian, depicted as a weeping exile

---

9. Ibid., 6.1–2, Nixon and Saylor Rodgers, 198–99, my italics. The dates are unclear since neither Fausta's date of birth nor that of Constantine have been established. She may have been barely five years old upon her engagement to Constantine, who was her senior by some twelve years. J.-P. Callu, "Le prince charmant: quelques prodromes antiques," in *L'éloge du prince: de l'antiquité au temps des lumières*, ed. I. Cogitore and F. Goyet (Grenoble 2003), 125–35, repr. in J.-P. Callu, *Culture profane et critique des sources de l'antiquité tardive* (Rome 2006), 583–93.

10. Merobaudes, *Carmen* 1 (fragmentary), above n. 1, with *PLRE II*, 756–57 (Merobaudes). My interpretation relies primarily on Matthews, *Laying Down the Law*, 4, which differs considerably from that of Clover and others.

11. Medallion portraits of the two also graced the mosaic painting that Galla commissioned for the church of John the Evangelist in Ravenna; Rebenich, "Gratian," 372–73, and below.

seeking assistance from his formidable relatives.[12] If correctly read, he would have been a toddler at that point (423) in the pictorial reconstructed sequence. His age was hinted at through the exceptional depiction of Galla as a doting mother.

Merobaudes's poem recaptured the history of the western imperial family between two turning points, its nadir with the arrival of the exiled Galla and her young children in Constantinople in 423, and its apogee with Valentinian's wedding to Licinia Eudoxia and the birth of Placidia, their first child, in 438/439. The verses re-created the tension between the moment of despair, when the fate of Galla, Valentinian, and Honoria hung in precarious balance, and the time of surpassing happiness, an unexpectedly joyful, even romantic end. Women dominate the picture— Eudocia, Licinia Eudoxia, Galla, Honoria, Placidia, each presumably depicted according to her significance but none existing outside the male nexus. Three mother-daughter pairs, Eudocia-Licinia, Galla-Honoria, and Licinia-Placidia, celebrate the founding myth of men. Bearers of dynastic legitimacy and continuity, the women verify the bridegroom's lineage and parentage.

Besides the two imperial families, now linked yet again, no other figure features in the surviving lines of Merobaudes's poem. Nor is it possible to gauge its original length—was the *ekphrasis*, like that of 307, a brief excursion into the past within a much longer composition? Whatever the main subject would have been, the omission of the two consuls of 437 from a description of the wedding would have been striking. They included the poet-soldier's own patron, Aetius, and Sigisvult, another general of the western Roman army whom Galla had sent to deal with the alleged revolt of Boniface in 430. Merobaudes could have made much of the exceptional nature of a year made so distinguished not only by an imperial wedding and by Valentinian's coming of age but also by a joint consulate of two westerners, both famous military men. Such an appointment was unprecedented, suggesting an unwonted concession on the part of the eastern court. Merobaudes could have also paid poetic homage to the senators whom Galla empowered to negotiate the royal wedding. Men like the enormously influential Volusianus and Anicius Acilius

12. Here lies the most radical departure from most interpreters of Merobaudes's words, who ordinarily assign the role of the exiled protagonist to Huneiric the Vandal, whom Valentinian engaged to his daughter in 442/443.

Glabrio Faustus, and up-and-coming provincial aristocrats like the young Gallic noble Consentius whose command of Latin and Greek rendered his presence invaluable in any diplomatic dealings with the eastern court.[13]

We can only speculate on the manner in which a panegyrist would have presented Theodosius's unique gift to his recently acquired son-in-law. The parting present was an imposing copy of a text, a legal code authorized by the eastern emperor and designed to lay down the law for both parts of the empire. When Faustus presented the Theodosian Code to his fellow senators at Rome in 438, the preface provided the clearest articulation of the purpose of the compilation:

> The felicity which emanates from our immortal emperors proceeds in its increase to the point that it arrays with the ornaments of peace those whom it defends in the fortunes of war. . . . The most sacred emperor, our lord Theodosius, desired . . . that regulations established by his order should be observed throughout the world. . . . The immortal emperor, our Lord Valentinian, with the loyalty of a colleague and the affection of a son, approved this undertaking.[14]

In so masculine an undertaking there was no specific reference to Galla, other than the appropriation of the title "son" for Valentinian by Theodosius, a forceful reminder of seniority. It is precisely how the "we" of men was expressed in this address, collegial and peremptory, that illustrates the transition from Galla's regency to her son's sole rule.

The universal validity that the Theodosian Code trumpeted confirmed an entrenched ideology of an indivisible empire: laws emanating from either part of the empire were always issued in the name of all the rulers. Imperial summons to ecclesiastical councils bore the names of all the reining monarchs, regardless of location, and even petitions from remote provincial towns to their emperor politely addressed all the legitimate emperors.[15] The letter of amnesty that restored the good name

13. *PLRE II*, 307–8 (Consentius II).

14. *CTh. Gesta Senatus* 2, trans. Pharr, slightly modified.

15. As that from Syene in southern Egypt to Constantinople that begins with: "to the masters of land and sea and of every nation and race of men, Flavius Theodosius and Flavius Valentinianus, Eternal Augusti," *Fontes Historia Nubiorum* III, 314, ed. T. Eide et al., Eng. trans. Millar, *Greek Roman Empire*, 63. Millar, 57, on the 430 letter of Theodosius summoning the Council of Ephesos, with *ACO* I.1.1. para. 25.

of the elder Flavianus in 431, undoubtedly Galla's initiative, duly listed Theodosius II as the senior emperor and Valentinian as coemperor.[16]

Although the Theodosian Code was an exclusively eastern enterprise, its antecedents had been planted in the west. In addition, the idea of instilling order in the chaos that governed judicial decisions and precedents had already occurred to Galla. When Theodosius II announced, in 429, his intent to gather laws issued by all the Christian Roman emperors since Constantine, the committee he appointed spent nearly a decade (429–437) gathering thousands of imperial regulations. Most of the laws came from western archives, especially those of Africa, Gaul, and Italy. Yet the last western law that found its way into the Theodosian Code was issued in 432, half a decade before the code's final redaction.[17] Of the laws issued in the west during Galla's regency (425–437), only twelve passed the editorial committee of the code. Are we to believe that Galla never troubled to govern via laws? If the number accurately represents the scope of her legal activities, it would amount to a single law per year, a striking aberration in view of an average of some twenty laws per regnal year (based on a total of some 2,500 laws spread over some 125 years). Moreover, seven laws, namely more than half of those issued from the western chancellery between 425 and 437, belonged to a single year (428–429), the year of Volusianus's prefecture (of Italy). We are then left with an average of a single law every other year.[18] Should one surmise that Galla appointed quaestors who were exceptionally idle? Should we conclude that no petitions or other matters requiring imperial pronouncements reached the court during those years? Were no copies available to be collected, or did Theodosius's legal experts decide to deliberately ignore the laws that Ravenna issued on Galla's instructions? Was this a legal limbo?

At the dawn of her regency, Galla lavished a great deal of attention on legislation. In late 426 an exceptionally lengthy law in the shape of an oration to the Roman senate (known as the Law of Citation after one of its surviving components) enunciated rules and remedies on astonishingly disparate matters. Reconstructed from twelve excerpts, the law addressed a crisis of jurisprudence that had hampered the administration

16. See ch. 4, also for the dispatch of Aspar, one of Theodosius's generals, not only to fight John in 425 but also to stem the seemingly unstoppable Vandals in 431. Aspar remained in this part of Valentinian's realm for three years.

17. *CTh* 6.23.3, March 432.

18. Honoré, *Law in the Crisis of Empire*, 248–57, for overview and statistics.

and the execution of justice for decades.[19] It articulated two principles of arbitration based on a hierarchy of juristic opinions to be consulted and cited (namely, whose sentence was to take precedence in case of disagreement among experts); and on criteria regarding "general laws" (namely, which imperial pronouncement would have universal validity and widest application). In addition, the 426 legal oration addressed family matters, such as testamentary law, and law of property relating to gifts and transfers, important issues in themselves whose relevance to the Law of Citations remains tenuous at best. In fact, the very comprehensiveness of Galla's 426 legislation points to an attempt to embark on precisely the same kind of legal venture that Theodosius II was to hijack. Put otherwise, we need not discount the possibility that Galla's court planned to launch its own "Valentinian Code," forestalling the Theodosian Code.

That the western legislation of 426 served as a cornerstone of the Theodosian Code itself is beyond doubt.[20] Nor was it the sole legal compilation that can be associated with Galla's early days. A collection of imperial regulations dealing with ecclesiastical matters, labeled by its modern collector the Sirmondian Constitutions, can be assigned to the mid-420s.[21] It contained twenty-one laws issued primarily between the late fourth and early fifth centuries. The last datable law in the collection (no. 6), addressed to the praetorian prefect of Gaul, dated to 425.[22] Like the Law of Citation, it, too, grouped distinct issues intended to address, and redress, regulations issued during John's usurpation (423–425). Among other stipulations, the law restored privileges to churches and clergy that had lost them under John. It also included a provision that allowed Bishop Patroclus of Arles to expel those he deemed "heretics and schismatics"; and it denied Jews and pagans access to law courts. Ten of the twenty-one Sirmondian

19. *CTh* 1.4.3, 4.1.1, 5.1.8, 8.18.9–10, 8.13.6, 8.19.1; *CJ* 1.14.2, 1.19.7, 1.22.5, 6.30.8, with Honoré, *Law in the Crisis of Empire*, 124–25, 248–57, esp. 250; Matthews, *Laying Down the Law*, 24–26, who further objects to the oft-quoted assumption of an eastern initiative and influence at work on the *oratio* of 426, contra Honoré, *Law in the Crisis of Empire*, 124. Millar, *Greek Roman Empire*, 56.

20. Honoré, *Law in the Crisis of Empire*, 124.

21. Matthews, *Laying Down the Law*, 121–67, for detailed discussion of the genesis of the Sirmondian Constitutions and for textual comparisons with the *CTh*'s versions. It is unclear when and where, exactly, the Sirmondian originated, nor how many imperial constitutions had been included; my attribution to 425 is based on the date of its last law. See also E. Magnou-Nortier, "Autour des Constitutions Sirmonidiennes," in *Traditio Iuris: Permanence et/ou discontinuité du droit romain durant le haut Moyen-âge* (Lyon 2005), 105–197, for text (of eighteen constitutions), translation, and introduction; and J. Rougé and R. Delmaire, *Les lois religieuses des empereurs romains II* (SCh 531) (Paris 2009), 429–539, for text (of sixteen constitutions), translation, and introduction.

22. Matthews, *Laying Down the Law*, 155–60.

Constitutions were incorporated in the Theodosian Code, with signifi-cant editorial revisions.[23]

Between the two legal ventures of 425, the Law of Citation and the Sirmondian Constitutions, Galla and her advisors appeared ready to undertake a major reform of Roman law. It never happened. Perhaps the mammoth project was hindered by troubles in Spain, Africa, and Gaul. Perhaps an admonitory word from Theodosius's court quenched the plan. Galla could ill afford to ignore the wishes of the emperor whose troops secured the installation of her young son as emperor of the western Roman provinces. Be that as it may, when in 438 Valentinian and his entourage returned to Ravenna after wintering with his bride in Thessa-lonike, they had a copy of the Theodosian Code. It was carried by Faustus, newly appointed praetorian prefect of Italy, Illyricum, and Africa, who presented it with great pomp and ceremony in late 438 to his senatorial colleagues in Rome.[24]

What matching gift could the bridegroom's mother give to a girl who had it all? Another luxury codex, carefully selected to reflect Galla's own preferences and status, would have been a perfect match, it seems. That empresses were in the habit of showering books on young relatives is a custom that cannot be proven. We know that Eusebia, wife of Con-stantius II, sent Julian, who indeed was an avid reader, many books to enliven the winter days of his Gallic campaign.[25] Licinia Eudoxia had grown up in a household full of pious and powerful women. In 437, the year of her wedding, her mother, the empress Eudocia, hosted Melania the Younger, the famed ascetic and erstwhile Roman aristocrat.[26] After "talking theology from dawn to dusk" to the ladies of the court, Melania herself fell ill.[27]

I believe that to match a law code issued by the bride's father and containing the best of imperial Christian legislation, Galla presented her daughter-in-law with a text of divinely given laws. This could only have been the laws of ancient Israel, the Torah (the Pentateuch, the first five books of the Hebrew Bible). As described by a poet who lived a century before the wedding, a solemn presentation of such a luxury edition with

23. Raising the question of who took from whom and which version bore the name of the original addressee and correct date. I leave these matters for another study.
24. See ch. 4 on the acclamations that accompanied the reception of the code.
25. Julian's oration of thanks to Eusebia (*Or.* III), 126b.
26. *VM* (Gr.) 50 (Gorce); Eng. trans. Clark, *Melania*.
27. *VM* 54 (Eng. trans. Clark).

appropriate illustrations would have been accompanied with suitable verses honoring donor, recipient, and gift:

> Muse who once used to put poetry in Augustus's hands,
> decked out in a handsome book, gleaming all over in purple,
> written in characters gleaming with silver and gold, had
> marked my words in a painted path. Finely crafted by the hand
> of the copyist, with a pleasing and appropriate sheen, suitable
> for the sacred eyes of *our lady and mistress.* . . . From here you
> make for the venerable court with trembling foot.[28]

We have, in fact, just such an example, the so-called Ashburnham Pentateuch, now at the French National Library in Paris. Its most recent investigator has proposed a date in the second quarter of the fifth century, tentatively pointing even to a possible link with Galla herself.[29]

The Ashburnham Pentateuch: A Woman's Bible Fit for a Bride?

The Ashburnham Pentateuch (hereafter AP) stands out on several accounts. It is the earliest extant illuminated Latin Pentateuch known. It contains a remarkable number of surviving pages, 143 folios of text and nineteen miniatures. And its history seems as adventuresome, inventive, and self-inventive, as that of Galla herself.[30] The names of either donor or dedicatee have disappeared, as have those of the scribes and

---

28. Publilius Optatianus Porfyrius, *Carmen* 1, cited with translation in A. Cameron, "Petronius Probus, Aemilius Probus and the Transmission of Nepos: A Note on Late Roman Caligraphers," in Carrié and R. Lizzi Testa, *Humana Sapit*, 123. The italics are mine; the original is couched in masculine terms.

29. B. Narkiss, *El Pentateuco Ashburnham* (Valencia 2007), 311. This is a beautiful multilingual edition designed to accompany the beautiful facsimile of the text. Especially welcome are the redrawings that accompany each of the illuminated pages, highlighting the order of each of its components.

30. Ibid., on previous scholarship. I am grateful to have had the privilege of "conversing Galla" with Professor Narkiss in Jerusalem shortly before his death. I have also benefited from e-mail correspondence with Larry Nees, who naturally is not in the least responsible for my views. My own analysis deliberately avoids consideration of style and iconography, both domains of art historians. I note, however, the curious if not striking visual similarities between the AP and the fifth-century illustrated *Ravenna Annals*, especially the arrangement of text and picture; Bischoff and Koehler, "Ravennater Annalen" (ch. 4 n. 49), 125–38. On the migration of images in late antiquity from one context (e.g., illustrated chronicles) to another (e.g., biblical exegesis), K. Weitzmann, "Illustrations for the Chronicles of Sozomenos, Theodoret and Malalas," *Byzantion* 16 (1942/1943), 87–134. I owe this reference to Roger Scott.

illuminators who toiled over its text and images.[31] Its sources of artistic inspirations have become a subject of lively debate among art historians.[32] Its provenance has proven to be another bone of scholarly contention.[33] Its date has been ascribed, solely on paleographical grounds, to the early seventh century (or late sixth at the earliest). But this, too, no longer bears scrutiny.[34] The earl of Ashburnham, who gave his name to this unusual book, possessed the manuscript for merely forty years (in the second half of the nineteenth century). Most of its long life the AP passed in the town of Tours, whence it was stolen and sold to the earl. In 1887 the manuscript returned to France. Commissioned for a specific event, this lavishly annotated Bible for private consumption celebrated class, rank, wealth, and piety.

The majority of the AP's surviving miniatures relate to Genesis stories. The full list of illuminated folios is:

A. Genesis
  1. Creation
  2. Adam, Eve, Cain, and Abel
  3. The Flood
  4. The end of the Flood
  5. Abraham, Lot, Abimelech, Hagar
  6. Abraham's servant and Rebecca
  7. Isaac, Rebecca, and sons
  8. Issac, Rebecca, and sons

31. The precise relationship between donor and artists remain elusive in spite of the endearing image of a bishop's wife engaged in reading the Bible aloud for the benefit of the craftsmen (artists?), Greg. Tur., *HF* 2.59; see H. L. Kessler, "Pictures as Scripture in Fifth Century Churches," *Studia Artium Orientalis et Occidentalis* II (1985), 17–31.

32. Narkiss, *El Pentateuco Ashburnham*, passim, on Jewish Aramaic as the oldest interpretative layer; K. Schubert, "Jewish Traditions in Christian Painting Cycles: The Vienna Genesis and the Ashburnham Pentateuch," in H. Schreckenberg and K. Schubert, *Jewish Historiography and Iconography in Early and Medieval Christianity* II (Assen 1991), 211–60, esp. 235ff.; J. Lowden, "The Beginnings of Biblical Illustration," in *Late Antiquity and Medieval Art of the Mediterranean World*, ed. E. R. Hoffman (Malden 2007), 117–34; J. Lowden, "The Beginnings of Biblical Illustration," in *Imaging the Early Medieval Bible*, ed. J. Williams (University Park 1999), 9–59, to mention but a few.

33. On the production of illustrated books, like the *Notitia Dignitatum*, in Ravenna as soon as the court moved there in the first decade of the fifth century, G. Cavallo, "La cultura scritta a Ravenna tra antichità tarda e alto medioevo," in *Storia di Ravenna II.2: dall'età bizantine all'età ottonia*, ed. A. Carile (Venice 1992), 79–125.

34. See the decisive comments of A. Cameron, "Vergil Illustrated between Pagans and Christians: Reconsidering 'the Late-4th C. Classical Revival,' the Dates of the Manuscripts, and the Places of Production of the Latin Classics" (review of D. H. Wright's *The Vatican Vergil*, and *The Roman Vergil*), *JRA* 17 (2004), 502–25, esp. 518, who reopens the question of Lowe's paleographical dating of the illustrated manuscripts of late antiquity and the early Middle Ages.

A cursory glance reveals an astonishing ubiquity of women, some whose presence would have been substantiated by Scripture, others a figment of artistic imagination. Genesis 24 provides an instructive example of gender choices and techniques. The story, beautifully narrated, relates a search for a suitable bride. Preliminaries include lengthy instructions given by Abraham to a trusted emissary, his personal slave (Gen. 24:1–9). None is illustrated. The illuminated folio begins with Genesis 24:10, the journey from Canaan to Mesopotamia of the slave and ten laden camels. The latter, increased in number from ten to eleven, occupy a substantial portion of the picture.[35] Genesis 24:11–28, dealing with the initial encounter of Abraham's slave and Rebecca in her hometown, is faithfully if somewhat erratically translated into a sequence of images: the slave meets Rebecca at the well; he asks her for water for himself and for his camels; she promptly and graciously fulfills his wishes; the slave presents her with a gift of jewelry, asks for her name, and requests a place to stay. She invites him to her parents' home. Genesis 24:29–60 takes place at Rebecca's parental home. The domestic scene includes a retelling of the story, beginning with Abraham's injunctions and ending with the meeting at the well (Gen. 24:34–49). The folio dispenses with this repetition. It condenses the exchange between the three men (Abraham's slave and Rebecca's father and brother) and the questioning of the girl herself into a single illustration that indicates a universal consent to the proposed match. Genesis 24:61–67 follows the bride's journey to

---

35. The following is roughly based on Narkiss's presentation of folio 21, from 21a to 21k, *El Pentateuco Ashburnham*, 348–50.

Canaan, the meeting between Rebecca and her intended (Isaac), her ruse (concealing her face with a veil), and their reunion, all elements that the painter included in the illuminated folio.

Throughout the illustrated narratives, captions identify places, protagonists, actions, and reflections. The brief phrases provide a simplified summary of the intricate and often repetitive biblical original with none of its subtleties. The pictured well is identified as the place where "Abraham's slave sees Rebecca" (*hic puer Abrahae ubi vedet Reveccam*), and where he "considers her silently" (*puer Abrahae ubi considerat Reveccam tacite*).[36] The exchange of water for jewelry receives the self-explanatory comment: "Abraham's slave offering Rebecca earrings" (*servus Abrahae offeret inaures ad Reveccam*). At Rebecca's home her father, presumably having heard of the encounter at the well, addresses his daughter: "Bethuel asks his daughter where is the man" (*Betuhel dicit fili[a]e su[a] e ubi est vir*) and then turns to the stranger: "Laban says: come in, blessed by Our Lord" (*Laban dicit ingrede benedicte DN*). At Rebecca's home, captions name Rebecca's father (Bethuel) but identify her mother as "his wife" (*uxor*), and Abraham's messenger as slave (*puer*). Back in Canaan, this time with ten camels, the images recall Rebecca's ruse upon beholding Isaac: "Rebecca is covered/concealed by her overgown" (*Revecca operitur pallio*), although the picture shows neither a veil nor a veiled woman. She is welcomed by Abraham into his home, a gesture not recorded in Genesis 24. The happy ending shows a woman, identified as Isaac's wet nurse (*nutrix*), who embraces Rebecca while a third woman, identified as Rebecca's own nurse, watches with approval.

Women, women everywhere.[37] Their ubiquity provides, I maintain, clues to conformity and congruity, to patrons and purpose. They underline an uneasy alliance between the biblical text and the text of the captions. The illuminated folios include women even when their presence was not warranted by Scripture. In the animated Genesis 24 women are as central as, paradoxically, the camels that dominate both corners of

---

36. The *Vetus Latina* translation, here used, designates the slave as *puer* (literally a child), a term that Jerome's Vulgate amended to *servus*. The Hebrew text designates the man as the oldest and most trustworthy of all Abraham's slaves.

37. Cf. the sizable portion devoted in early Christian Syriac literature (fourth–sixth centuries) to biblical stories featuring women, including the composition of long and elaborate speeches and dialogues to be put in the mouths of female characters to whom the Bible rarely granted a tongue of their own; S. Ashbrook Harvey, "Revisiting the Daughters of the Covenant: Women's Choir and Sacred Song in Ancient Syriac Christianity," *Hugoye* 8 (2005), 13.

the folio. The latter represent the "orient," a remote and exotic terrain, complementing the projection of women's perpetual foreignness.

United through the biblical text, the illustrations of Genesis 24, as of the entire AP, re-create biblical women and environments by eliminating the radical separation between the domestic (female) and public (male) spheres. At stake in the biblical narratives were survival of the (male) name and genealogy. Couples, whether well or badly matched, inscribed their origins into a religious space. Creation itself, according to its illustration, was molded to suit the coupling paradigm. The first folio depicted not a single God of the Creation, as Genesis 1 does, but a divine creative pair composed of a bearded God the Father and a clean-shaven Son, each designated as "almighty" (*omnipotens*).[38]

An emphasis on illustrated wet nurses in the folio accompanying Genesis 24 is especially instructive. Wet nurses are rarely referred to in the Bible. Barring Rebecca's wet nurse, who is mentioned twice (Genesis 24:59, and Genesis 35:8 where she is even named), there are only two other wet nurses in the Hebrew Bible. These are Moses's wet nurse, in reality his mother disguised as a hired hand in order to enter the palace (Ex. 2:7–9), and the woman who nursed King Joash (2 Kings 11:2–3; 2 Chron. 22:11–12), the sole surviving scion of the Davidic dynasty.[39] Sarah had nursed Isaac without the aid of a wet nurse (Gen. 21:7–8). So evidently did most other biblical women unless they belonged to royalty. Rebecca remains an inexplicable exception. The appearance of not one but two wet nurses in the AP's illustrated version of Genesis 24 seems deliberate.

When Melania the Younger arrived in Constantinople to convert to Christianity her uncle Volusianus, whom Galla had entrusted with the marital negotiations, both uncle and niece fell sick.[40] The ground for so radical a change had been prepared by Paulinus of Nola, Melania's relative and Galla's erstwhile connection.[41] In Melania's absence, the empress

38. Narkiss, *El Pentateuco Ashburnham*, 329–30, 402–12, on "binity" creation, at the expense of the Holy Spirit in John's Gospel.

39. C. Meyers et al. (eds.), *Women in Scripture*: A Dictionary of Named and Unnamed Women in the Hebrew Bible, the Apocryphal/Deuterocanonical Books, and the New Testament (Boston 2000), 65–66 (Deborah, Rebecca's wet nurse), 277–77 (Joash's wet nurse).

40. *VM* 54 (Gorce) and above. A. Chastagnol, "Le sénateur Volusien et la conversion d'une famille de l'aristocratie romaine au Bas-Empire," *REAug* 58 (1956), 241–53, repr. in A. Chastagnol, *L'Italie et l'Afrique au Bas Empire* (Lille 1987), 235–47.

41. Chastagnol, "Le sénateur Volusien," 252–53, on Volusianus as the addressee of Paulinus's *Carmen ad Antonium (poema ultimum)*, which he assigns to a date between 410 and 436.

(Eudocia) sent Eleuthera, a wet nurse, to attend to Volusianus's spiritual and physical needs. The woman had nursed Licinia Eudoxia, Valentinian's intended bride.[42] Eleuthera accomplished what sickness had prevented Melania from doing, namely "liberating" Volusianus from his pagan past. The final step of Volusianus's desired conversion is ascribed by her biographer to Melania herself, who recovered just in time to watch her uncle receiving deathbed baptism. Perhaps, then, the ubiquity of wet nurses in the artistic rendering of Genesis 24, another story of marital negotiations and a bride from afar, was due to the prominence of these women at the courts of Constantinople and Ravenna. Galla herself would have met in Constantinople the Iberian prince Nabarnugios (later known as Peter the Iberian), whose wet nurse was the first to inculcate Christian tenets in him and whose memory he carried with him all his life.[43]

A Pentateuch, then, the definitive divine laws that had guided the history of ancient Israel, provided a perfect balance in an exchange intended to proclaim each side's commitment to a Roman Christian empire. It affirmed its patron's commitment to a Christian reading of the Law of Israel, just as the Theodosian Code acknowledged Theodosius's debt to his Christian predecessors. Both codices were unique in their completeness, one incorporating all five books of the Torah, the other all Christian imperial laws of universal validity.

If, as I maintain, the Ashburnham Pentateuch was likely commissioned by Galla for Licinia Eudoxia, and presented at her wedding with Valentinian, this "feminist" interpretation of Genesis served to forge a bond between (the absent) mother-in-law and the new empress of the western Roman Empire. A "Woman's Pentateuch" of this sort suggests choices carefully calculated to highlight a community of interest and experience among women. These images expressed issues central to Galla's, Valentinian's, and Theodosius's regimes, namely uncompromising commitment to orthodoxy, and acknowledgment of the role that

---

42. *VM* 55 (Gorce). Is she to be identified with Eleuthera, one of Pulcheria's attendants who became a solitary (*PLRE II*, Eleuthera)?

43. On Zuzo, Peter's wet nurse, *Vita Petri Iberi* 6 (Raabe), Eng. trans. C. Horn and R. R. Phenix, *John Rufus: The Lives of Peter the Iberian, Theodosius of Jerusalem and the Monk Romanus* (Atlanta 2008). Peter reached the capital at age twelve; his date of birth is unclear (409, 412, 417). I prefer 412, a date that would bring Peter to Constantinople in 424/425, precisely when Galla resided in the city. On Peter, C. Horn, *Asceticism and Christological Controversy in Fifth Century Palestine: The Career of Peter the Iberian* (Oxford 2006).

the collectivity of women had in promoting the dynasty and its credal ideology. These principles would be put to the test in the late 440s when the harmony hovering over the painted Ravenna banquet of Mero-baudes turned to discord.

Odd as the journeys of the Theodosian Code and the Ashburnham Pentateuch between east and west may appear, they were hardly a novelty. In 388/389 Achantia carried all the way from Constantinople back to her Spanish homeland a corpse and a text. The former belonged to her husband, the Spaniard Maternus Cynegius, who had served Galla's father (Theodosius I) as praetorian prefect of the east.[44] The latter was a Latin recension of consular annals (*descriptio consulum*), which had, in fact, originated in the 340s in the west, in the Gallic city of Trier. During its eastern "residence" in Contantinople, the original text was augmented. It was one of these later expanded compilations (known as *Consularia Constantinopolitana*, the Constantinopolitan consular annals) that Achantia carried back to the west with her. And it is to her pen, or rather to her inspiration, that the surviving manuscripts owe an unusually long entry devoted to Cynegius, as well as a reference to herself. In fact, besides Helena, Constantine's mother, Achantia is the only woman mentioned in the entire compilation.[45] Her Spanish version of the consular annals enjoyed a long afterlife—it was copied and dispatched from Spain to every corner of the western empire.

Rome: Empress and Pope

> It is appropriate, most holy and venerable daughter Augusta,
> that piety should prevail. Therefore, may your clemency, in
> accordance with the catholic faith, once again share our
> objectives along with us, as it always has been, so that whatever
> was done at that disorderly and most wretched council should
> by every effort be subverted. Regarding the issues remaining in
> suspense, the case of the episcopal see [Constantinople] should
> be referred to the Apostolic see [Rome] in which the blessed

---

44. See ch. 2 n. 18. The lady allegedly even walked all the way from Constantinople.

45. R. M. Errington, *Roman Imperial Policy from Julian to Theodosius* (Chapel Hill 2006), 306–7, n. 65; R. Burgess, *The Chronicle of Hydatius and the Consularia Constantinopolitana* (Oxford 1993), 215–45.

Peter, the first of the Apostles, who also held the keys of the
heavenly kingdoms, was the prince of bishops. For we ought in
all things, in our immortal conduct, to yield the primacy to
that city which filled the whole world with the domination of
its own *virtus*, and committed the globe to being governed and
preserved by our empire.[46]

These are Galla's last recorded words. They were addressed, in a letter,
to Pulcheria, her niece and Augusta of the Eastern Roman Empire. The
message read plainly—the orthodox credentials of neither empress
(Galla) nor bishop of Rome (Leo) could be held to higher standards.
Underlying such open assertions was a presentation of symbolic comparisons, between Galla's and Pulcheria's strength of Catholic conviction, and between the status of the bishops of the old and the new
imperial capitals. No other document reflected more fully the reinven-
tion of Galla. None showed more clearly her open alliance with the
most elevated ecclesiastical position in her realm. By early 450, the
metamorphosis that obliterated Galla's early escapades had been complete.[47] The Galla who set out to lend the power of her pen and imperial
authority to the pope had cast herself as guardian of imperial morality
and universal orthodoxy.

In the background was a dispute that, at first glance, had nothing
whatsoever to do with the west, or with either Galla or the pope. In 448
Eutyches, an influential abbot at Constantinople, sought input from Leo
at Rome regarding the dogmatic debates (mostly over the nature of
Christ) that then raged in the east.[48] Before Leo had a chance to delve
into the intricacies of the issues raised by Eutyches, the latter was deposed
on the initiative of Flavian, patriarch of Constantinople. A council summoned in Ephesos in 449, however, reversed decisions, reinstating
Eutyches and deposing Flavian. The reversal was engineered by the

46. Leo, *Ep.* 58 = *ACO* II.3.1.18, trans. Millar, *Greek Roman Empire*, 37.

47. An anonymous chronicler described Galla's later life as "irreproachable" following her
"conversion" (*conversio*), *Chron. Galla.* s.a. 452, 136 (*Chron. Min.* I, 662), and below ch. 7.

48. Leo, *Ep.* 20 (*ACO* II.4.3). What follows is largely based on R. Price, "The Council of Chalcedon (451): A Narrative," in *Chalcedon in Context: Church Councils 400–700*, ed. R. Price and M.
Whitby (Liverpool 2009), 70–91; and on G. E. M. de Ste. Croix, "The Council of Chalcedon with
Addition by Michael Whitby," in *Christian Persecution, Martyrdom, and Orthodoxy* (Oxford 2006),
259–319. See also Jalland, *Life and Times of St Leo*, 205–398, for great detail on Leo and the churches
of the east; and R. Price and M. Gaddis, *The Acts of the Council of Chalcedon*, vol. 1 (Liverpool
2005), 1–85 for general introduction, and 86–107 for Leo's feverish exchange of letters in 450–451.

bishop of Alexandria, who presided over the proceedings at Ephesos, and countenanced by the emperor himself (Theodosius II). Still, Eutyches had powerful patrons at the imperial court, chief among them Chrysaphius, the chamberlain whose influence over the emperor even neutralized the powerful Pulcheria.[49]

Directly following his condemnation in 448, Eutyches addressed appeals to both Leo of Rome and Peter (Chrysologus), bishop of Ravenna. He had hoped, it seems, to gain the ear of the western court (which was, as he well knew, closely related by blood to Theodosius II) through the bishop of the western capital.[50] Peter preferred words to action and merely admonished Eutyches to heed Leo's words, warning the appellant of the dangers of speculation in the hidden mystery of the Incarnation.[51] Since Peter was also legalistically minded, he added a clever comment on the endless appetite of his eastern colleagues for delving into matters that should have been resolved centuries before:"Human laws remove human questions after thirty years; the birth of Christ, which was written in divine law and cannot be expressed in words, is after so many centuries being tossed about in reckless disputes."[52]

The trenchant response to Eutyches's plea reflected both deference to the authority of the apostolic see and the court's cautious neutrality.[53] Leo, addressing Flavian of Constantinople, reminded his eastern colleague of Rome's role as the guardian of "what the venerable fathers have decided and divinely sanctioned," namely the doctrines of the Council of Nicaea (325), by then over a century old.[54] Leo also dispatched Hilary, his trusted deacon (and later pope), to Ephesos to attend the 449 council. The assembled eastern bishops elected to ignore Leo's aspirations to exert papal authority as arbiter of universal orthodoxy and conformity, which the pope had eloquently articulated in a long letter to Flavian (later made famous as the "Tome of Leo"). Onsite at Ephesos, Hilary's

49. *PLRE II*, 295–97.

50. D. M. Gwynn, "The Council of Chalcedon and the Definition of Christian Tradition," in Price and Whitby, *Chalcedon in Context*, 13 [7–26], on doctrine. T. Jalland, *Life and Times of St Leo*, 219; and S. Wessel, *Leo the Great and the Spiritual Rebuilding of a Universal Rome* (Leiden 2008), 276, on the appeal to Peter Chrysologos.

51. Leo, *Ep.* 25 (Peter to Eutyches), with Jalland, *Life and Times of St Leo*, 219–20.

52. Leo, *Ep.* 25.1, trans. Wessel, *Leo the Great*, 276.

53. Wessel, *Leo the Great*, 276, nor was Peter authorized to hear such cases without the consent of the bishop of Rome.

54. Leo, *Ep.* 23, Eng. trans. E. Hunt (The Fathers of the Church 34).

protestations remained likewise unheeded.[55] Even Pulcheria, to whom Leo dispatched a letter on the day he wrote to Flavian, could not alter the council's decisions (and Flavian's deposition).[56] Pope Leo and Valentinian III rejected both the dogma and the decisions reached at Ephesos. By contrast, Theodosius II, in whose domain all these events had taken place, insisted that the deposed bishop of the capital was "chief cause of contention" and that his removal contradicted neither faith nor justice.[57] Schism between east and west seemed in the air.

At the beginning of 450 the imperial household relocated from Ravenna to Rome.[58] The imperial entry into the ancient capital coincided with the feast commemorating the establishment of St. Peter's episcopacy in Rome (*cathedra Petri*).[59] Leo could not resist the opportunity to present to the court an account of the sorry state of affairs in the other imperial capital (Constantinople). The dramatic scene at St. Peter's was described by Galla in a letter to her nephew, Theodosius II:

> When on our very arrival in the ancient city [Rome], we were engaged in paying our devotion to the most blessed Apostle Peter, at the martyr's very altar, the most reverend bishop Leo, waiting behind for a while after the service, uttered laments over the catholic faith to us. Calling as witness the chief of the Apostles himself, whom we had just approached, and surrounded by a number of bishops whom he had brought together from numerous cities in Italy by the authority and dignity of his position, adding tears to his words, Leo called upon us to join our moans to his own.[60]

Galla's letter signaled the start of an exceptional wave of communications between the two branches of the Theodosian dynasty. Of the seven

55. On the "Tome" and its rather convoluted history, B. Green, *The Soteriology of Leo the Great* (Oxford 2008), 188–247. Hilary fled just in time to avoid subscribing to Ephesos's dogmas, acknowledging the indispensable assistance of John the Evangelist, to whom he, like Galla, later dedicated a chapel in the Vatican, *LP* 242–48, with Mackie, *Early Christian Chapels*, 195–211. *ILCV* 980 for the dedicatory inscription.

56. Leo, *Ep.* 31, with Green, 203.

57. Leo, *Ep.* 62–64, with Ste. Croix, 277.

58. On the relocation of the court to Rome as "the precise moment when a truly 'Roman' empire was reestablished," Millar, *Greek Roman Empire*, 55.

59. Leo, *Ep.* 55.1, with Gillett, "Rome, Ravenna," 147. Pietri, *Roma Christiana*, I, 382.

60. Leo, *Ep.* 56, Eng. trans. NPN (available on the Internet). Price and Gaddis, *Acts of the Council of Chalcedon*, 160 n. 6, note that Galla erroneously referred to the canons of Nicaea, rather than to canon 4 of the 343 council of Sardica, as the measure authorizing an appeal from the Constantinopolitan bishop to the pope at Rome. The error was in all likelihood Leo's.

letters sent from Rome in support of Leo's stand (449/450), five were written by or addressed to women, including two written by Galla and one addressed to her:

1. Galla Placidia to Theodosius II
2. Licinia Eudoxia to Theodosius II
3. Galla Placidia to Pulcheria
4. Theodosius to Galla Placidia
5. Theodosius to Licinia Eudoxia[61]

Leo had hoped that a combined western appeal, from aunt, daughter, and son-in-law, would convince Theodosius II to reverse, yet again, a synodal decision and to reinstate Flavian. The appeals that Leo elicited from Galla, Valentinian III, and Licinia Eudoxia were to be simple and straightforward: the decisions of Ephesos were illegal; only Leo, and a council on Italian soil, had the power to decide matters pertaining to the faith.

The letters provided an opportunity for women of the western court to demonstrate their own commitment to orthodoxy as defined by the papacy on their very territory. Repetition proved essential. Galla's letter to Pulcheria described yet again the scene in St. Peter's:[62]

> Because of sadness interspersed with sighs, Leo was scarcely able to convey his request in words. The constancy of priestly wisdom having the upper hand, he contained his tears long enough to deliver, as vindicator of the faith so violated [at Ephesos] a clear sermon. . . . [We] recognized that at the council in Ephesos, where no one guarded either the order or standard of the priesthood, everything was executed with such lack of consideration for the divinity that obstinacy and injustice were said to prevail throughout.[63]

Moving from drama to dogma, Galla urged Theodosius II, her nephew, to heed the advice of the pope, reminding the emperor of the deference due to Rome itself:

---

61. Leo, *Ep.* 56, 57, 58, 63, 64; Millar, *Greek Roman Empire*, 231. For a full exposé of the letter collections that circulated with the Acts of Chalcedon, including the letters penned by the members of Galla's family, Price and Gaddis, *Acts of the Council of Chalcedon*, vol. 3, 157–79.

62. A message that "retains its significance as the only example from classical antiquity of a letter from a woman to a woman on a major matter of public policy," Millar, *Greek Roman Empire*, 231.

63. Leo, *Ep.* 58 (Galla to Pulcheria), Eng. trans. Wessel, *Leo the Great*, 262, modified.

The faith . . . has been recently muddied by the will of a single man [Dioscorus, bishop of Alexandria] who at the synod of Ephesos was said to have incited hatred and contention, intimidating Flavianus, the bishop of the city of Constantinople, by the presence and the fear inspired by the soldiers because he had sent a petition to the apostolic see . . . wherefore let your grace resist such illegality and ordain that the true faith of the catholic religion may be preserved inviolate to the end that, in accordance with the letter and decision of the Apostolic see, which we all alike honor as the first of all, Flavian may remain in all respects secure in the rank of the episcopate, and the case may be referred to the synod of the Apostolic see, in which he who was deemed worthy to receive the keys of heaven was the first to be awarded the office of the chief bishopric: since it is fitting that in all things we should show respect for this glorious city which is the mistress of the whole earth.[64]

She also called on Pulcheria, whose power at the court at that point she misjudged, to dismiss the case against Flavian.[65] At the same time Licinia Eudoxia demanded that her father hold a new synod to review the decisions reached at the 449 Council of Ephesos.[66]

Form and contents of the letters posed "a direct challenge, transmitted through the channels of familial relationships, to the authority of the eastern imperial court and its capacity to participate in ecclesiastical affairs."[67] Theodosius's reply to Galla reflected both his grasp of the singularity of her statements and his displeasure, insisting on his uncompromising orthodoxy:

By this letter we declare what has often been written about thoroughly and clearly . . . that at Ephesos we have neither defined nor decreed nor understood anything beyond the faith of the fathers, the divine dogmas, or the definitions of the most reverend fathers who had been in Nicaea under the auspices of

64. Leo, *Ep.* 56 (Galla to Theodosius), Eng. trans. Wessel, *Leo the Great*, 262, slightly modified, and Jalland, *Life and Times of St Leo*, 265.
65. Pulcheria withdrew from the court following Chrysaphius's attempt to ordain her; Theophanes, *AM* 5940, with Holum, *Theodosian Empresses*, 192f.
66. Leo, *Ep.* 57 (Licinia Eudoxia to Theodosius), *Ep.* 58. Wessel, *Leo the Great*, 263.
67. Wessel, *Leo the Great*, 261.

Constantine. . . . This alone we had bidden—that all those who harm the holy churches by their attacks be removed in a fitting manner.[68]

Yet imperial women had been active and visible promoters of Christianity already at the dawn of the fourth century. The travels of Helena, mother of Constantine, throughout the Mediterranean to the Holy Land were not only a mission of piety but also "a public act of state."[69] Along her journeys Helena affirmed dynastic commitment to Constantine's newly adopted creed, as well as to the ideology of divine investment in him as the sole ruler of the Roman Empire.[70] Justina, Galla's grandmother, clashed with Ambrose, bishop of Milan, over the rights of Arians to worship openly in the imperial capital (Milan, at that point) and in their own church.[71] Even with such precedents, Galla's readiness to enter the fray of complex and often impenetrable politics of dogma highlights a novel aspect of fifth-century imperial politics.

In 418/419, not yet an Augusta, Galla intervened in disputes over papal succession. In 421 Honorius, who was the senior emperor between 408 and 423, did not hesitate to counter the claims of Constantinople to exert patriarchal jurisdiction over Illyricum, a territory officially within the domain of the Eastern Roman Empire, although subjected to papal jurisdiction.[72] The correspondence between Honorius and Theodosius II in the early 420s, as well as Honorius's insistence on the inviolable rights of Pope Boniface in Illyricum, accompanied the emergence of a close community of interests between popes and emperors in the west, a solidarity that reemerged in Galla's letters to Pulcheria and to Theodosius II.[73]

Few chapters in the history of church and state provoked so vividly a sense of the vigor of imperial women as the correspondence between the two courts residing at Rome and Constantinople in the early months

68. Leo, *Ep.* 63 (Theodosius to Galla), Eng. trans. Wessel, *Leo the Great*, 267, modified.
69. Hunt, *Holy Land Pilgrimage*, 35, for the citation.
70. Ibid., 34.
71. See ch. 4.
72. Coleman-Norton, *Roman State*, no. 375, for English translation of the letters and the law; Millar, *Greek Roman Empire*, 53–54. See also Wessel, *Leo the Great*, 114–21, for a brief overview of the vicariate of Illyricum and its vicissitudes.
73. For a recent discussion of the vexed question of the affiliation of Illyricum in the fifth century, MacGeorge, *Late Roman Warlords*, 32–39, 64, reaching a conclusion that only a part of the diocese was formally ceded in the 430s (p. 38) and that it mattered little to each side, since much of it had been out of imperial control anyway and run by various barbarian invader-settlers.

of 450. Leo's request to hold an arbitrating council in Italy presented an opportunity to bolster the credentials of both pope and court as prime proponents of universal orthodoxy. Although the imperial letters failed to achieve their purpose, the collaboration between court and pope, likely inspired by Galla, crystallized her full and final reintegration into the political fabric. Her support of papal ambitions, and the manner in which she communicated Leo's desires, evocative yet authoritative, conformed to the system and confirmed her belonging. Applying the lesson learned from Justina's bitter encounters with Ambrose of Milan, Galla knew how wise it was under the circumstances to avoid confrontation with a powerful and ambitious prelate. Nor could she afford to pick a quarrel with the bishop of Rome, the city she now selected as her new residence.

CHAPTER SIX

Between Rome and Ravenna

(438–450)

Time to Remember: Theodosius III at Rome

Galla's last public appearance was at a funeral in Rome in the year 450. It was a conspicuous public affair, full of pomp and ceremony and attended by pope and senate.[1] The funerary procession came to a halt at St. Peter's. A tiny corpse, covered with a gold cloth and carried in a cypress wood coffin sheathed in silver, was solemnly deposited in a marble sarcophagus of surpassing beauty.[2] The weight of the dead baby, whom none of the accompanying dignitaries had known in person, must have been as light as a feather. He had been dead for more than three decades. Nor did he pass away in Rome, nor even in Italy, but in Spanish Barcelona.

The dead infant has been identified as Theodosius III, son of Galla and Athaulf.[3] He was born in late 414 or early 415 in Barcelona, died shortly afterward, and was interred on Spanish soil.[4] The imperial mausoleum at Rome where his sarcophagus was placed occupied a reassuring space beside St. Peter himself. A circular building crowned by a

---

1. Prosper, *Chron. Reich. Add.* 12 (s.a. 450): "Theodosius cum magna pompa a Placidia et Leone et omni senatu deductus et in mausoleo ad apostolum Petrum depositus est." S. I. Oost, "Some Problems in the History of Galla Placidia," *CP* 60 (1965), 7–8; Mackie, *Early Christian Chapels*, 177–78. The absence of Valentinian III from the funeral seems pointed unless glossed over by the chronicler, below.

2. Cf. the golden bier that bore the corpse of the young Pulcheria, daughter of Theodosius I and half sister of Galla; Gregory of Nyssa, *Oratio*, see ch. 2 n. 74.

3. Oost, *Galla Placidia*, 134.

4. When the corpse first reached Italy remains unclear, perhaps already in 415. At any rate, Theodosius III featured with two other imperial boys who died in infancy, Gratian and John, on the mosaic at the church that Galla dedicated to John the Evangelist, around 430; see below.

dome, the structure sported architecture fit for royal blood, a deliberate counterpart to the splendid mausoleums at the Church of the Holy Apostles in Constantinople where emperors from Constantine onward had been buried.[5] The location at Rome had been chosen originally by Anastasia, sister of the emperor Constantine, as her own tomb.[6] It had served as the last resting place of several members of Galla's family, including Honorius, her half brother, his two wives, Maria and Thermantia, and Constantius III, Galla's husband.[7] The addition of Galla's long-deceased son to the distinguished dead reminded the audience, if they cared to speculate, of what could have been had Theodosius III survived. Would he have become the first half-barbarian to rule Rome as its lawful emperor?

Of all the imperial cities, Rome provided an ideal stage on which to engage in funerary displays. A series of suburban cemeteries, often dotted with sumptuous chapels commemorating those who had died for the faith, encircled the city. Rome's periphery had become focal points of Christian worship, private and public. Beyond the walls and along the roads that led to and from the city, it was possible to pay homage to the dead as well as to one's favorite martyr, be it St. Agnes on the Via Nomentana, St. Lawrence on the Via Tiburtina; SS. Marcellinus and Peter on the Via Labicana, St. Sebastian on the Via Appia, or St. Paul (S. Paulo fuori le mura) on the Via Ostiene, not to mention St. Peter himself.[8] Worship at these *martyria* provided respite, a moment to remember the dead and the holy.[9]

5. G. Downey, "The Tombs of the Byzantine Emperors at the Church of the Holy Apostles in Constantinople," *JHS* 79 (1959), 27–51; P. Grierson, "The Tombs of Obits of the Byzantine Emperors (337–1042)," *DOP* 16 (1962), 1–63. But see also D. Woods, "On the Alleged Reburial of Julian the Apostate in Constantinople," *Byzantion* 76 (2006), 364–71.

6. Mackie, *Early Christian Chapels*, 59. Note the diffusion of the name Anastasia in the family of Constantius I (Constantine's father) and its allied clan of the Seneciones Albini, as well as the various additions and alterations at St. Peter's connected with the other Anastasiae, esp. a granddaughter of Constantine; Chausson, "Une soeur de Constantin," 131–55, esp. p. 146 for putative family trees, and p. 147 for the inscription of Gallus, *Anastasiae natus (ICUR* 4122 = *ILCV* 1759) at St. Peter's; and Chausson, *Stemmata aurea*, passim.

7. M. J. Johnson, "On the Burial Places of the Theodosian Dynasty," *Byzantion* 61 (1991), 338.

8. R. Lim, "People as Power: Games, Munificence, and Contested Topography," in *The Transformation of Urbs Roma in Late Antiquity*, ed. W. V. Harris (*JRA* supp. 38) (Portsmouth 1999), 265, and 277 on the informal character of martyrs' celebration as opposed to the official *feriae publicae* of Sundays and other Christian high holidays (265–81), with C. Pietri, *Roma Christiana*, 2 vols. (Rome 1976), I, 3–77. On the debate regarding the location of Peter's bones, H. Chadwick, "St. Peter and St. Paul in Rome: The Problem of the *memoria apostolorum ad catacumbas*," *JTS* 8 (1957), 31–52.

9. M. Salzman, "The Christianization of Sacred Time and Sacred Space," in Harris, *Transformation of Urbs Roma*, 126–27, on the explosion in numbers of martyrs and bishops recognized and honored in and around Rome.

Within Rome's massive walls, imperial and papal endeavors gradually baptized spaces sacred to ancient divinities. Under Constantine such enterprises were grand in scale yet discreet in location. The Lateran complex and the Church of the Holy Cross (Santa Croce in Gerusalemme) were tucked away on the side of imperial palaces, "striving for splendor" amid private mansions and gardens.[10] Constantinian princesses made Rome their burial place of choice, a place where they expected to be remembered for all eternity, like the saints to whose *martyria* they joined their own mausoleums. The mausoleum of Constantina (S. Costanza), Constantine's daughter, on the Via Nomentana outside the walls, joined the shrine dedicated to St. Agnes, "the victorious virgin," on land owned by the imperial family. When Constantina died far from Rome in 354, in Bithynia, her corpse was taken to Rome to be buried in her appointed mausoleum.[11] The body of her sister, Helena, who died in Gaul in 360, was likewise dispatched to Rome to occupy its own space in the same funerary structure.[12] Citizens of Rome who came to pay their respects to Agnes, or to their own dead, could admire in addition the stunning mosaics that embellished the walls of the imperial mausoleum. These bore twenty-four biblical scenes, a dozen from the Hebrew Bible and a matching dozen from the New Testament, each intended to intercede on behalf of the dead and to ensure their salvation.

Saintly proximity, secured by a timely donation, had already dictated the selection of grounds for another imperial mausoleum, built for Helena, the first Christian empress, by her son Constantine. Erected atop a cemetery that had served the imperial horse guard, the mausoleum was adjacent to a basilica built in honor of those who had died for the faith during an era of persecution (SS. Marcellinus and Peter).[13] The complex, like that of Agnes, Constantina, and Helena, had been strategically located along a highway, the Via Labicana, southeast of the Porta

10. R. Krautheimer, *Rome: Profile of a City, 312–1308* (Princeton 1980), 24; H. Brandenburg, *The Ancient Churches of Rome from the Fourth to the Seventh Century*, trans. A. Knopp (Turnhout 2005), 253, for cited phrase.

11. *ILCV* 1768, with Brandenburg, *Ancient Churches*, 70; in general on S. Costanza, ibid., 69–86. Mackie, *Early Christian Chapels*; M. J. Johnson, *The Roman Imperial Mausoleum in Late Antiquity* (New York 2009), 139–56.

12. Amm. 21.1.5.

13. Brandenburg, *Ancient Churches*, 55–60, esp. 59, on the belated identification of the shrine with Marcellinus and Peter; Mackie, *Early Christian Chapels*, 56–57; Johnson, *Roman Imperial Mausoleum*, 110–18.

Praenestina (Sessoriana). Upon its completion, Constantine, "for love of his mother and to honor the saints," endowed her mausoleum and the basilica with precious gifts of a gold paten, chalices, a chandelier, pitchers, silver candelabra, and an altar cast in pure silver, as well as with landed properties yielding substantial annual incomes, a worthy accompaniment to the imposing porphyry sarcophagus where Helena was laid to rest.[14]

It seemed inevitable that sooner or later the great site of St. Peter on the Vatican Hill would receive its own imperial dynasty. The appropriation of space next to the basilica by Galla's family was first recorded in 450, when she conducted the internment of her son Theodosius. Planted challengingly within a stone's throw of the city walls, Constantine's monumental church never stopped growing. From its very beginnings it attracted extensions that included fountains, monasteries, baptisteries, triumphal arches, colonnaded streets, and even protective walls of its own, all financed by emperors, popes, and wealthy individuals.[15] In 359 the stunning sarcophagus of Junius Bassus, who died during his prefecture of the city of Rome, was placed only a few feet away from that of St. Peter himself, as though the apostle and the noble administrator continued to discuss weighty matters beyond the grave. Three decades later the monumental sarcophagus of another distinguished senator, Petronius Probus, was placed not in the church itself but in a mausoleum abutting the apse of St. Peter's. Such aristocratic manifestation of "territorial piety" rendered Rome and St. Peter paradigmatic, a majestic backdrop for ceremonial displays of newly found credal affinity between the Roman senatorial nobility and the great apostle.[16]

A funeral march in 450 through Rome, from the palace to St. Peter's, would have been an opportunity for princess and pope to unite all Rome in mourning. The stately procession would have been a compelling demonstration of Galla's dynastic claims and an affirmation of her staying power. For Pope Leo the moment provided a public stage for his conviction of the role of St. Peter's see in rejuvenating Rome's claim to be

14. *LP* 26 (Davis); Johnson, *Roman Imperial Mausoleum*, 116.
15. Brandenburg, *Ancient Churches*, 91–102.
16. J. Matthews, "Four Funerals and a Wedding: This World and the Next in Fourth Century Rome," in *Tranformations of Late Antiquity: Essays for Peter Brown*, ed. P. Rousseau and M. Papoutsakis (Farnham 2009), 129–46, 137 for the cited expression.

"head of the world" (*caput mundi*). A funeral of a dead prince was as good a reminder as any that it was neither the empire's military might nor imperial laws that made Rome the hub of the world, but Peter, the rock of the church and fountainhead of her rulers.[17]

Because Rome's primacy was challenged, not the least in the recent Council of Ephesos (449) when papal protests were ignored, the united funerary front of empress, senate, and pope at Constantine's St. Peter's bolstered Rome's aspiration to be the supreme judge in all matters, doctrine and ecclesiastical discipline.[18] That the pleas issued in 450 by Galla, Valentinian III, and Licinia Eudoxia to Theodosius II were ignored could not have compromised the solemnity of the ceremony. Rather, the belated internment would have served as a reminder of fruitful collaboration between papacy and imperial court. In 440 Leo, then deacon, had been entrusted with negotiating a discreet settlement of a dispute that Valentinian's court was unable to resolve. Details are scanty. Apparently a quarrel had flared suddenly between Aetius and Albinus, then the two men in charge of military and civil affairs, respectively, in Gaul.[19] Only two years before, in 438, Albinus and his senatorial colleagues at Rome lauded Aetius with repeated acclamations, thanking him for his military labors.[20] The senate even voted a bronze statue in Aetius's honor, to be placed directly behind the curia, the senate's venerable meeting place. The inscription designated him as "guarantor of [senatorial] liberties."[21]

Little in such amicable proceedings appeared to predict a rift. But the 440 breach of *amicitia* between Albinus and Aetius—perhaps over taxing the aristocracy, a group notoriously reluctant to saddle extra charges, perhaps over Aetius's initiative of minting coins for his troops, a measure solely at the discretion of the civil authorities—threatened the stability of the throne itself.[22] The selection of Leo as mediator may

17. Leo, *Sermo* 82, 83; Krautheimer, *Rome*, 46.

18. Wessel, *Leo the Great*, 296–97, and see ch. 5.

19. *PLRE II*, 53 (Albinus 10) proposes to identify him with Albinus 7, *praefectus urbis Romae* in 414, possible but doubtful.

20. *CTh* (*Gesta senatus*), with Matthews, *Laying Down the Law*, 41–42.

21. *Année epigraphique* 1950, 15; Coulon, *Aetius*, 195. This was perhaps the occasion of the delivery of Merobaudes's first panegyric of Aetius, pace *PLRE II*, 25–26.

22. The sole source is Prosper s.a. 440. Coulon, *Aetius*, 194 (table) appears to indicate that with the exception of Albinus's open hostility to Aetius, perhaps representing the mood of his clan, the Caeionii, it is difficult, if not downright impossible, to determine the precise degree of enmity or friendship between Aetius and members of the Roman senate. Twyman, "Aetius," passim.

have been due to Galla.[23] She had recognized quite early on the value of ecclesiastical intervention. In 427 she had sent Maximinus, a seasoned bishop, in addition to an army, to quell, successfully, a rebellious general in Africa.[24] Her joint appearance at Rome in 450 with Leo and the senate, including perhaps Albinus, who had just completed a six-year tenure as the praetorian prefect of Italy, Illyricum (now rather reduced), and Africa (now mostly under Vandal control), at the funeral of a half-barbarian-Arian child, would have been an exceptional moment of unity of the western court, the senatorial aristocracy, and the papal establishment.[25]

Time for Reflection?

Had there been a Claudian, or even a Merobaudes, to hail the senate at the 450 funeral, a sense of senatorial dignity and ideology would have emerged:

> All the nobles, offspring of the Tiber and Latium, throng the
>   consecration.
> Gathered in one are all the great ones of the earth
>   that owe their rank to you and to your father.
> Many a consular surrounds you,
>   the consul whose good pleasure it is to associate the senate
>   in your triumph,

23. In fact Leo, who was close to Pope Sixtus III and became his immediate successor, appears an odd choice if Albinus had been a party to accusations brought against Sixtus. The accusations and the subsequent inquiry are related in a document, *Gesta de Xysti purgatione*, now edited by E. Wirbelauer, *Zwei Päpste in Rom: der Konflict zwischen Laurentius und Symmachus (498–514)* (Munich 1993), deemed a forgery produced c. 500 but perhaps anchored in an authentic core; *PLRE II*, 53 (Albinus 10), with *LP* (Duchesne), I, 232; and J. D. Mansi, *Sacrorum Conciliorum Nova et Amplissima Collectio* V (Florence 1761), 1167, against Barnes, "Patricii," 163–65, who dismisses the *Gesta* altogether. That Auchenius Bassus, whose career prospered during Galla's regency (PPO in 426 and 435; cos. in 431; *PLRE II*, 220–21, below), was evidently a coaccuser further suggests tension between the papacy and the senatorial aristocracy of Rome. On the *Gesta* as a narrative reflecting competition between popes and aristocrats, K. Sessa, "Domestic Conversion: Households and Bishops in Late Antique 'Papal Legends,'" in Cooper and Hillner, *Religion, Dynasty, and Patronage in Early Christian Rome*, 91–96.

24. See ch. 4.

25. P. Wormald, "The Decline of the Western Empire and the Survival of Its Aristocracy," *JRS* 66 (1976), 217–26; C. Wickham, *Framing the Early Middle Ages: Europe and the Mediterranean 400–800* (Oxford 2005).

the nobles of Spain, the wise men of Gaul, and the senators
of Rome, all throng around you.[26]

What the senators, members of Rome's oldest and most venerable insti-
tution, indeed a relic of its spectacular longevity, would have thought
about the return of the court in 450 to the ancient capital is difficult
to gauge.[27] Rome had been left without resident emperors around 300
to become an arena where senators and popes either collaborated or
clashed. The "pervasive continuity of aristocratic influence in late Roman
life" was apparent through initiatives like the endorsement of usurpers
(the senator Attalus in 408 and the notary John in 423) or through the
rehabilitation of dead and condemned senators.[28] The appearance of
Galla in public with both senate and pope signaled the court's awareness
of Rome as the center of senatorial and papal power.

A poem commemorating the funeral would have registered senatorial approbation of the court's policy of filling the higher civilian offices
with scions of the great senatorial families. This policy, launched by
Galla during her regency, marked a departure from Honorius's practice
of filling the same positions with men who had worked their way from
modest beginnings.[29] By 450 she could reflect on the lot of her senatorial
appointees, who by then had retired, had died, or had been shunned in
favor of others, men like Flavius Anicius Auchenius Bassus, son of the
consul of 408 and grandson of the city prefect of 382, who had been
comes rei privatae (treasurer of the imperial privy purse) in 426 and consul in 431, and who disappeared from view in 435 upon terminating his
praetorian prefecture of Italy.[30] Bassus's administrative career lasted
about a decade, a fairly brief span. Did he elect to retire early or was he
deliberately ignored in favor of others? His family's heyday seemed to
have been over with the transition from Galla's to Valentinian's regimes.

The spectacular career of Rufinus Anonius Agrypinius Volusianus
had been launched upon Galla's return to Italy with the prefecture of
Rome (417–418).[31] In 428–429, soon after Galla was restored to Ravenna

26. Claudian, *De IV Cons. Hon.* 578–83, Eng. trans. Platnauer (Loeb).
27. Gillett, "Rome, Ravenna," 147–48, correctly notes that the court relocated from Rome to
Ravenna before Italy was geared for Attila's attacks, hence a "relocation" rather than a "retreat."
28. Matthews, *Western Aristocracies*, 386, for the quote. See ch. 4 for the 431 rehabilitation of
Flavianus.
29. Jones, *Later Roman Empire*, I, 177. Ibid., I, 550–51, on the stratification of the senatorial class.
30. *PLRE II*, 220–21 (Bassus 8), and Bassus 7, esp. on the (hypothetical) family tree.
31. *PLRE II*, 1184–185 (Volusianus 6). On his deathbed baptism, see ch. 5.

by Theodosius II, Volusianus became praetorian prefect of Italy. In 436 he represented the Ravenna court at Constantinople, conducting the delicate negotiations of the proposed nuptials between Valentinian III and Licinia Eudoxia. Volusianus's deathbed baptism (January 437), orchestrated by his niece Melania and executed by Licinia's wet nurse, corrected a rightful sense of incongruity. The pagan aristocrat finally gave up his gods, bowing to the pressure of the correct creed.

In 430 a man named Theodosius held the office of praetorian prefect of Italy and Africa.[32] He, too, would have been one of Galla's appointees. In 426, as chief notary, Theodosius solemnly presented, no doubt to considerable applause, the imperial law that remitted the *aurum oblaticium*, the obligatory contribution that the affluent senators were expected to offer on the occasion of the accession of a new emperor.[33] If this Theodosius is to be identified with Macrobius Ambrosius Theodosius, it seems that after five years of administrative responsibilities he promptly elected to retire to a life of luxury and literary leisure. A year after his retirement he had already produced the *Saturnalia*, a banqueting discourse of aristocratic nostalgia, followed by grammatical treatises and commentaries on classical authors. His friend and successor in the prefecture, Nichomacus Flavianus (the younger), embarked, conversely, on the longest career possible. In his teens, he had been governor of Campania, perhaps in the late 370s under the emperor Gratian.[34] By 431, when he successfully rehabilitated the name of his father, Flavianus the younger had ascended the administrative ladder via the proconsulship of Asia (382–383) and the prefecture of Rome (three times, including one under a usurper). The crowning gem of his exceptionally lengthy career came with the praetorian prefecture of Italy, Illyricum, and Africa under Galla in 431.[35] He would have been about ninety years old at that point. The younger Flavianus indulged in literary aspirations while vacationing on his African estates.[36] By 450 he must have been deceased.

Still during Galla's regime (425–437), another aristocratic scion three times occupied the "more or less ornamental office of the prefect

---

32. *PLRE II*, 1101 (Theodosius 8) to be plausibly identified with Macrobius Ambrosius Theodosius (*PLRE* 1102–103, Theodosius 20), author of the Saturnalia.

33. *CTh* 6.2.25, with Matthews, *Western Aristocracies*, 356.

34. He had been born c. 358, pace Hedrick, *History and Silence*, 27. Matthews, *Western Aristocracies*, 26, on the probable date of governorship.

35. *PLRE I* (Flavianus 4). On Macrobius and Flavianus, see ch. 4.

36. Matthews, *Western Aristocracies*, 374.

of the city" of Rome.[37] This was Anicius Acilius Glabrio Faustus, who reached the consulship in 438 (or 439).[38] In 437–438 he held the praetorian prefecture of Italy, in which capacity he attended Valentinian's wedding in Constantinople and received a copy of the Theodosian Code, which he presented to the senate at his own home on December 25, 438. Faustus also weathered the transition from Galla's to Valentinian's sole rule—his last recorded office was the prefecture of Italy, for the second time, in 442. By 450 he would have been either too old to attend the funeral of Galla's infant son or perhaps dead.

Flavius Albinus, who rose to the urban prefecture in 426, disappeared from the rosters of Galla's regency only to reappear in 440 as the praetorian prefect of the Gallic dioceses and as the praetorian prefect of Italy throughout most of the 440s (443–449).[39] In 444 he was consul. When in Gaul, Albinus clashed with Aetius, then the general in charge of the troops stationed there. A quarrelsome man, Albinus was also involved in allegations leveled against Pope Sixtus III in the 430s. If he is to be identified with Caecina Decius Acinatius Albinus, who had been the urban prefect in 414, he was a well-connected man.[40] Nor did his clash with Aetius hamper his career. By 450 Albinus, who may have been of Galla's age, would have perhaps retired, to emerge, albeit briefly, to take part in the 450 ceremonies with Galla and Leo, the cleric who had reconciled him to Aetius back in 440. His appearance at the internment would have been a touching demonstration of loyalty to Galla, his patroness.

Senatorial destinies could also lead to murder. Another of Galla's aristocratic contemporaries, Petronius Maximus, ended up as killer of her son.[41] Of noble origins, Maximus had held the office of treasurer (*comes sacrarum largitionum*) in "extreme youth," thence proceeding to hold, twice, the prefecture of Rome (in 420–421 and 439), and once of the west (c. 440). Maximus held the consulship twice, in 433 and 443, an exceptional honor for a civilian, even a well-connected one. In spite of

---

37. Jones, *Later Roman Empire*, I, 177, for the quote. The three prefectures are unclear: I. 408 (or 423), II. 425, and III. 437, pace *PLRE* (below), 421/423 for the first of the three, pace Matthews, *Western Aristocracies*, 356.

38. *PLRE II*, 452–54 (Faustus 8).

39. *PLRE II*, 53 (Albinus 10). But see R. J. Weber, "Albinus: The Living Memory of a Fifth Century Personality," *Historia* 38 (1989), 472–97, on difficulties of identification.

40. *PLRE II*, 50–51 (Albinus 7).

41. *PLRE II*, 749 (Maximus 22). He was born in the late 380s.

the fact that Maximus did rather well under the combined patronage of Honorius, Galla, and Valentinian III, he murdered Valentinian in 455, inheriting both throne and wife. His reign lasted two months. His murderous accession emphasized the tension that must have lurked under the cordiality that Galla, who had died in November 450, had established with the senate of Rome.

The singularity of the process of divesting or investing Galla's senatorial nominees highlights the absence of Aetius from the 450 ceremonies at St. Peter's.[42] Had he been present, he would have been placed right next to the princess and the pope, ahead of the senators who had been both consuls and patricians. Aetius's prominence would have been guaranteed both by his powerful position as the supreme commander of the western army and by a law, issued under Galla, on the order of precedence of dignitaries on public occasions.[43] The law ranked former consuls according to temporal seniority, regardless of second consulships and regardless of the acquisition of the title of *patricius*. Among contenders for the first place in the 450 public procession would have been Bassus, who had been consul in 431, a year before Aetius became consul for the first time (432) and two years before Petronius Maximus was granted his first consulship (433). The other contender for the same ceremonial honor, in the absence of both Bassus and Aetius, was Petronius Maximus.[44]

Had Aetius been present at Rome in 450, the reinternment of Theodosius III would have been an apt moment for reflection on his remarkable career and relations with Galla. According to one assessment, their fates were intrinsically intertwined:

> He [Aetius] had been the guardian of Placidia, who was the
> mother of Valentinian, and of her son when he was a youth,
> through his connection with the barbarians. He had made war

42. This is of course a conjecture. The year 450 had no record at all for Aetius, as is also reflected in the chronological table reconstructed by Coulon, *Aetius*, 343–45, where no activity is listed for that year. See also T. Stickler, *Aëtius: Gestaltungsspielräume eines Heernmeisters im ausgehenden Weströmischen Reich* (Munich 2002).

43. *CJ* 12.3.1, dated by Seeck, *Regesten*, to 426 but by Barnes, "Patricii," 167–68, to 437. I tend to follow the former.

44. Perhaps Sigisvult was in attendance at the internment. In this case the *Nov. Val.* 11 would have given Petronius Maximus precedence over him in spite of Sigisvult's acquisition of both consulate (437) and the title *patricius*; Barnes, "Patricii," 158–59.

on Boniface when he crossed from Libya with a great force, so that he [Boniface] died by disease under the burden of his cares, and Aetius became master of his wife and property. He had killed by craft Felix, who had held the generalship with him, when he found out that at Placidia's instigation this man was making preparations for his removal. He had warred with the [Visi]Goths of western Galatia who attacked the territories of the Romans [and had their kingdom in Gallic Aquitania since 418]. He had also subdued the Aemorichians [of Brittany] who were hostile to the Romans. To put it briefly, he had wielded the greatest power so that not only kings but even nations dwelling nearby came at his orders.[45]

Were Aetius and Galla sworn enemies, as has been asserted?[46] What role did memory play in establishing or maintaining dependence? Boniface, who emerged in the early 420s as Galla's sole champion, had fought, successfully, against her first husband, Athaulf, in southern Gaul (413).[47] Given a chance, she believed that Boniface would become a turncoat. In this light, it would not be wise to underestimate the mystifying effect of shifting alliances. Once Boniface was dead and Aetius in control of military affairs (in 432), further opposition on Galla's part to the latter would have been deemed futile. No other generals were apparently available or ready to assume the responsibilities that Aetius shouldered.[48] Moreover, during much of his career Aetius kept busy in Gaul and along the frontiers, away from Ravenna and Rome. Had he attended Valentinian's wedding in Constantinople in 437, as has been conjectured, Aetius's (unlikely) presence would have reflected the court's official discourse of reconciliation and unanimity.[49] Both were fixtures of the political tradition established by Theodosius I, and both required constant reshaping, particularly during regimes headed by women and by meek emperors.

---

45. John of Antioch, fr. 201.3, trans. in C. D. Gordon, *The Age of Attila* (New York 1960), 50.
46. Oost, *Galla Placidia*, passim.
47. Olympiodorus, fr. 22.2 (Blockley).
48. It is curious that Sigisvult retained his titles of *comes* and *magister utriusque militiae* until at least 448, although after his African mission of 427 only one military venture is associated with his name, the organization of coastal defenses against the Vandals in 440, *Nov. Val.* 9.
49. Barnes, "Patricii," 168, and n. 68.

At the 450 gathering around the coffin of Theodosius III, the absence of the infant's half sister, Iusta Grata Honoria, Galla's only daughter, would have been as remarkable as that of Aetius. In 449 Honoria's activities hastened a Hunnic invasion of the west, a threat that accounted for Aetius's absence from the Roman funerary ceremonies.[50] At thirty-one in 450 (she was born in late 417 or 418) Honoria had been a celibate, probably vowed to perpetual virginity, as had been her aunts at the court of Constantinople. Galla had little reason to consult Honoria's own desires. Yet the mother possibly overestimated the profession of virginal vocation as quencher of worldly ambitions or of sexual drives:

> Honoria, although of royal line and herself possessing the symbols of authority [i.e., the rank of Augusta], was caught going secretly to bed with a certain Eugenius, who had the management of her affairs. He was put to death for this crime and she was deprived of her royal position and betrothed to Herculanus, a man of consular rank and of such good character that it was not expected that he would aspire to royalty or revolution. She brought her affairs to disastrous and terrible trouble by sending Hyacinthus, a eunuch, to Attila so that for money he might avenge her marriage. In addition she also sent a ring pledging herself to the barbarian, who made ready to go against the western empire. He wanted to capture Aetius first for he thought he would not otherwise attain his ends unless he put him out of the way. When Theodosius learnt of these things he sent a message to Valentinian to surrender Honoria to Attila. Valentinian arrested Hyacinthus and examined the whole matter thoroughly. After inflicting many bodily tortures on him, he ordered that he be beheaded. Valentinian granted his sister Honoria to his mother as a boon, since she persistently asked

50. The date of Honoria's affair and the subsequent invitation to Attila has been established by J. B. Bury, "Justa Grata Honoria," *JRS* 9 (1919), 1–13, in spite of an entry in the chronicle of Marcellinus Comes that assigns the affair to 434, followed by Holum, *Theodosian Empresses*, and by Croke, editor and translator of Marcellinus. A date earlier than 449 would have rendered the tale's fictionality instantly apparent.

for her. And so Honoria was freed from her danger at this time.[51]

As a background to Attila's invasion of Gaul and the battle of the Catalaunian Plains in 451, the story of a disgruntled princess appeared to have digressed from facts to fiction. The depiction of Honoria as a woman driven by exceptionally selfish motives may have derived its force from two sources: the idolization of a feminine model followed by the ascetic princesses at the court of Constantinople, and a critique of Galla. The mother in the story used her power to protect a favorite daughter from the justifiable wrath of her brother, having failed to protect the same young woman's virtue and reputation, not to mention the empire itself.

Although the verisimilitude of the story has never been doubted, only a few details inspire confidence.[52] Its accuracy appears compromised by the striking similarity it bears to Galla's own history, and by an underlying comparison with Julia, Augustus's disgraced daughter. Furthermore, the bipolar categorization of female behavior, either chaste and prudent, like the Constantinopolitan royal ladies, or lewd and impudent like Honoria, and possibly like Galla in her early incarnation, undermines the veracity of the tale. It is as though the western branch of the Theodosian dynasty was plagued with illicit love affairs, adventuresome princesses, and short-tempered monarchs. When such unruly characters intersected with crafty and ambitious barbarians like Attila (or vice versa), a scandal was imminent. So alluring and lurid a tale renders difficult the deciphering of the social and political realities lurking behind the reports.

Pieced together, the story of Honoria began with a simple case of sex between unequals. She carried on a clandestine relationship with a

---

51. John of Antioch, fr. 199.2, Eng. trans. Gordon, *The Age of Attila*, 104–5; for text and trans. see also Blockley, 300–302 (= Priscus, fr. 17).

52. It is narrated as fact in practically all modern accounts that touch on Attila (e.g., Halsall, *Barbarian Migrations*, 252). The only scholar who gave it short schrift was O. J. Maenchen Helfen, *The World of the Huns: Studies in Their History and Culture* (Berkeley 1973), 130. Attila's blazing appearance on the western horizon inspired numerous fantasies, not the least a lengthy narrative on the miraculous escape of Ravenna from a fierce siege due to John, the city's half-legendary bishop; Agnellus, *LPR* 37–38, translation and commentary in J. M. Pizzaro, *Writing Ravenna: The Liber Pontificalis of Andreas Agnellus* (Ann Arbor 1995), 101–19. On the heroic mold in which biographers cast bishops, especially when dealing with fierce barbarian monarchs, compare Constantius on Germanus of Auxerre, below, and A. Gillett, *Envoys and Political Communication in the Late Antique West, 411–533* (Cambridge 2003), 115–37.

man of inferior social status, perhaps even a slave or a freedman. Penalties attendant on the discovery of such affairs had been spelled out by a law of the emperor Constantine: "If any woman is revealed to have dealings with [her] slave in secret, she shall undergo a capital penalty, and the worthless scoundrel should be handed over to the flames."[53] Valentinian applied the letter of the law to his sister's lover, who was executed. By the same law, Honoria would suffer the same fate but was saved by Galla's intervention. An imaginary conversation between mother and son would have resuscitated the memory of Julia, Augustus's daughter, whose mother accompanied her to the location of exile selected by Julia's father:

> That very year at Rome a calamity occurred in Caesar's household, loathsome to report and dreadful to recall. His daughter Julia, utterly indifferent to her great father and to her husband, left no wanton or lustful disgrace undone that any woman could inflict or suffer, and measured the greatness of her fortune by her license in sinning, claiming whatever she fancied as permissible [list of alleged lovers and their fate]. . . . Julia was relegated to an island, removed from the sight of her country and family. But Scribonia [her mother] accompanied her there as a willing companion in her exile.[54]

If exile had been discussed as Honoria's suitable lot, the option would have confronted Galla with a difficult choice between son and daughter. Would Galla and Valentinian have considered the dour court at Constantinople as a suitable punishment for an unruly princess? Perhaps, but in 449 and 450 the eastern emperor was fully occupied with unraveling ecclesiastical knots. The compromise reached deprived Honoria of her honored title of Augusta.[55] In addition, Valentinian, possibly with Galla's consent, selected Flavius Bassus Herculanus, a staid senator, as

53. *CTh* 9.1.1, with J. Evans Grubbs, "Marriage More Shameful Than Adultery: Slave-Mistress Relationships, 'Mixed Marriages,' and Late Roman Law," *Phoenix* 47 (1993), 125–54.

54. *Vell. Pat.* 2.93, trans. in E. Fantham, *Julia Augusta: The Emperor's Daughter* (Abingdon 2006), 139, and in general on Julia's history, adultery, and exile. See ch. 3 for another appearance of Julia in Macrobius's *Saturnalia*.

55. Conferred by Valentinian or Theodosius II, *PLRE II*, 568, argues for a date "not earlier than 439." In the inscription that Galla had placed in the church dedicated to John the Evangelist to commemorate the salvation of the family from the storms of the sea, Honoria is designated as Augusta. The date of either structure or inscription is unclear but could have been as early as 425, below.

Honoria's future husband. Herculanus's appeal, at least in Valentinian's eyes, consisted of suitable nobility and wealth, the man's readiness to marry a wayward princess, and his notable lack of ambition.

A happy end, it would appear. But appearances tend to be deceptive. Resentful of lost privileges and proposed marriage, Honoria sent a trusted eunuch to Attila with a large enough bribe to tempt the Hun to action. She added a ring, an item that Attila chose to interpret as a marriage proposal. Her timing was impeccable. Attila had been weighing options of advancing his troops farther into Roman territory. With Honoria's alleged backing, he demanded his Roman bride and her share of empire, promising revenge if the lady were ill treated.[56] Theodosius II evidently advised his younger imperial colleague to concede to the dispatch of his sister to the Hunnic camp. Perhaps he believed that such an experience would sober Honoria, as it had her mother. Nor were marital schemes of this sort exceptional. Valentinian himself had betrothed his own daughter, Eudocia, to Huneric, son of the Vandal king Geiseric, in 442/443. Marriage between Attila and Honoria could have bought peace, at least for a while.[57] But Valentinian had his own idea of how to handle his sister's overtures. He had her emissary executed and would perhaps have considered execution for Honoria as well. Galla had to intervene yet again.[58] Honoria's subsequent fate remains unknown.

When Attila decided to attack, he marched westward, to Gaul, to confront Aetius, the man he probably feared most, rather than to rescue his alleged bride. The excuse used to switch courses was a quarrel among the heirs to the Frankish throne, and when battle was joined, at the Catalaunian Plains in 451, Aetius and his Visigothic allies won. Because the story of Attila's invasion of the west has acquired legendary proportions, with popes courageously facing the barbarous Huns and bishops valiantly defending their cities against huge odds, the role of Honoria as an accomplice of a barbarian monarch bent on Rome's ruin would have been subjected to a similar mythification. There were other precedents, besides Galla's. Already in 410 the name of Proba, a venerable Roman aristocrat, was coupled with that of Alaric—she reputedly opened to

56. This is as much as can be gleaned from John of Antioch, fr. 199.2, and Priscus, fr. 20–22 (Blockley).

57. It is unclear whether Honoria was also packed off to Constantinople, an option that Oost, *Galla Placidia*, 283, favors but that is rejected by most modern commentators, *PLRE II*, 568.

58. The precise sequence is unclear. Attila's demands would have been issued on several occasions, once at least before Galla's death in November 450, and another time in 451.

him the gates of Rome, taking pity on the city's starved residents.[59] In 455 it was allegedly Licinia Eudoxia, Honoria's sister-in-law and Valentinian's wife, who invited Geiseric the Vandal to sack Rome. In her case, the invitation was issued to avenge the murder of her husband by Petronius Maximus, who forced her into marriage.[60]

Examined soberly, Honoria's story provides comments on two major aspects of life of aristocratic women in late antiquity—on breakable religious restraint, and on commitment to rank and vocation. Its outline established opposition between the valued and the forbidden, between vows to perpetual virginity and adulterous behavior. Beyond this opposition, the story drew distinctions between royal women of the eastern and the western courts as it aimed to account for the Hunnic invasion of the west. The tale as it was (re)cast by contemporaries lent literary cohesion to a profusion of factors not otherwise easily explained.

It is worth dwelling briefly on the report of the ring. John of Antioch (above) regarded the ring as an additional bribe, and no more.[61] In Priscus's account the ring was instrumental in serving to substantiate Attila's demand for bride and dowry. Rings appeared to play considerable roles in sinister affairs of the heart, hastening the end of the Theodosian dynasty in the west. A few years after Galla's death, her son used a ring as a ruse when attempting to seduce a married woman.[62] She believed that the ring had been sent by her husband, Petronius Maximus. Confronting the latter after her seduction, the violated wife accused Maximus of betraying her trust. The enraged husband killed the imperial adulterer, whose throne he proceeded to occupy and whose wife he married.[63] By then the wife had obligingly vanished to make room for Valentinian's widow. Licinia Eudoxia, clearly unhappy, apparently invited her in-law the Vandal king Geiseric to eliminate her unwanted new spouse. Geiseric arrived with a fleet and proceeded to sack Rome (455), precisely as

59. Olympiodorus, fr. 11.3 (Blockley).

60. John of Antioch, fr. 200 = Priscus 30 (Blockley).

61. An exchange of gifts between an affianced couple after the betrothal agreement but before the wedding was not uncommon, with the *sponsus* (groom-to-be) sending the *sponsa* (bride-to-be) a ring as a pledge of his intentions and fidelity; Evans Grubbs, *Law and Family in Late Antiquity*, 142; L. Anné, *Les rites des fiançailles et la donation pour cause de mariage sous le Bas-Empire* (Louvain 1941), 5–62. In Honoria's tale the opposite is stipulated, namely the *sponsa* sending a ring to the *sponsus*.

62. John of Antioch, fr. 200.1; Eng. trans. Gordon, *Attila*, 51. Date is 455.

63. A narrative molded along the lines of the tale of Lucretia and the end of the Roman monarchy.

Alaric had done in 410. A dramatic sequence infused by raging women, rapacious barbarians, and deceiving Romans—in brief, a perfect literary paradigm to account for the end of an era.

Rome and Ravenna

Galla's divisive family may have been in evidence at Rome in 450 precisely because of the absence of both the emperor and the disgraced sister from the funeral of their older and long gone half brother. The presence of the pope, on whose behalf Galla had just written two trenchant letters to her eastern relatives, evoked the transformation of Rome itself from pagan metropolis to a Christian city worthy of an ambitious pope and a pious empress.[64] This was "a new Rome, Christian and classical, the capital of the pope as spiritual leader of the west and as Peter's successor."[65] This was a city where even church decoration was directly related to the politics of power. At St. Maria Maggiore the church's mosaics were invested with double-edged imagery—a Jesus enthroned with four angels that distinctly recalled a young emperor attended by chamberlains; and a Virgin decked in a manner that echoed an empress ready to meet a reception committee that had come to greet her.[66] The program for this mosaic may have been drawn up by the man who stood next to Galla at the 450 funeral, Pope Leo himself.[67] It was Leo's idea to cover the walls of Rome's great basilicas, St. Peter's, S. Paolo fuori le mura, the Lateran, and St. Maria Maggiore, with biblical scenes drawn from the Hebrew Bible and the New Testament.[68] And it may have been under his inspiration that Galla commissioned a Pentateuch for the wedding of her son with Theodosius's daughter.

Rome provided a ready recipient of imperial construction endeavors, and Galla was set to resume Constantinian traditions. At S. Paolo fuori le mura, on the road from Rome to Ostia, she repaired and completed the structure that her father had started as a replacement of the Constantinian church.[69] In 441, following an earthquake or fire, Galla undertook

---

64. Curran, *Pagan City and Christian Capital,* passim.
65. Krautheimer, *Rome,* 46.
66. Ibid., 49, on St. Maria Maggiore of the early 430s.
67. Suggestion made by Krautheimer, Ibid., 51.
68. Ibid., 52.
69. Ibid., 42.

repairs and redecoration, an endeavor duly commemorated in mosaic inscriptions that were prominently placed. These recorded an ongoing dynastic investment in honor of the apostle, beginning with Galla's father, continuing with her brother Honorius, and culminating in Galla's own commitment and her "rejoicing that the whole beauty of her father's work is resplendent through the zeal of the pontiff Leo."[70]

The wording invited reflection on Galla's new vocation as a pious donor, a performer of acts of magnanimous charity in perfect accord with venerable dynastic traditions. When her father Theodosius, shortly after accession in 379, undertook the remodeling of the church of St. Paul, the endeavor was calculated to insert the new imperial family into the raw fabric of Christian Rome, linking it with both Constantine, the founder of the church, and with the apostle himself:

> Upon consideration of the veneration already sacred from
> ancient times, we desire to adorn the basilica of Paul the
> Apostle for the sake of sanctity of religion and to enlarge it in
> proportion to the number of the assemblage, to exalt it on
> account of zeal for devotion. . . . [H]ence, after consultation
> with the venerable priest [the pope], we [command that] you
> [the urban prefect of Rome] shall arrange the plan for the
> future basilica.[71]

Galla's own donation of 441 would have been perceived as a palliative to the papacy. That same year Valentinian issued a lengthy law that curtailed exemptions that clergymen had thus far had from public burdens.[72] The Vandals' conquest of Carthage in 439 and their subsequent control of Rome's major grain supplies necessitated far-reaching adjustments. Citing current hardships, the law abolished tax immunities, including those customarily accorded to the imperial household itself. Pope Leo may have protested about the curtailed clerical privileges. Four years later Valentinian III conferred on the papacy jurisdiction over all the churches of the western Roman Empire, including Gaul, where the see of Arles had long claimed sole primacy.[73] The words of the

---

70. *LP* 47.6. For the date, Krautheimer, *Rome*, 43.
71. *CSEL* 35.46–47 (*Coll. Avell.* 3), Eng. trans. Coleman-Norton, II, 412–13, slightly modified.
72. *Nov. Val.* 10.
73. *Nov. Val.* 17. Wessel, *Leo the Great*, 53–136, on the complex relationship between Gallic sees, especially the see of Arles under Hilary and the papacy under Leo, esp. 85–86 on Valentinian's law; and Mathisen, *Ecclesiastical Factionalism*, 165–66.

445 concession, preserved in a law addressed to Aetius, were later echoed in Galla's letters to Pulcheria and Theodosius II. All three texts insisted on the intimate link between Christian creed and Roman commonwealth; all three extolled the status of St. Peter and the concomitant standing of the papacy; and all three emphasized the rank of Rome as the Eternal City and privileged papal residence.

At Portus, Rome's port, Galla's name was linked with a colonnaded street (the so-called Porticus Placidiana).[74] Less tangible is Galla's hand in the 429 donation that Felix, chief of staff in the late 420s, and his wife Padusia, her confidante, had made toward a mosaic at the Lateran cathedral, or in the extensive remodeling of Constantine's baptistery at the Lateran and the erection of its palatial papal residence in the 430s, during the papacy of Sixtus III (432–440).[75] She may have encouraged her daughter-in-law, Licinia Eudoxia, to launch her charitable career with the reconstruction of a church dedicated to Paul and Peter on the exclusive Esquiline Hill (Basilica Eudoxiana, now San Pietro in Vincoli).[76] These would have been, in the words of Symmachus, "decorous manifestations of munificence."[77]

On the whole Galla's imprint on Rome, via charitable investments such as the mosaic at Santa Croce, appears limited.[78] It pales by comparison with the recorded donations of wealthy individuals like Vestina, a *femina illustris* otherwise unknown, who endowed the papacy under Pope Innocent (401–417) with substantial properties centering on a church honoring the martyrs Gervasius and Protasius.[79] Nor could Galla's Roman charitable endeavors compare with those of Demetrias, the Anician heiress who had vowed perpetual virginity in 414, and who endowed a church on her estate in honor of St. Stephen during Leo's

74. *ILS* 805; Oost, *Galla Placidia*, 278.

75. *ILS* 1293; Krautheimer, *Rome*, 54.

76. *ILS* 819; Oost, *Galla Placidia*, 248. The basilica dates to 438–440, the last years of Pope Sixtus III. R. Krautheimer, *Corpus basilicarum Christianarum Romae: The Early Christian Basilicas of Rome (IV–IX Centuries)* (Rome 1937–), IV.179–234.

77. Symmachus, *Relat.* 12.3 (384–85), with L. Cracco Ruggini, "Rome in Late Antiquity: Clientship, Urban Topography, and Prosopography," *CP* 98 (2003), 375–76.

78. For the Roman Santa Croce, see ch. 4. *LP* 46 records that Pope Sixtus (432–440) urged Valentinian to present the churches of St. Peter and St. Paul with valuable gifts. If these can be dated to the early years of Sixtus, then one should probably accredit Galla with these extravagant gestures.

79. *LP* I.221 (Duchesne), but see H. Hillner, "Families, Patronage," in Cooper and Hillner, *Religion, Dynasty, and Patronage in Early Christian Rome*, 232, 241, on the rarity of such endowment foundations; and ibid., 225 n. 3, listing twelve major donations of notable individuals.

pontificate.[80] Between popes and pious individuals, Rome in the second quarter of the fifth century was rising with vigor from the debris of Alaric's sack of 410.[81]

Galla spent the better part of her regency (425–437/438) in Ravenna.[82] The youngest of all imperial capitals, Ravenna had been a veritable Theodosian foundation since Honorius moved there in 402. The change catapulted a small town, its adjacent harbor (Classis, where the imperial navy had been based since the first century), and the area between town and port (Caesarea) to prominence, adding territory, a palace, churches, and chapels. Today a tourist who survives the tedious train ride between Rome and Ravenna needs a great deal of imagination to conjure the grandeur of an imperial capital. As imperial capital in the fifth century Ravenna had two distinct advantages over Rome and Milan—it was safely ensconced behind walls and marshes; and it faced eastward, making it relatively easy, if need be, to leave Italy in a hurry by boarding a ship heading due east to Greece. To Honorius and Galla, Ravenna further presented a tabula rasa, a space on which they could leave their individual imprints while dreaming of a city rivaling the great Constantinople.[83]

The presence of an orthodox court did not necessarily ensure the Christianization of Ravenna. The city's first cathedral had been a creation of the early fifth century, perhaps an outcome of collaboration between Honorius and Ursus, the town's bishop between 405 and 431.[84] In the 440s, the new year, coupled with the nomination of the new consuls, was celebrated with pomp and processions that mobilized "an entire factory of idols," to use the words of Ravenna's shocked bishop.[85]

80. *LP* I.238; and *ILCV* 1765.
81. For a description of the Christianization of Rome's urban landscape, in and outside the walls, and of the Romanization of Christianity, Krautheimer, *Rome*, 33–58.
82. Gillett, "Rome, Ravenna," 142–43, for list of attested residences and dates. On the history of the city, see D. M. Deliyannis, *Ravenna in Late Antiquity* (Cambridge 2010).
83. R. Farioli Campanati, "Ravenna imperiale all'epoca di Galla Placidia," *Ravenna: Studi et ricerche* 1 (1994), 177–88, on the deliberate imitation of Constantinopolitan monuments in Ravenna; and R. Farioli Campanati, "Ravenna, Costantinopoli: aspetti topografico-monumentali e iconografici," in *Storia di Ravenna*, ed. A. Carile (Venice 1992), III.2, 127–57.
84. Agnellus, *LPR* 23, with detailed description of its décor and donors. On the adjacent housing complex for the bishops, M. C. Miller, "The Development of the Archiepiscopal Residence in Ravenna 300–1300," *Felix Ravenna* 141–44 (1991–1992), 154.
85. Peter Chrysologus, *Sermo* 155bis, 1, with P. Brown, *Aspects of the Christianisation of the Roman World: The Tanner Lectures on Human Values* (Cambridge 1993) (available via the Internet), 120–30.

Men dressed as the mighty planets, representing the old gods of Rome, swirled solemnly through the Hippodrome of Ravenna, reenacting the promise of renewal.[86] Peter, Ravenna's scandalized bishop, could do little to stem the enthusiasm on such occasions. His counterpart in Constantinople, more conversant with realities, put a stop to monkish protests against the celebration of the Olympic games in Constantinople in 434–435.[87] Even at the heart of the capitals of the most Catholic of emperors, it would have been futile to attempt to cut ceremonies that bore witness to Rome's "eternal energy."[88]

From the vantage point of Agnellus, a ninth-century Ravennate monk, Galla's contributions to the Christian landscape of Ravenna were as significant as those of Honorius, if not more so.[89] Ravenna allowed Galla to advance an ideology of unity between the imperial family and its new capital. There the conjunction of a resident pious empress, an ambitious local prelate, and a territory ready to be molded at will and by wealth, produced a highly charged new discourse. To a significant extent the history of Ravenna in the early fifth century was also the story of Galla.

Equally remarkable appears to have been the close association between Galla and Ravenna's Peter Chrysologus, a bishop whose long episcopate (c. 425–450) witnessed the rise of the city to the rank of metropolitan (c. 430). In the first sermon delivered after his consecration, Peter depicted Galla, in her presence, in glowing terms:

> Also present is the mother of the Christian, eternal and faithful
> Empire herself, who by following and imitating the blessed
> church in her faith, her works of mercy, her holiness, and in
> her reverence for the Trinity, has been found worthy of
> bringing to birth, embracing, and possessing an august
> trinity.[90]

---

86. Brown, *Aspects of the Christianisation*, 130.

87. Callinicus, *Via Hypatii* 33, with Brown, *Aspects of the Christianisation*, 164.

88. Brown, *Aspects of the Christianisation*, 130, for the expression.

89. On Agnellus, see the introduction in Deliyannis, *Agnellus*; and J. M. Pizarro, *Writing Ravenna: The Liber Pontificalis of Andreas Agnellus* (Ann Arbor 1995). On Galla's churches in Ravenna, see Deliyannis, *Ravenna*, 62–84. On the development of the city in late antiquity, see also F. W. Deichmann, *Ravenna: Haupstadt des spätantikes Abendlandes*, 2 vols. (Wiesbaden 1969–1989); and the various volumes in *Mirabilia Italiae* dedicated to specific monuments.

90. Peter Chrysologus, *Sermo* 130.3, Eng. trans. W. B. Palardy, *St. Peter Chrysologus*, Vol. 3 (Fathers of the Church) (New York 2005).

No specifics are given regarding the nature of Galla's universal maternity, nor information about her contribution to Ravenna's landscape. Four centuries after Peter, Agnellus cast Galla as the city's architectural apostle:

> In the church of the blessed John the Evangelist, because of his sanctity, Galla Placidia ordered that the apostle's image in mosaic should adorn the lower wall of the apse, behind the back of the bishop, over the seat where the bishop sits. The image [*effigies*] was constructed in the following manner: it had a long beard, extended hands as though singing the mass, with an angel of the Lord facing the altar as though receiving his prayers. During that time Galla also offered many gifts to the church of Ravenna. She had a lamp made with a candelabrum of the purest gold weighing, as some say, seven pounds, made into one with her own likeness imprinted in a medallion surrounded by an inscription that read: I will prepare a lamp for my Christ.[91]

She also added an inscription within the apse, above the heads of emperors and empresses, that commemorated the dedication of the church (below). The list of Galla's architectural endeavors in Ravenna, as remembered and recounted in the ninth century, further consisted of providing labor and finances for a church honoring Zacharias while enhancing its endowment with a golden chalice. She added a church in honor of the Holy Cross, which she further endowed with a candelabrum. Even in Rimini, a town south of Ravenna, Galla dedicated a church in honor of St. Stephen.[92] It may be noted that the list of Galla's projects between 425 and 450 was inserted, erroneously, into a biography of John, bishop of Ravenna between 477 and 494. John's episcopacy coincided with the establishment of the Ostrogoths under Theodoric in Ravenna. Although the Goths were Arian and hence deemed heretic, even the orthodox Agnellus could ill afford to ignore Ravenna's efflorescence under the Goths.[93] In some ways Theodosian Ravenna, as shaped by Honorius, Galla, and Valentinian III, was eclipsed by the splendor of Gothic Ravenna. The misplacing of Galla's projects would have served as

91. Agnellus, *LPR* 27, trans. Deliyannis, modified, recorded by Agnellus under the heading of Peter's episcopate, c. 430–50.
92. Agnellus, *LPR* 41–42, Eng. trans. Deliyannis, modified.
93. Deliyannis, *Ravenna*, 106–200.

a bizarre balance of the projects financed by Theodoric, the first Gothic king of Ravenna.

Of Galla's projects in Ravenna, the Church of John the Evangelist, erected in the imperial quarter, highlights how the court set out to entrench its own image of profound piety on the topography of the capital.[94] Through pictures and texts, the church's triumphal arch conveyed multiple messages, all proclaiming Galla's attachment to her imperial ancestry and to orthodoxy.[95] At the center of the arch the Lord was seen delivering a book to John the Evangelist, the latter identified by name (*sanctus Iohannes Evangelista*).[96] Both figures were surrounded by apocalyptic symbols. Flanking this central imagery was the history behind the building—how John saved Galla and her children from the storms of the sea. The inscription along the arch extolled John and reminded the beholder that the church demonstrated the fact that Galla discharged her debt to the saint both for the favor shown to her and for the general good (*pro se et his omnibus*), as though public safety on earth depended on the Augusta's correct if not cordial relations with the powers that be.[97]

Ten medallion portraits of imperial figures were displayed below the inscribed arch. These named Valentinian, Gratian, Constantinus (or Constantius), a second Gratian, and Ioannes on one side; and Constantine, Theodosius, Arcadius, Honorius, and a second Theodosius on the other side. All ten figures were males with whom Galla claimed connection, through either blood or marriage, and all, by 425, were deceased. Besides her own maternal grandfather (Valentinian I) and the grandfather of her aunt by marriage (Constantine I, 306–337), the list numbered Galla's father (Theodosius I, 379–395), her half brothers (Arcadius, 395–408, and Honorius, 395–423), her half uncle (Gratian, 375–383), and possibly her own second husband (Constantius III, 421).[98] Three other

94. For recent detailed analyses of the contents and message of the basilica, V. Zangara, "Una predicazione," *AT* 8 (2000), 265–304; and A. Amici, "Imperatori Divi nella decorazione musiva della chiesa di San Giovanni Evangelista in Ravenna," *Ravenna: Studi et Ricerche* 7 (2000), 15–55. See also Deliyannis, *Ravenna*, 63–70. On the impossibility of locating Galla's palace, Deichmann, *Ravenna*, II, 3, p. 49; with Zangara, "Una predicazione," 278.

95. Nothing survived but we have several descriptions of the decoration; Rebenich, "Gratian," 373, for list of sources.

96. Ibid.

97. On Ambrosian echoes, Zangara, "Una predicazione," 282–83.

98. I agree with Holum, *Theodosian Empresses*, 178 n. 14, that neither Arcadius on the arch is an otherwise unknown son of Theodosius II.

names have baffled modern interpreters—Theodosius, Gratianus, and Ioannes, each designated as *nep*, a royal descendant (*nepos*) or a prince (*nobilissimus puer*). Theodosius *nep*. possibly alluded to Galla's son by Athaulf. The two others may have been Galla's brothers, sons of Galla and Theodosius I who, like Theodosius III, died in infancy.[99]

The list was highly selective. It omitted Valentinian II, Galla's maternal uncle (388–393), and Valens, her uncle (364–378), as well as a host of imperial women including her own mother, Galla, and her grandmother, Justina. The list's theme, if indeed a genealogy of Nicene orthodoxy, the brand of Christianity endorsed by Theodosius I, would account for some but not all omissions. That such indeed had been the message invested in the imagery could be deduced from the picture embossed on the vault of the church—Christ seated on his throne, surrounded with twelve sealed books and holding a book inscribed with the fifth beatitude (Matthew 5.7).[100] This was Christ as both the ultimate judge and the master legislator, an image that conveyed Galla's own commitment to the law, whether divinely conferred (like the Pentateuch) or issued by the imperial consistory.[101]

The dedicatory inscription, a morsel of history that explained the reason for the building, was carefully placed just below Christ and the books, possibly at the most accessible level for viewers, right above the bishop's throne. Between the text and the throne was a scene of celebration featuring either the bishop conducting the Mass or, less likely, the biblical Melchizedek celebrating the Eucharist.[102] On both sides of this scene were four more imperial portraits, this time arranged in couples and identified as Theodosius and his wife Eudocia on one side, and Arcadius and his wife Eudoxia on the other, the latter a dead couple, the former very much alive and very much the senior rulers of the Roman realm.[103] The portraits were accompanied by a biblical verse from Psalms 67:28–29 that referred to the Temple in Jerusalem.

---

99. Zangara, "Una predicazione," 285, for summary of views. I prefer the reading of Oost, *Galla Placidia*, 274–75.

100. On the language of the inscription, which differs from the Vulgate, Zangara, "Una predicazione," 294.

101. Ibid., 294–97, for iconographic exegesis, esp. 296 on the link with Leo's homily 11.1.

102. Zangara, "Una predicazione," 297, for the latter; all other commentators for the former.

103. The fact that Arcadius and possibly Theodosius appear twice has raised problems. Galla herself is recorded twice as well.

Politically minded readers of such a profusion of images and texts on the triumphal arch of the church would have shared readily in the exaltation of Christ and of John the Evangelist. Historically minded observers would have acknowledged the divine intervention that engineered the restoration of the Theodosian dynasty to the west in 425. Back then John had saved Galla and Valentinian from dying at sea. Had they died, their death would have spelled the demise of the Theodosian dynasty in the west. John's miracle had been aided by the instrumental role of the earthly power of the Constantinopolitan court. The indispensable assistance of the eastern branch of the dynasty, headed by Theodosius II, as restorer of legitimacy was clearly proclaimed both in the Church of John the Evangelist and at the palace, in pictures described by Merobaudes. Between these texts and images Galla's brand of patriotism emerged. It was profoundly Christian and specifically Ravennate.

The story attached to the foundation of St. Zacharias in the city is likewise highly instructive. According to Agnellus, a lady named Singledia had a dream in which she was instructed by a bearded man to build him a church at a location where she was to find a cross drawn on the ground and according to his plan.[104] Singledia, who, Agnellus claimed, was Galla's niece, requested the empress to lend her builders, and the structure was completed in thirteen days! The narrative of this uncommonly rapid chain of events brought together a woman (otherwise unattested), a nightly vision (apparently corroborated by foundations dug by unknown hands), saintly auspices (of one who identified himself in a dream as the holy Zacharias), and imperial permission (granted by Galla). The corpse of the dedicatee, Zacharias, father of John the Baptist, had been discovered in 415, the year when the body of Stephen the first martyr was likewise unearthed in Palestine.[105] Relics, especially of Stephen, were promptly dispersed all over the Mediterranean. At Constantinople, Pulcheria adopted Stephen, building a chapel to house his arm in the palace complex (421 C.E.).[106] Galla

---

104. Agnellus, *LPR* 41.

105. Mackie, *Early Christian Chapels*, 28, dating the enterprise to the late 410s, following the discovery of Zacharia's tomb in 416, a date that would cast Galla as the pioneer of placing relics from the Holy Land in an appropriate context. On the discovery of Zacharia's grave, Sozomen, *HE* 9.16–17, who couples it with that of Stephen as twin pillars of divine favor vis-à-vis the empire. Hunt, *Holy Land Pilgrimage*, 212.

106. Theophanes a.m. 5920. On the possible representation of the arrival of the relics and their reception by Pulcheria on the Trier ivory, see ch. 3. On the discovery of Stephen, Sivan, *Palestine in Late Antiquity*, passim.

must have visited the church during her Constantinopolitan exile. That she deliberately imitated Pulcheria by adopting another Palestinian saint in order to enhance Ravenna's standing as capital of equally pious Theodosians revealed a competition rooted in time and tradition.

Presided over by an empress who reputedly passed entire nights in praying on a cold pavement in a church, Galla's court personnel followed suit.[107] In 435, Lauricius, a eunuch holding the eminent position of *cubicularius* (in charge of the palace affairs), dedicated a funerary chapel to Stephen, Protasius, and Gervasius, the last two Italian saints, and all three appointed guardians of Lauricius's tomb.[108] Lauricius's successor in this palace position, Acolius, together with Galla and Peter (Chrysologus), Ravenna's bishop, organized a warm welcome for Germanus, the saintly bishop of Gallic Auxerre, when he came to Ravenna to plead for the Gauls.[109] Through Germanus's appearance at Ravenna it is possible to perceive how outsiders observed the court in action and how royalty and commoners interacted. According to Constantius, Germanus's Gallic biographer, palace and people conspired to defy Germanus's intention to enter Ravenna incognito. Led by Galla, Valentinian, Peter (Chrysologus) the bishop, and nobles of the court, the entire congregation escorted Germanus from the gate to his modest lodgings.[110]

At Ravenna an early morning walk took the visiting Gallic dignitary through the streets past the prison where Germanus stopped to demand the liberation of prisoners about to be executed.[111] Whenever he appeared in public, crowds pressed upon him with requests. And since he was invariably accompanied by other bishops, the prelates would witness Germanus's miraculous power of healing and of redressing social wrongs.[112] For Galla, Germanus's visit presented an opportunity to display exceptional generosity. She sent a huge silver dish to his

107. Agnellus, *LPR* 42.
108. Agnellus, *LPR* 35, with *PLRE II*, 659–60.
109. Constantius of Lyon, *Vie de Saint Germain d'Auxerre (Vita Germani)*, ed. and trans. R. Borius (SC 112) (Paris 1965). English translation of the life in T. Noble and T. Head (eds.), *Soldiers of Christ: Saints' Lives from Late Antiquity and the Early Middle Ages* (State College 1994), 75–106. The date of the Ravenna visit, 445 or 448 (Oost, *Galla Placidia*, 265) has been shifted to 437 by E. A. Thompson, *Saint Germanus of Auxerre and the End of Roman Britain* (Woodbridge 1984), 68–70, with persuasive arguments. But see also Gillett, *Envoys*.
110. Constantius of Lyon, *V. Germani*, 35.
111. Ibid., 36.
112. Ibid., 37.
113. Agnellus, *LPR* 51 (Barbatianus); Constantius of Lyon, *V. Germani*, 44 (Germanus).

lodgings. In return the saint sent her a tiny wooden plate.[113] When Germanus died unexpectedly while still in Ravenna, Galla and Acolius paid for a lavish funeral.[114] As a corpse, Germanus proved even more useful to the court. Galla and Peter Chrysologus apparently had an amicable quarrel over Germanus's possessions. In the words of Germanus's biographer, the saint's heritage was to be divided between *imperium* (state) and *sacerdotes* (church), with Galla appropriating the box containing Germanus's relics, and Peter taking possession of Germanus's hood.[115]

On a more sober note, as the funerary cortege of Germanus made its ponderous way from Ravenna all the way back to Gallic Auxerre, the saint's Gallic admirers had to fix the roads and mend the bridges that carried his corpse at their own expense. Germanus's biographer interpreted the enterprise as homage to his hero.[116] Less sanguine observers would have reflected on the dramatically different fate of the provinces of the western Roman Empire in the second quarter of the fifth century, and on the role of the Ravenna court in its crafting. In the course of his career Germanus traveled twice to Britain, as papal envoy charged with quelling heresy on the island, and in response to pleas issued by Britons under attack by invading Saxons and Picts (429? 447?).[117] On the latter occasion, Germanus had to institute himself as a general, leading the locals against the barbarians with chants of "alleluia," and winning a victory by the power of his piety alone.[118] The bloodless battle was a sad comment on the impotence of Galla's and Valentinian's government, which never managed to reconnect Britain to the empire after Honorius withdrew the imperial troops in 410. Whatever opposition the locals marshaled against invaders had to be organized by self-appointed leaders, local militias, and imported Gallic bishops.

Galla's Gallic subjects, by contrast with the Britons, directly experienced the heavy-handed manner in which the court handled provincial affairs. Germanus traveled to Ravenna in the wake of clashes between the inhabitants of Armorica (Brittany), conveniently labeled "bandits"

114. Constantius of Lyon, *V. Germani*, 39, 44.

115. Ibid., 43.

116. Ibid., 46.

117. Thompson, *Saint Germanus*, passim, for vexed chronology of fifth-century Britain; see also I. Wood, "The End of Roman Britain: Continental Evidence and Parallels," in *Gildas: New Approaches*, ed. M. Lapidge and D. Dumville (Woodbridge 1984), 1–25.

118. Constantius of Lyon, *V. Germani*, 3.

(*bacaudae*), and Alanic (barbarian) troops employed by Aetius, the commander in chief of the Roman army.[119] To regain control (and taxes), Aetius punished those who resisted the Alans. Germanus was asked to intercede with the Ravenna court, and with the king of the Alans, on behalf of the beleaguered Romans of Armorica. The bishop, now patron of Gauls far from his own see of Auxerre, undertook this rather unpalatable task, successfully. Neither Galla nor her imperial son could afford to ignore Germanus's request. When the mediator between "rebellious" Romans in Gaul and the demonstrably pious court was a bishop with remarkable orthodox credentials, Galla adopted with zeal a public discourse of exemplary generosity.

119. J. F. Drinkwater, "The *Bacaudae* of Fifth-Century Gaul," in *Fifth-Century Gaul: A Crisis of Identity?*, ed. J. F. Drinkwater and H. Elton (Cambridge 1992), 208–17; and J. F. Drinkwater, "Patronage in Roman Gaul and the Problem of the Bagaudae," in *Patronage in Ancient Society*, ed. A. Wallace-Hadrill (London 1989), 189–203.

CHAPTER SEVEN

Conclusion

Critical reading of the primary sources relating to the first half of the fifth century has been caught in an obvious dilemma—hindsight. Whether looking back at Ravenna from the vantage point of sixth-century Justinianic projects, or of a ninth-century monastery, whether assessing the in/ activities of the western branch of the Valentinian-Theodosian dynasty from the height of a throne occupied by barbarian kings after 476, or looking down from the haughty mansions of the powerful and literate Roman aristocrats who continued to dominate the landscape of Italy well beyond the "demise" of the empire in the west, the categorical decisiveness of assessing these trends reveals the ambivalence of contemporary discourse.

A quick arithmetic would result in an intriguing result—the combined reigns of members of the Valentinian and Theodosian dynasties in the west, beginning with Valentinian I (364–475), Galla's maternal grandfather, and ending with Valentinian III (425–455), her son, amounted to ninety, by far the longest-lasting period of all the clans that ruled the empire. Even the Constantinian dynasty, beginning with Constantius I, Constantine's father (293–305), and ending with Julian (361–363), did not last as long. Only the Julio-Claudians enjoyed similar longevity (31/27 B.C.E.–68 C.E.). Taking into account that the empire itself lasted barely another twenty years after the murder of Valentinian III in 455, who ascended the throne at age six and never led an army in the three decades of his real rule, this would appear a remarkable feat.

To what extent the delicate act of balancing barbarians with Romans, papal aspirations with provincial needs, and of treading water among powerful generals without whom the dynasty could not survive, of sustaining

the loss of key provinces, and of maintaining control over what was left under
Ravenna's direct rule was directly due to Galla's dozen years of regency is
difficult to assess (425–437/438). At the dawn of her regency the government of the western Roman Empire emerged from two years of usurpation (423–425). When her son reached a formal majority, with a wedding
and a sole rule in the late 430s, the future seemed less promising than it
had been when his father, Constantius III, restored order in Gaul and
Spain in 420. That the transition in 425 from a usurper back to a legitimate
emperor was peaceful suggests that Galla was fully aware of the stakes.

That Valentinian III was able to remain on the throne, nominally for
no less than three decades (425–455), is astonishing, especially in view of
the dominant and often rivaling presence of powerful generals, ostenta-
tious aristocrats, and ambitious popes. The absence of an open rift
between the throne and the top military brass, until Valentinian threw a
spear at Aetius in 454, could not have been solely due to Aetius's laudable restraint during his ascendancy in the 430s and 440s, or to Aspar's
prudence back in 425. Both generals maintained that the throne of the
empire should be occupied by a full-blooded Roman, not to mention a
legitimate scion of emperors. That throughout Valentinian's reign the
regime maintained correct, if not cordial, relations with the Roman senatorial aristocracy and close contact with the papacy at Rome should
endorse, if not as positive an evaluation of Galla as the one that Oost
generously provided, at least an appreciation of the alternatives.[1]

Recent biographies of Aetius and Valentinian III, whose activities
and reign span the precise same period (425–454), take readers back to
the terrain of positivist and reassuring history.[2] Their erudite authors
have produced an orderly review along chronological lines of domestic
and foreign policies, of economy and society, surveying in due course
the troubles that beset the western provinces, religious and legal policies, wars with barbarians, and relations with the aristocracy, all themes
of great importance. Although the body politic of the western (and eastern) Roman Empire in late antiquity continued to be characterized by
an indivisible and often invisible unity, these modern presentations lend
an artificial order to the chaos of history dictated by divisions, human

1. And probably not as severe as Burgess's sweeping judgment of Pulcheria, and by extension
of other Theodosian empresses, as "a mere tool in the dynastic plans of men"; R. Burgess, "The
Accession of Marcian in the Light of Chalcedonian Apologetic and Monophysite Polemic," *Byz.Z*
86/87 (1993–1994), 47–68.
2. F. Elia, *Valentiniano III* (Catania 1999); D. Coulon, *Aetius* (Villeneuve d'Ascq 2003).

passions, and inexplicable movements. In these studies, as in books that set out to record the history of the Roman Empire in late antiquity, Galla is marginal, often reduced to a single footnote.[3]

One remarkable aspect of the Galla case is to be found in the threads that intertwined her personal story with the personal histories of the figures who dominated the annals of the western empire in the fifth century. When compared with Aetius she seems less of an aberration. She spent five years in the Gothic camp, as hostage and as bride. Aetius, the realm's most famous, ferocious, and longest-lasting military commander, had been hostage twice, once to the Goths and another time to the Huns. Galla was married to a Gothic king and bore him a child. Aetius married a Gothic princess, producing a son whom he planned to marry to Galla's granddaughter. Galla died in peace at Rome; Aetius was murdered by Galla's son likewise in the city.

How paradigmatic was such a course? I have tried to illuminate expectations and representations of women, dealing with women as patronesses, as politicians, and as pious individuals. I have assessed women's strategies of survival whether menaced or pampered, whether at home or on the throne, investigating how they bonded with society, how they crossed the threshold into marriage, and how they made themselves heard. Through Galla I traced how women functioned in environments that kept redefining themselves, and how practice and theory generated or limited their authority.

A contemporary assessment of Galla, in fact no more than an entry in a chronicle that listed her death in 450, described her life as "irreproachable," following her "conversion."[4] One can easily assume that her son would have provided for a lavish funeral, as well as commissioning a lengthy funeral oration. Had such a speech survived (and it has not), it would have emphasized Galla's noble origin, her remarkable ancestry, and how, against all odds, she secured the throne of the western empire for her only son back in 424–425. Such a discourse would have further referred to her marriage (with Constantius but probably not with Athaulf), to her excellent relations with the papacy, even venturing to

---

3. I wonder whether the trend had been set by Bury's magisterial survey (J. B. Bury, *History of the Later Roman Empire* [London 1923], now available over the Internet), who titled one of his chapters "The Dismemberment of the Empire in the West" (ch. 8), devoting a single subsection to the "regency of Placidia and the defense of Gaul, 425–30" [sic].

4. *Chron. Gall.* 452, s.a. 450: *vita irreprehensibilis.*

describe her regency (425–437), or rather the means by which she secured the realm for her son during his minority. Above all, the declaimer would have extolled Galla's Christian piety, her endeavors on behalf of popes and orthodoxy, and how she brought up a son worthy of ruling a Christian commonwealth.

Perhaps such an oration would also have reflected on the splendor of the sole monument that has been linked with Galla's name, the Mausoleum of Galla Placidia in Ravenna. Still standing, and frequently visited by tourists, the mausoleum is a small and well-proportioned structure, cruciform shaped, and remarkable for its mosaic decoration.[5] An enterprising orator at Galla's state funeral in 450 would have relished an artful description of these mosaics. They stud the mausoleum's dome in a manner designed to reflect heaven itself, with blazing blue and golden tesserae (mosaic pieces). In the sky hovers a huge gold cross. The vault is "carried" by winged figures, beasts of the apocalypse, each with a symbol of the four evangelists (lion, ox, eagle, and man). On the upper walls, pairs of male figures (the same evangelists?) point their right hands toward the domed cross. Doves, vases, and shells accentuate the centrality of the cross. Below the dome, one panel depicts a seated Christ, dressed in gold and imperial purple, as the Good Shepherd, tending to six sheep. Another shows a man carrying a cross and a book, apparently heading straight to a central grill lit by flames (St. Lawrence?). And yet another depicts a cupboard with four books, each bearing the names of the four evangelists.

With the mausoleum the panegyric could reach a peak, a touching yet stunning example of the power of female piety. Was the mausoleum, as its current name indicates, conceived as a funerary chapel intended as resting place for Galla's Spanish son (Theodosius III), or for Galla herself? One possible clue is linked to the identification of the mosaic panel depicting a man next to the flaming grill. He could have been the Spanish Saint Vincent (of Saragossa). Such a connection would have enabled an orator at Galla's funeral to discourse on the land (Spain) that had bred Galla's father and her firstborn, as well as men like Vincent, ready to die for the faith. An inventive panegyrist could have further re-created an imaginary journey of both the dead baby and the martyred saint from Spain to Ravenna, the one (Theodosius III)

5. Mackie, *Early Christian Chapels*, 179–94, for detailed description, survey of scholarly theories, and own interpretation. Deliyannis, *Ravenna*, 74–84, for the most recent assessment.

to be laid to rest by his grieving, dutiful, and pious mother next to her own palace, the other (Vincent) to grace the mosaics of the mausoleum with his exemplary story.

There are no surviving contemporary tributes to Galla, whose death in 450 was recorded in several contemporary chronicles. Less than a century after her demise, Cassiodorus, an eminent Italian senator serving at the Gothic court of Theodoric in Ravenna, compared Galla, unfavorably, with his own queen, the Gothic Amalasuintha, daughter of Theodoric the Great, king (of the Ostrogoths, 489–526), and mother of Athalaric, king (of the Goths, 526–534). Cassiodorus rated Galla's regency as a nadir of imperial fortunes, going so far as to accuse her of reducing the size of the empire:

> Had revered antiquity achieved the like [of Amalasuintha's capabilities]? There is Placidia, with a famous reputation in the world: we have learnt that she was glorious for her descent from various emperors and cared for her imperial son. But we know that the empire she slackly ruled for him was shamefully diminished. Eventually she purchased a daughter in law by the loss of Illyricum: rulers were united but the provinces were lamentably divided. Moreover, she weakened the soldiery by too much peace . . . but under this queen [Amalasuintha] with God's help our army will terrify foreign powers. Prudent and nicely calculated policy ensures that it is neither worn down by continuous fighting nor enervated by prolonged peace.[6]

What Cassiodorus perceived were superficial similarities between the biographies of Amalasuintha and Galla. Both women were regents, the former for her ten-year-old son, Athalaric, in 526, the latter for her six-year-old son, Valentinian, in 425.[7] Both gave their sons a classical education. In Galla's Ravenna, such a pedagogy was acceptable since Valentinian was not required to lead armies in person. In Gothic Ravenna the Gothic army objected to "Roman" education, requiring instead a militarily coached prince. Amalasuintha, ruling over a military

---

6. Cassiodorus, *Variae*, 1.1.9: "Placidiam mundi opinione celebratam aliquorum principum prosapia gloriosam purpurato filio studuisse percepimus, cuius dum remisse administrat imperium, indecenter cognoscitur imminutum . . . militem quoque nimia quiete dissolvit." Eng. trans. Barnish.

7. P. Amory, *People and Identity in Ostrogothic Italy 489–554* (Cambridge 1997), 9–10, 155–59.

aristocracy, had to bow to pressure, and Athalaric was joined to the camp where he died, at eighteen, of immersion, surprisingly not in military strategies but in the sensual pleasures indulged in by the Gothic top brass.

Upon Athalaric's death, Amalasuintha was coerced into taking her cousin as coregent, but fearing for her life she asked Justinian, emperor of the Eastern Roman Empire, to come to her aid. Constantinople, it may be noted, continued to feature as a chief source of support for western rulers in trouble. Her murder provided Justinian with an excuse to mount a major campaign of "reconquering" Italy. No such dramatic course had developed a century before when Theodosius II restored Galla and her children to Italy in 425. Galla was clearly more fortunate than her Gothic "sister."

Cassiodorus, who weathered not only the demise of his Gothic patrons but also the fall of their kingdom, accredited Amalasuintha with singular achievements. Among these he singled out the preservation of the kingdom from enemies and the classical upbringing of her son, heir to the Ostrogothic throne. Had there been a Cassiodorus to hail Galla in similar terms, perhaps a more judicious assessment would have been forthcoming. Ironically, the greatest tribute that Cassiodorus handed to Galla was precisely what he invoked to malign her—the characterization of her regency as a peaceful period.

Cassiodorus's unflattering portrayal of Galla was shared by an-other sixth-century historian, Procopius, who recorded Justinian's (or rather Belisarius's) Italian campaigns against the Goths. Procopius blamed Galla for her son's dissipation and for the resultant loss of Africa to the Vandals, the reconquest of which by Justinian was another subject of Procopius's "history of the wars": "Placidia, Valentinian's mother, had reared this emperor and educated him in an altogether effeminate manner, and in consequence he was filled with wickedness from childhood."[8] Peter Chrysologus, Ravenna's bishop and Galla's contemporary, provided a different perspective on Galla and the imperial family. Citing her faith, piety, and generosity, Peter advanced a sphere of ideas remarkably remote from the militant realm of Gothic Ravenna:

> Standing here is the most pious imperial family, serving the
> One, so that they may reign over all; bowing their heads to

8. Procopius, *Bell. Vand.* 1.3.10–13 (Loeb trans.).

God, so that all nations may bend their necks to them; offering
gifts to God alone, so as to obtain tribute from all peoples.
They are here, strong in faith, secure in their innocence,
prudent in their simplicity, rich in mercy, wealthy in love,
awesome in their kindness, and what matters most, reigning
thanks to their unchangeable communion.[9]

Peter avoided definitions in political terms. The familial rather than the
individual, faith rather than strength of arms, became principles of organization in Peter's projected universe. The evaluation of the dynasty as
first in piety, rather than in military feats, accorded well with his presentation of Galla as the mother of the empire.[10] She, and her family of faith,
became paradigmatic citizens and cornerstone of a system constructed
on religion alone. Without Galla, the quality of imperial blood could not
be perfect. She transmitted legitimacy. Yet interwoven into Peter's picture of a perfect earthly family was the figure of Galla in an equivocal
position of a woman acting in place of a man, a mother standing in for
a father. Replacing an essentially masculine model, Peter proposed a
model of behavior that accorded to perfection with Galla's projected
public image.

Such contrasting assessments reflect less Galla's own personality
and deeds than they do the formulaic framework of late ancient writ-
ings. Neither Cassiodorus, an Italian aristocrat by birth, a literary man
of no mean achievements, highly placed in the civil administration of
Gothic Italy, nor Procopius, a well-educated Palestinian, well placed at
the court of Justinian and Theodora in Constantinople, had a reason to
flatter either Galla or the Theodosian dynasty. Cassiodorus represented
their indirect (Gothic) successors in Italy; Procopius praised Justinian,
the restorer of Roman legitimacy to the west.

Local Ravennate (Catholic) traditions, then, as propounded and
preserved in ecclesiastical circles, advanced an image of Galla as a generous and pious empress, donor to the church and promoter of saints
and holy men. Yet to locate the reality lurking behind this rhetoric,
whether laudatory or condemnatory, one needs to assess the imaginary
and the concrete about the lives of women in antiquity. This is what I
have done in this book by way of exploring the stage on which women
like Galla were placed.

9. Peter Chrysologus, *Sermo* 85.3 (Eng. trans. W. B. Palardy).
10. Peter Chrysologus, *Sermo* 130, see ch. 6.

Appendixes

A. Maps: Galla's Life in Cartography

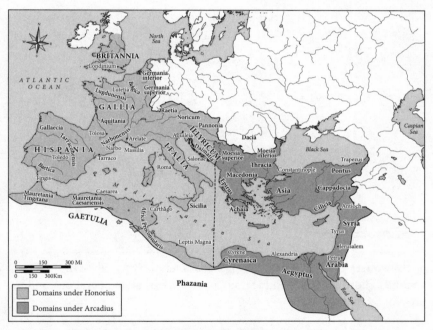

1. The Roman Empire at Galla's birth (c. 395) showing the domains under Honorius (western provinces) and Arcadius (eastern provinces), Galla's half brothers.

2. The western Roman Empire during Galla's lifetime (first half of the fifth century), showing Galla's Gothic trail (410–416), barbarian migrations, and areas of settlement.

North Sea

BRITANNIA
Anglo-Saxons
449

ATLANTIC OCEAN

Franks

GERMANIA

Armorica

Huns
451

GALLIA

Burgundians
443

Ostrogoths
454

Suebi
411

Visigoths
418

LUSITANIA

456

HISPANIA

ITALIA

CORSICA

SARDINIA

Alans
409

SICILY

AFRICA

Vandals
429–439

Mediterranean Sea

0   150   300 Mi

0   150   300 Km

3. The Roman Empire at Galla's death (450).

B. Time Line

364: Valentinian I, founder of a new imperial dynasty and Galla Placidia's maternal grandfather, is elected to the imperial throne after the death in quick succession of the emperor Julian, last scion of the dynasty of Constantine, and of Jovian, his short-lived successor. Valentinian marries twice, fathering Gratian, Valentinian II, and Galla (who will become Galla Placidia's mother). He rules the west while his brother, Valens, rules the eastern empire.

375: Valentinian's death and the accession of his sons, Gratian (by his first wife) and Valentinian II (by his second wife, Justina) to the throne of the western Roman Empire.

About 375? Gratian marries Constantia, great-granddaughter of Helena, granddaughter of the emperor Constantine, and posthumous daughter of the emperor Constantius II (precise date of nuptials remains unknown). Execution of Theodosius Comes, paternal grandfather of Galla Placidia, father of Theodosius I.

379: Theodosius I, Galla Placidia's father, becomes emperor of the eastern Roman provinces after the death of Valens, Valentinian I's brother, on the battlefield in 378. Theodosius is married to Flaccilla, by whom he fathers two sons, Arcadius and Honorius, and one daughter.

About 380? Gratian marries Laeta. Precise date unknown, perhaps when he moves from Gallic Trier to Milan in 382.

383: Murder of Gratian and accession of the Spaniard Magnus Maximus to become colleague of Valentinian II.

388–389: Theodosius (by now a widower) in Italy, defeating Maximus and marrying Galla, Justina's daughter by the emperor Valentinian I. Galla gives birth to two sons who die in infancy and to a baby girl.

About 390? Birth of Galla Placidia (precise date remains unknown; speculations range between 388 and 392).

392: Valentinian II is found dead in Gaul. His chief of staff, Arbogast, elevates Eugenius to the throne of the western Roman Empire. Galla Placidia and her mother in Constantinople, Theodosius's capital.

394: Theodosius I in Italy, defeating Eugenius and Arbogast. Galla, his wife and Galla Placidia's mother, dies in childbirth.

395: Theodosius dies. His sons by his first marriage succeed to the imperial thrones, with Arcadius as emperor of the eastern provinces (capital in Constantinople) and Honorius as emperor of the western provinces (capital in Milan).

395–408: Stilicho, a half-Vandal general, husband of Serena, niece of Theodosius I and aunt to Galla Placidia, is the power behind Honorius's throne. He and Serena father three children, Galla Placidia's cousins. Their two girls, Maria and Theramentia, are married off to Honorius; their son, Eucherius, is slotted to wed Galla Placidia.

408–410: The Goths, led by Alaric, their king, and Athaulf, his brother-in-law, besiege the city of Rome after the murder of Stilicho in 408. Galla Placidia colludes with the senate of Rome in the execution of Serena. In 410 the city is sacked by the Goths. In Constantinople the emperor Arcadius, son of Theodosius I and Galla's half brother, dies in 408, to be succeeded by his infant son, Theodosius II, whose older sisters, primarily Pulcheria, rule the eastern court.

410–416/417: The throne of Honorius, Galla's half brother and emperor of the western Roman Empire, is constantly threatened by the rise of local leaders or usurpers in Britain, Gaul, and Spain. Constantius is appointed his chief of staff and leads the Roman army, now consisting largely of barbarians, in a series of campaigns against usurpers and rebellious barbarians.

410–412/413: Galla, captive (?) in the Gothic camp, meanders in the company of the Goths, who are headed by Athaulf, elected king after the death of Alaric in 410. The Goths try, in vain, to cross over to North Africa via Sicily, and then turn back north.

412/413–414/415: The Goths, with Galla Placidia in their train, are in southern Gaul.

414: In January, Galla Placidia, half sister of the ruling emperor of the west and aunt of the ruling emperor of the east (Theodosius II), and Athaulf the Gothic king are married in the city of Narbonne in southern Gaul, not far from the Mediterranean and the Pyrenees. The Goths, and Galla, are driven to Spain by Constantius, who blockades Narbonne.

415–416: Galla and the Goths are in Spanish Barcelona. Galla loses her firstborn child, a son named Theodosius (III), and her husband.

417: Galla and Constantius are married in Ravenna.

418/419: Galla and Constantius intervene in disputes over papal succession in Rome. Two of Galla's letters on that occasion are preserved, one of which is addressed to Paulinus, a Gallic nobleman who lived with his wife, a Spanish heiress, in Barcelona in the early 390s and moved to Italy in 395, to settle in Campania (Nola), where he was elected bishop. The Goths are brought back to Gaul, to settle in the southwest (Aquitania) under their new king, Theodoric I.

421: Constantius becomes coemperor, with Honorius, of the western Roman Empire. He and Galla have two children, Iusta Grata Honoria and Valentinian (III). Constantius dies after a few months on the throne.

422/423: Galla and Honorius quarrel and Galla has to leave the court.

423–424: Galla in Constantinople, at the court of Theodosius II, now married to Eudocia. Her sole supporter in the west, Boniface, controls the valuable resources of the North African provinces.

423–425: Honorius dies in 423 in Ravenna. John becomes emperor. Theodosius II decides to send Galla and her children back to the west, with an army. John is defeated (424). His general, Aetius, is pardoned and asked to serve the new emperor, the child Valentinian III, who ascends the throne in Rome in a ceremony attended by the senate, the emissary of Theodosius II, and Galla.

425–438: Galla, during the minority years of her son, controls the court while the supreme command of the army is disputed between Boniface and Aetius, to the detriment of the empire.

429: The Vandals cross from Spain to North Africa, conquer the rich provinces that had supplied Italy with precious grain, and establish their capital in Carthage from 439. All subsequent attempts to eject them fail.

431: Galla extends posthumous pardon to the noble Flavianus, an old favorite of her father yet a supporter of Eugenius.

437: Galla's son, Valentinian III, marries his cousin, Licinia Eudoxia, daughter of Theodosius II and Eudocia, in a well-attended ceremony in Constantinople. Galla apparently not in attendance.

438: The Theodosian Code, the first imperial law code to include legislation of emperors from Constantine to Theodosius II, is presented at Rome. Valentinian's marriage and the code provide a prelude to his sole rule. By that date, the Visigoths had been in Aquitaine for two decades; the Vandals in Africa for a decade; Britain had been left out of the imperial sphere for four decades; and the Suevi and Alans were still in Spain, as were the Burgundians in Gaul.

440–450: Galla resides at Ravenna and Rome. At Rome she and Pope Leo I maintain cordial relations, culminating in an exchange of letters between Galla and her relatives at the eastern court in an effort to promote papal interests and to legitimize papal intervention in the ecclesiastical affairs of the Eastern Roman Empire. We have three of Galla's letters (to Pulcheria and to Theodosius II).

450: Galla dies, probably at Rome, after attending a reburial ceremony for her first child, Theodosius III.

450–455: The last years of the Valentinian-Theodosian dynasty in the west. Attila at the gates of Rome claiming Galla's daughter as his bride. Valentinian III kills Aetius (454) and is killed in turn (455) by one of Aetius's supporters. His death is followed by twenty years of instability, a series of short-lived emperors, and the dominance of the military.

C. Family Tree

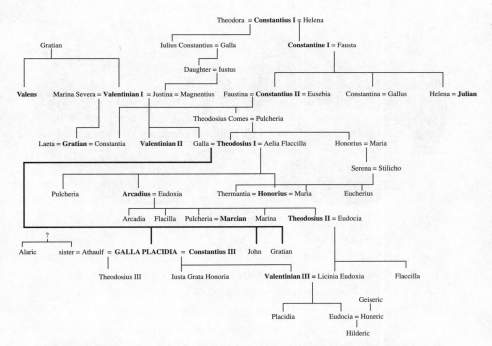

The Valentinian-Theodosian Dynasty and Its Constantinian Connections

D. Images

1. Constantine I (306–337), the first Christian emperor and Galla's ancestor through her grandmother Justina and her half brother Gratian. The emperor is shown laureate, helmeted, wearing a cuirass, shield, and spear, ready to lead armies to victory. The reverse shows the emperor standing with a signum (military standard) in each hand. [Permission of Classical Numismatic Group Inc.]

2. Constantius II (337–361), son of Constantine and ultimately sole emperor of the Roman Empire, shown wearing a pearl diadem, draped, and wearing a cuirass. The reverse refers to the celebration of the thirtieth year of his elevation. Related to Galla through his posthumous daughter, Constantia, whom Gratian, Galla's half brother, had married. [Permission of Classical Numismatic Group Inc.]

3. Valentinian I (364–375), Galla's maternal grandfather, ruler of the western Roman Empire, shown wearing a pearl diadem and a cuirass. The reverse reads *pax perpetua* (eternal peace) inscribed on a shield held by a seated figure of Victory, goddess of triumphs. This type will later appear on coins even of empresses. It mattered little that the presiding divinity was traditional rather than Christian. [Permission of Numismatica Ars Classica.]

4. Gratian (375–383), Galla's half brother, son of Valentinian I by his first wife, Marina Severa. Gratian wears the same pearl diadem as his father. The reverse shows two seated emperors under the wings (literally) of Victory, probably Gratian himself and his younger half brother, Valentinian II (383–388). [Permission of Heidelberger Münzhandlung Herbert Grün.]

5. Theodosius I (379–395), Galla's father, here shown with the familiar imperial diadem. The reverse shows the emperor holding a military standard and a globe, with an enemy trodden under his feet. The legend, *virtus exerciti* (the might, virtue, prowess of the army), another traditional feature of Roman imperial coins, extols the army, which, under Theodosius, excelled mostly in civil wars. [Permission of Helios Numismatik.]

6. Arcadius (395–408), Theodosius's eldest son by his first marriage to Aelia Flaccilla, emperor of the eastern Roman provinces and Galla's half brother. He is shown full faced, with the familiar pearl diadem but also helmeted, with a cuirassed bust, shield, and spear. The shield depicts a horseman thrashing an enemy. The reverse shows the familiar Victory. These military and triumphant themes are traditional yet somewhat ironic when attached to an emperor who never led an army in his life. [Permission of Numismatica Ars Classica.]

7. Honorius (395–423), Theodosius's younger son by his first marriage to Aelia Flaccilla, emperor of the western Roman provinces, and Galla's half brother. He is shown, like his brother, donning both a diadem and a helmet, while the reverse sports the emperor holding a spear mounted with the Christian Chi-Rho symbol. Note the hand of God above his head, a popular motif on the coins of the empresses of the Theodosian dynasty, and the lion under his right foot. The coin was minted in Ravenna, Honorius's capital since 402 and Galla's main residence. [Permission of Chaponnière & Hess-Divo-AG Coins and Medals.]

8. Honorius, here shown full face, helmeted and diademed. Note the shield inscribed with the Christian Chi-Rho symbol. The reverse shows Rome and Constantinople, the two great cities of the empire, one the capital of the eastern Roman Empire, the other the old (but no longer) capital of the Roman Empire. [Permission of Classical Numismatic Group.]

9. Theodosius II (408–450), emperor of the eastern Roman Empire, son of Arcadius and Eudoxia, shown with the diadem and the helmet. The reverse shows two seated emperors, the larger figure that of Theodosius II, the smaller that of Valentinian III, Galla's son, whom the senior emperor restored to the west in 425. The common legend *salus reipublica* hails the integrity of the deeply divided empire. [Permission of Numismatik Lanz.]

10. Constantius III (421), Galla's second husband and coemperor of the western empire (with Honorius). Minted in Ravenna. Constantius is shown with a diadem and a cuirass, the reverse depicting him with a foot placed on a captive, holding a standard and a Victory on a globe. Unlike his brother-in-law, Constantius was a military man, the chief commander of the Roman army for a decade, to whom Honorius largely owed the preservation of his throne in the uneasy years that began in 406 with the Rhine crossing of barbarians. [Permission of Freeman & Sear.]

11. Valentinian III (425–455), Galla's son and emperor of the western Roman Empire. Here shown with the traditional imperial attributes, with the reverse depicting him atop a horse, with his cloak flowing behind him, and the familiar legend of the *Victoria Auggg* (triumphant emperors), perhaps issued in 437 at Thessalonike to mark his presence in the city on the occasion of his wedding with Licinia Eudoxia. [Permission of Numismatica Ars Classica.]

12. Valentinian III. This magnificent gold coin commemorates the wedding of Galla's son in 437 with the daughter of the emperor Theodosius II. The obverse shows the young emperor with the usual diadem and helmet. The reverse, which is duplicated on contemporary coins of Theodosius II, shows the couple linking their right arms (the traditional *dextarum iunctio* gesture symbolizing the unification of the couple) with the father-in-law placing his hand on Valentinian's shoulder. Minted in Thessalonike in late 437 or early 438, possibly in conjunction with the coin depicting a riding Valentinian. The legend, *felicite nubtiis*, blesses the marriage. [Permission of A. Tkalec AG.]

13. Attalus, the unfortunate senator who was elevated to the throne of the
western Roman Empire by Alaric, brother-in-law of Athaulf (Galla's first
husband). The coin, in the best tradition of Roman imperial coins, shows
Attalus wearing a pearl diadem, with his name inscribed around his head
(Priscus Attalus Augustus). The reverse shows the goddess Roma in all her
glory, seated on a throne and holding a Victory on a globe and a spear. The
legend (*Invicta Roma Aeterna*), the invincible eternal city, reminds beholders
of better days as well as of Attalus's intimate connections with both Rome and
its senate. This is a highly rare gold coin (solidus) struck in 409 or 410. Once
Honorius's government reached an agreement with the Goths who held both
Attalus and Galla, the ex-emperor was exiled to an isolated island, after his
right thumb and forefinger had been cut off. [Permission of Numismatica
Ars Classica.]

14. Sebastianus, brother of Jovinus, one of the Gallic noblemen who aspired to the throne during Honorius's reign. Sebastianus, whose elevation by Jovinus as coemperor antagonized Athaulf and resulted in Jovinus's defeat, is shown with traditional imperial attributes on the obverse, while the goddess Roma, seated on the curule chair and holding Victory on a globe and a spear, hails a wished-for triumph of the Gallic brothers over their enemies. This is an extremely rare coin, minted in Arles, not before Athaulf captured and beheaded Sebastianus. [Permission of Numismatica Ars Classica.]

15. Boniface (Bonifatius), *comes Africae* 422–431, Galla's ardent supporter and Aetius's ardent enemy. Controlled the rich provinces of Roman Africa while the throne of the western empire shifted from Honorius to John. Rewarded but later suspected of treachery. His colorful history, not the least "bequeathing" his wife to Aetius, illustrates the vagaries of power and of the military during Galla's lifetime. The coin was minted in Carthage and shows Boniface with a pearl diadem and a cuirass, both traditional imperial attributes, while the legend reads *dominis nostris* (to our masters), reflecting, it seems, his loyalty to Theodosius II and Valentinian III. [Permission of Classical Numismatic Group.]

16. Helena. Shown in the customary profile, Constantine's mother, who became the model for imperial women in late antiquity, wears a diadem, while the reverse shows a modestly draped woman holding two branches while the legend proclaims imperial security (*securitas reipublicae*), a much desired state of affairs achieved with the greatest difficulty after several bloody civil wars won by her son. [Permission of Helios Numismatik.]

17. Fausta, Constantine's wife and Helena's daughter-in-law, who came to grief and was executed (326). Shown here without imperial attributes, the reverse depicts a draped woman holding two infants. The legend (*spes reipublicae*) highlights the hope invested in mothers as producers of dynastic security and guarantors of continuity. [Permission of Helios Numismatik.]

18. Aelia Flaccilla, first wife of Theodosius I (Galla's father), the "mother" of all Theodosian empresses and a model of Christian piety. She is wearing a diadem and is richly clad, her title of Augusta carefully noted. The obverse shows the familiar type of a seated Victory holding a shield bearing the Christian Chi-Rho symbol. The legend is the equally monotonous "safety of/for the state" (*salus reipublicae*). Both bust and reverse hark back to coin types of Helena and Fausta while, in turn, shaping the iconography of all coins minted by the daughters and granddaughters of Theodosius I. Even her name, Aelia, was adopted by them as a token of status. [Permission of Numismatica Ars Classica.]

19. Galla Placidia. Solidus (gold coin), minted in Ravenna. Galla is draped and bejeweled. Her shoulder ornament bears the cross, a type that became solely hers. She is crowned by the hand of God, while on the reverse Victory is standing, holding a large jeweled cross. [Permission of Dr. Constantine Marinescu, Vilmar.]

20. Galla Placidia. A similar obverse, but the reverse shows a seated victory with a shield inscribed with a large Christogram and the legend "universal security" (*salus reipublicae*). Galla's coinage fits seamlessly into types seen on coins of both male and female members of the Theodosian dynasty. [Permission of A. Tkalec AG.]

21. Eudoxia, wife of Arcadius, here with the "Aelia," a name component adopted from Aelia Flaccilla. Diademed and draped like all other empresses, and crowned by the hand of God. The reverse shows the city of Constantinople enthroned, holding a globe and a shield. [Permission of Dr. Constantine Marinescu, Vilmar.]

22. Pulcheria, daughter of Arcadius and Eudoxia, sister of Theodosius II, for many years the dominant figure at the court of Constantinople. Shown here with a richly decorated diadem as the hand of God above holds her crown. The reverse shows Constantinople holding a globe mounted by a huge cross while her other hand holds a scepter and a shield. [Permission of Gorny & Mosch Giessener Münzhandlung.]

23. Eudocia, wife of Theodosius II. Her bust depicts a very youthful face, with the inevitable "Aelia," while the reverse shows a large cross within a wreath. Eudocia, who had been born in Athens to a philosopher father who believed in the old gods, converted to Christianity upon her marriage to the emperor. The size of the cross seems reassuring. [Permission of Numismatica Ars Classica.]

24. Licinia Eudoxia, wife of Valentinian III and Galla's daughter-in-law. Daughter of Theodosius II and Eudocia, she married Valentinian in 437. Her youthful, even childish face is mounted with an elaborate hairdo and a crown. The reverse shows what may be her enthroned holding a globe surmounted by a cross, and a scepter likewise mounted by a cross, with the familiar legend of "safety and security" (*salus*). [Permission of Fritz Rudolf Künker GmbH & Co. KG, Osnabrück; Lübke & Wiedemann, Stuttgart.]

Bibliography

Agnellus of Ravenna, *The Book of Pontiffs of the Church of Ravenna*, trans. with introduction and notes by D. M. Deliyannis (Washington, DC 2004).

Amici, A., "Imperatori Divi nella decorazione musiva della chiesa di San Giovanni Evangelista in Ravenna," *Ravenna. Studi et Ricerche* 7 (2000), 15–55.

Amory, P., *People and Identity in Ostrogothic Italy* (Cambridge 1997).

Angelide, C., *Pulcheria: la castità al potere* (Milan 1998).

Anné, L. (ed.), *Centcelles. El monumento tardoromano: iconografía y arquitectura* (Rome 2002).

———, *Les rites des fiançailles et la donation pour cause de mariage sous le Bas-Empire* (Louvain 1941).

———, "The Urban Domus in Late Antique Hispania: Examples from Emerita, Barcino and Complutum," in *Housing in Late Antiquity*, ed. L. Lavan et al. (Leiden 2007), 305–36.

———, "La villa romana de Carranque (Toledo, España): identificación y propietario," *Gerión* 21 (2003), 15–27.

Ariès, P., *Centuries of Childhood: A Social History of Family Life*, trans. R. Baldick (New York 1962).

Arjava, A., "A Bibliography on Women and the Family in Late Antiquity and the Early Middle Ages (2nd to 7th Century AD)." http://www.nipissingu.ca/department/history/muhlberger/orb/arjava3.htm.

———, *Women and Law in Late Antiquity* (Oxford 1996).

Ashbrook Harvey, S., "Revisiting the Daughters of the Covenant: Women's Choir and Sacred Song in Ancient Syriac Christianity," *Hugoye* 8 (2005), 13, www.syrcom.cia.edu/Hugoye.

Bagnall, R. W., et al., *Consuls of the Later Roman Empire* (Atlanta 1987).

Balmelle, C., *Les demeures aristocratiques d'Aquitaine: Société et culture de l'Antiquité tardive dans le Sud-Ouest de la Gaule* (Bordeaux-Paris 2001).

Barbet, A., *La peinture murale en Gaule romaine* (Paris 2008).

Barnes, T. D., "Ambrose and Gratian," *AT* 7 (1999), 165–74.

———, "Patricii under Valentinian III," *Phoenix* 19 (1975), 155–70.

Beaucamp, J., *Le statut de la femme à Byzance, 4e-7e siècle*, 2 vols. (Paris 1990–1992).

Bek, L., "'*Quaestiones conviviales*': The Idea of the Triclinium and the Staging of Convivial Ceremonies from Rome to Byzantium," *Analecta Romana* 12 (1983), 81–107.

Beltrán de Heredia Bercero, J. (ed.), *From Barcino to Barcinona: The Archaeological Remains of Plaça del Rei in Barcelona* (Barcelona 2001).

Beltrán de Heredia Bercero, J., and C. Bonnet, "Nouveau regard sur le groupe épiscopal de Barcelone," *Rivista di Archeologia Cristiana* 80 (2004), 137–58.

Bermond, I., and C. Pellecuer, "Recherches sur l'occupation des sols dans la région de l'étang de Thau: son apport à l'étude de la villa et des campagnes de Narbonnaise," *Revue archéologique de Narbonnaise* 30 (1997), 63–84.

Bischoff, B., and M. Koehler, "Eine illustrierte Ausgabe der spätantiken Ravennater Annalen," in *Medieval Studies in Memory of A. Kingsley Porter*, ed. W. Koehler (Cambridge, Mass. 1939), 125–38.

Blair-Dixon, K., "Memory and Authority in Sixth-Century Rome: The *Liber Pontificalis* and the *Collectio Avellana*," in *Religion, Dynasty, and Patronage in Early Christian Rome*, ed. K. Cooper and J. Hillner (Cambridge 2007), 59–76.

Blockley, R. C., *East Roman Foreign Policy: Formation and Conduct from Diocletian to Anastasius* (Leeds 1992).

Borowski, M J., *Pulcheria, Empress of Byzantium: An Investigation of the Political and Religious Aspects of Her Reign 414–453* (PhD, University of Kansas 1979).

Bowes, K., *Private Worship, Public Values, and Religious Change in Late Antiquity* (Cambridge 2008).

Bradbury, S., *Severus of Minorca: Letter on the Conversion of the Jews* (Oxford 1996).

Bradley, K., "The Roman Child in Sickness and in Health," in *The Roman Family in the Empire*, ed. M. George (Oxford 2005), 67–92.

Brandenburg, H., *The Ancient Churches of Rome from the Fourth to the Seventh Century*, trans. A. Knopp (Turnhout 2005).

Brown, P., "Aspects of the Christianization of the Roman Aristocracy," *JRS* 51 (1961), 1–11.

——, *Aspects of the Christianisation of the Roman World: The Tanner Lectures on Human Values* (Cambridge 1993).

——, *The Body and Society: Men, Women, and Sexual Renunciation in Early Christianity* (New York 1988).

——, "The Patrons of Pelagius: The Roman Aristocracy between East and West," *JTS* 21 (1970), 56–72.

——, "Pelagius and His Supporters: Aims and Environment," *JTS* 19 (1968), 93–114.

——, "Religious Coercion in the Later Roman Empire: The Case of North Africa," *History* 48 (2007), 283–305.

——, "The Rise and Function of the Holy Man in Late Antiquity," *JRS* 61 (1971), 80–101.

——, "Sorcery, Demons and the Rise of Christianity: From Late Antiquity into the Middle Ages," *Witchcraft Confessions and Accusations: Association of Social Anthropologists Monographs* 9 (1970), 56–72.

——, "The Study of Elites in Late Antiquity," *Arethusa* 33 (2000), 321–46.

Brubaker, L., "Memories of Helena: Patterns in Imperial Female Matronage in the Fourth and Fifth Centuries," in *Women, Men and Eunuchs*, ed. L. James (New York 1997), 52–75.

Buddensieg, T., "Le coffre en ivoire de Pola, Saint-Pierre et le Lateran," *Cahiers archéologiques* 10 (1959), 157–200.

Burgess, R., "The Accession of Marcian in the Light of Chalcedonian Apologetic and Monophysite Polemic," *Byz.Z* 86/87 (1993–1994), 47–68.

———, *The Chronicle of Hydatius and the Consularia Constantinopolitana* (Oxford 1993).

Burrus, V., *The Making of a Heretic: Gender, Authority and the Priscillianist Controversy* (Berkeley 1995).

Bury, J. B., *History of the Later Roman Empire* (London 1923).

———, "Justa Grata Honoria," *JRS* 9 (1919), 1–13.

Caffin, P., *Galla Placidia: la dernière impératrice de Rome* (Paris 1977).

Callu, J.-P., "Le prince charmant: quelques prodromes antiques," in *L'éloge du prince: de l'antiquité au temps des lumières*, ed. I. Cogitore and F. Goyet (Grenoble 2003), 125–35, repr. in J.-P. Callu, *Culture profane et critique des sources de l'antiquité tardive* (Rome 2006), 583–93.

Cameron, A., *Claudian: Poetry and Propaganda at the Court of Honorius* (Oxford 1970).

———, "The Date and Identity of Macrobius," *JRS* 56 (1966), 25–38.

———, "Flavius: A Nicety of Protocol," *Latomus* 47 (1988), 26–33.

———, "Petronius Probus, Aemilius Probus and the Transmission of Nepos: A Note on Late Roman Caligraphers," in *Humana Sapit: Études d'antiquité tardive offertes à Lellia Cracco Ruggini*, ed. J.-M. Carrié and R. Lizzi Testa (Turnhout 2002), 121–30.

———, "Vergil Illustrated between Pagans and Christians. Reconsidering 'the Late-4th Century Classical Revival,' the Dates of the Manuscripts, and the Places of Production of the Latin Classics," review of D. H. Wright's *The Vatican Vergil, and the Roman Vergil*, *JRA* 17 (2004), 502–25.

———, "Wandering Poets: A Literary Movement in Byzantine Egypt," *Historia* 14 (1965), 470–509.

Cameron, A., and J. Long, *Barbarians and Politics at the Court of Arcadius* (Berkeley 1993).

Carletti, C., "Aspetti biometrici del matrimonio nelle iscrizioni cristiane di Roma," *Augustinianum* 17 (1977), 39–51.

Carroll, M., *Spirits of the Dead: Roman Funerary Commemoration in Western Europe* (Oxford 2006).

Castelli, E. A., *Martyrdom and Memory: Early Christian Culture Making* (New York 2004).

Cavallo, G., "La cultura scritta a Ravenna tra antichità tarda e alto medioevo," in *Storia di Ravenna II.2: dall'età bizantine all'età ottonia*, ed. A. Carile (Venice 1992), 79–125.

Cazes, D., *Le Musée Saint Raymond: Musée des Antiques de Toulouse* (Toulouse 1999).

Cesa, M., "Il matrimonio di Placidia ed Ataulfo sullo sfondo dei rapporti fra Ravenna e i Visigoti," *Romanobarbarica* 12 (1992–1993), 23–53.

——, *Impero tardoancico e barbari: La crisi militare da Adrianopoi al 418* (Como 1984).

Chadwick, H., *Priscillian of Avila* (Oxford 1978).

——, "St. Peter and St. Paul [in Rome: The Problems of the *memoria apostolorum ad catacumbas*]," *JTS* 8 (1957), 31–52.

Chantraine, H., "Das Schisma 418/419 und das Eingreifen der kaiserlichen Gewalt in die römische Bishofwahl," in *Alte Geschichte und Wissenshcaftsge-schiche. Festschrift K. Christ*, ed. P. Kneissl and V. Losemann (Darmstadt 1988), 79–94.

Chastagnol, A., "Les Espagnols dans l'aristocratie gouvernementale de Théodose," in *Les empereurs romains d'Espagne* (Paris 1965), 269–307.

——, "Le sénateur Volusien et la conversion d'une famille de l'aristocratie romaine au Bas Empire," *REAug* 58 (1956), 241–53, repr. in A. Chastagnol, *L'Italie et l'Afrique au Bas Empire* (Lille 1987), 235–47.

Chausson, F., "Une soeur de Constantin: Anastasia," in *Humana Sapit: Études d'antiquité tardive offertes à Lellia Cracco Ruggini*, ed. J.-M. Carrié and R. Lizzi Testa (Turnhout 2002), 131–55.

——, *Stemmata aurea: Constantin, Justine, Théodose: revendications généalogiques et idéologie impériale au IV s. ap J.-C.* (Rome 2007).

Clark, E. A., *Jerome, Chrysostom and Friends: Essays and Translations* (New York 1979).

——, *The Life of Melania the Younger* (New York 1984).

——, "Theory and Practice in Late Ancient Asceticism: Jerome, Chrysostom, and Augustine," *Journal of Feminist Studies in Religion* 5 (1989), 25–46.

Clark, E. A., and D. F. Hatch, *The Golden Bough, the Oaken Cross: The Virgilian Cento of Faltonia Betittia Proba* (Chico 1981).

Clark, G., *Women in Late Antiquity: Pagan and Christian Life-Styles* (Oxford 1993).

Cloke, G., "Mater or Martyr: Christianity and the Alienation of Women within the Family in the Later Roman Empire," *Theology and Sexuality* 5 (1996), 37–57.

Clover, F. M., *Flavius Merobaudes: A Translation and Historical Commentary* (Philadelphia 1971).

Coleman-Norton, P. R., *Roman State and Christian Church*, 3 vols. (London 1966).

Collaci, A., *Galla Placidia: la vita e i giorni* (Firenze 1995).

Collins, R., "Review Article: Making Sense of the Early Middle Ages," *English Historical Review* 124 (2008), 641–65.

Collins, W., *Antonina: Or the Fall of Rome* (London 1875).

Connor, C. L., "Female Imperial Authority: Empresses of the Theodosian House: Galla Placidia," in *Women of Byzantium* (New Haven 2004), 45–72.

Consolino, F. E., "La 'santa' regina da Elena a Galla Placidia nella tradizione dell'Occidente latino," in *Vicende e figure femminili in Grecia e a Roma*, ed. R. Raffaelli (Ancona 1995), 467–92.

Coon, L., *Sacred Fictions: Holy Women and Hagiography in Late Antiquity* (Philadelphia 1997).

Cooper, K., *The Fall of the Roman Household* (Cambridge 2007).

———, "Insinuations of Womanly Influence: An Aspect of the Christianization of the Roman Aristocracy," *JRS* 82 (1992), 150–64.

———, "Poverty, Obligation, and Inheritance: Roman Heiresses and the Varieties of Senatorial Christianity in Fifth Century Rome," in *Religion, Dynasty, and Patronage in Early Christian Rome, 300–900*, ed. K. Cooper and H. Hillner (Cambridge 2007), 165–89.

———, *The Virgin and the Bride: Idealized Womanhood in Late Antiquity* (Cambridge, Mass. 1996).

Cooper, K., and J. Hillner (eds.), *Religion, Dynasty, and Patronage in Early Christian Rome* (Cambridge 2007), 190–224.

Coşkun, A., "Virius Nicomachus Flavianus, der Praefectus und Consul des *Carmen contra paganos*," *Vigiliae Christianae* 58 (2004), 152–78.

Coulon, D., *Aetius* (Villeneuve d'Ascq 2003).

Cracco Ruggini, L., "Fonti, problem e studi sulol'età di Galla Placidia," *Anthenaeum* 40 (1962), 373–91.

———, "Il paganesimo romano tra religione et politica (383–394 d.C.): per una reinterpretazione del *carmen contra paganos*," *Memorie dell' Accademia Nationale dei Lincei, Classe di scienze morali, storiche e filologiche*, ser. 8 vol. 23 (1979), 3–143.

———, "Rome in Late Antiquity: Clientship, Urban Topography, and Prosopography," *CP* 98 (2003), 366–82.

Croke, B., and J. Harries, *Religious Conflict in Fourth Century Rome* (Sydney 1982).

Curran, J., *Pagan City and Christian Capital: Rome in the Fourth Century* (Oxford 2000).

Dagron, G., *Naissance d'une capitale: Constantinople et ses insitutions de 330 à 451* (Paris 1974).

Davis, R., *The Book of Pontiffs* (Liverpool 2000).

de Filippo, R., "Le grand bâtiment du site de Larrey: la question palatiale," *Aquitania* 14 (1996), 23–29.

Deichmann, F. W., *Ravenna: Haupstadt des spätantikes Abendlandes*, 2 vols. (Wiesbaden 1969–1989).

De Imperatoribus Romanis: An Online Encyclopedia of Roman Rulers and Their Families, www.roman-emperors.org.

Delbrueck, R., *Die Consulardiptychen und verwandte Denkmäaler: Studien zur spätantiken Kunstgechichte* (Berlin 1929).

Deliyannis, D. M., *Ravenna in Late Antiquity* (Cambridge 2010).

Demandt, A., and G. Brummer, "Der Prozess gegen Serena im Jahre 408 n. Chr.," *Historia* 26 (1977), 479–502.

———, "The Osmosis of Late Roman and Germanic Aristocracies," in *Das Reich und die Barbaren*, ed. E. Chrysos and A. Schwarcz (Vienna 1989), 75–89.

Denzey, N., *The Bone Gatherers: The Lost Worlds of Early Christian Women* (Boston 2007).

de Ste. Croix, G. E. M., "The Council of Chalcedon with Addition by Michael Whitby," in *Christian Persecution, Martyrdom, and Orthodoxy* (Oxford 2006), 259–319.

Dewar, M., *Claudian: Panegyricus de sexto consulatu Honorii* (Oxford 1996).

Dixon, D. (ed.), *Childhood, Class and Kin in the Roman World* (London 2001).

Dolbeau, F., "Nouveaux sermons de saint Augustin pour la conversion des païens et des donatistes," *Revue des Études Augustiniennes* 37 (1991), 267–310.

———, *Vingt-six sermons au peuple d'Afrique* (Paris 1996).

Downey, G., "The Tombs of the Byzantine Emperors at the Church of the Holy Apostles in Constantinople," *JHS* 79 (1959), 27–51.

Drijvers, J. W., "Virginity and Aceticism in Late Roman Western Elites" in *Sexual Asymmetry*, ed. J. Blok and P. Mason (Amsterdam 1988), 241–73.

Drinkwater, J. F., "The *Bacaudae* of Fifth-Century Gaul," in *Fifth-Century Gaul: A Crisis of Identity?*, ed. J. F. Drinkwater and H. Elton (Cambridge 1992), 208–17.

———, "Patronage in Roman Gaul and the Problem of the Bagaudae," in *Patronage in Ancient Society*, ed. A. Wallace-Hadrill (London 1989), 189–203.

———, "The Usurpers Constantine III (407–411) and Jovinus (411–413)," *Britannia* 29 (1997), 269–98.

Dunbabin, K., *Mosaics of the Greek and Roman World* (Cambridge 1999).

Dunbabin, K. M. D., "Convivial Spaces: Dining and Entertainment in the Roman Villa," *JRA* 9 (1996), 66–79.

———, "Triclinium and Stibadium," in *Dining in a Classical Context*, ed. W. J. Slater (Ann Arbor 1991), 121–48.

———, "Wine and Water at the Roman Convivium," *JRA* 6 (1993), 116–41.

Dunn, G. D., "The Validity of Marriage in Cases of Captivity: The Letter of Innocent I to Probus," *Ephemerides Theologicae Lovaniensis* 83 (2007), 107–21.

Eisen, U. E., *Women Officeholders in Early Christianity: Epigraphical and Literary Studies*, trans. L. M. Maloney (Collegeville 2000).

Elia, F., *Valentiniano III* (Catania 1999).

Ellis, S. P., "Late Antique Dining: Architecture, Furnishings and Behaviour," in *Domestic Space in the Roman World: Pompeii and Beyond*, ed. R. Laurence and A. Wallace-Hadrill (*JRA* supp. 22) (Portsmouth 1997), 41–51.

———, "Power, Architecture and Décor: How the Late Roman Aristocrat Appeared to His Guests," in *Roman Art in the Private Sphere: New Perspectives on the Architecture and Décor of the Domus, Villa and Insula*, ed. E. Gazda (Ann Arbor 1991), 117–34.

Errington, R. M., "The Praetorian Prefectures of Virius Nicomachus Flavianus," *Historia* 41 (1992), 439–61.

———, *Roman Imperial Policy from Julian to Theodosius* (Chapel Hill 2006).

Evans, J. K., *War, Women and Children in Ancient Rome* (London 1991).

Evans Grubbs, J., *Law and Family in Late Antiquity: The Emperor Constantine's Marriage Legislation* (Oxford 1995).

———, "Marriage More Shameful Than Adultery: Slave-Mistress Relationships, 'Mixed Marriages,' and Late Roman Law," *Phoenix* 47 (1993), 125–54.

———, *Women and the Law in the Roman Empire: A Sourcebook on Marriage, Divorce and Widowhood* (London 2002).

Fabre, G., et al., *Inscriptions romaines de Catalogne IV: Barcino* (Paris 1997).

Fantham, E., *Julia Augusta* (Milton Park 2006).

Farioli Campanati, R., "Ravenna, Costantinopoli: aspetti topografico-monumentali e iconografici," in *Storia di Ravenna*, ed. A. Carile (Venice 1992), III.2, 127–57.

———, "Ravenna imperiale all'epoca di Galla Placidia," *Ravenna: Studi et ricerche* 1 (1994), 177–88.

Fasoli, A., "Il patrimonio della chiesa Ravennate," in *Storia di Ravenna*, ed. A. Carile (Venice 1991), 2.1, 389–400.

Fernández-Galiano Ruiz, D., *Carranque: Centro de la Hispania Romana: Catálogo de la Exposición* (Madrid 2001).

Fontaine, J., "Société et culture chrétiennes sur l'aire circumpyrénéenne au siècle de Théodose," *Bulletin de littérature ecclésiastique de Toulouse* 7–5 (1974), 241–82.

Frakes, J. F. D., *Framing Public Life: The Portico in Roman Gaul* (Wien 2009).

Frankfurter, D., "Review of L. Ciraolo and J. Seidel, Magic and Divination in the Ancient World," *BMCR* 2005.05.32.

Frier, B., "Roman Life Expectancy: The Pannonian Evidence," *Phoenix* 37 (1983), 328–44.

———, "Roman Life Expectancy: Ulpian's Evidence," *HSCP* 86 (1982), 213–51.

Frutaz, A., *Il complesso monumentale di sant'Agnese et di Santa Costanza*, 2nd ed. (Rome 1969).

Frye, D., "A Mutual Friend of Athaulf and Jerome," *Historia* 40 (1991), 507–8.

———, "Rusticus: Ein gemeinsamer Freund von Athaulf und Hieronymus? A Response," *Historia* 43 (1994), 504–6.

Funke, H., "*Univira*: Ein Beisiel heidnischer Gechichtsapologetik," *JAC* 8/9 (1965–1966), 183–88.

Giardina, A., "Carità eversiva: le donazioni di Melania la Giovane e gli equilibri della società tardoromana," *Studi Storici* 1 (1988), 127–42.

Gillett, A., "The Birth of Ricimer," *Historia* 44 (1995), 380–84.

———, *Envoys and Political Communication in the Late Antique West, 411–533* (Cambridge 2003).

———, "Rome, Ravenna and the Last Western Emperors," *PBSR* 69 (2001), 131–67.

Gordon, C. D., *The Age of Attila* (New York 1960).

Gourdin, H., *Galla Placidia: impératrice romaine, reine des Goths: biographie (388–450)* (Paris 2008).

Graumann, T., "Reading the First Council of Ephesos (431)," in *Chalcedon in Context: Church Councils 400–700*, ed. R. Price and M. Whitby (Liverpool 2009), 27–44.

Green, B., *The Soteriology of Leo the Great* (Oxford 2008).

Grierson, P., "The Tombs of Obits and the Byzantine Emperors (337–1042)," *DOP* 16 (1962), 1–63.

Grierson, P., and M. Mays, *Catalogue of Late Roman Coins in the Dumbarton Oaks Collection* (Washington, DC 1992).

Guarducci, M., *La capsella eburnea di samagher: Un cimelio di arte paleocristiana nella storia del tardo impero*, Atti e memorie della Società Istriana di archeologia et Storia 26 (Trieste 1978).

Gwynn, D. M., "The Council of Chalcedon and the Definition of Christian Tradition," in *Chalcedon in Context: Church Councils 400–700*, ed. R. Price and M. Whitby (Liverpool 2009), 7–26.

Hahn, J., "The Conversion of Cult Statues: The Destruction of the Serapeum and the Transformation of Alexandria into the 'Christ-Loving' City," in *From Temple to Church: Destruction and Renewal of Local Cultic Topograpy in Late Antiquity*, ed. J. Hahn et al. (Leiden-Boston 2008), 335–65.

Halsall, G., *Barbarian Migrations and the Roman West 376–568* (Cambridge 2007).

Harlow, M., "Galla Placidia: Conduit of Culture?" in *Women's Influence on Classical Civilization*, ed. F. McHardy (London 2004), 138–50.

Harlow, M., and R. Laurence, *Growing Up and Growing Old in Ancient Rome* (London 2002).

Heath, M., *Menander: A Rhetor in Context* (Oxford 2004).

Heather, P., and J. F. Matthews, *Goths and Romans 332–489* (Oxford 1991).

——, *The Goths in the Fourth Century* (TTH 11) (Liverpool 1991).

Hedrick, C. W., *History and Silence: Purge and Rehabilitation of Memory in Late Antiquity* (Austin 2000).

Herrin, J., "Book Burning as Purification," in *Transformations of Late Antiquity: Essays for Peter Brown*, ed. P. Rousssreau and M. Papoutsakis (Farnham 2009), 205–22.

Herzhaft, G., *Galla Placidia* (Paris 1987).

Holmes, W. G., *Age of Justinian and Theodora* (London 1912).

Holum, K. G., *Theodosian Empresses: Women and Imperial Dominion in Late Antiquity* (Berkeley 1989).

Holum, K. G., and G. Vikan, "The Trier Ivory, Adventus Ceremonial, and the Relics of St. Stephen," *DOP* 33 (1979), 115–33.

Honoré, T., *Law in the Crisis of Empire 379–455 AD* (Oxford 1998).

Hopkins, K., "On the Probable Age Structure of the Roman Population," *Population Studies* 20 (1966), 245–64.

——, "The Age of Roman Girls at Marriage," *Population Studies* 18 (1965), 309–27.

Hordern, P., and N. Purcell, *The Corrupting Sea: A Study of Mediterranean History* (Oxford 2000).

Horn, C., *Asceticism and Christological Controversy in Fifth Century Palestine: The Career of Peter the Iberian* (Oxford 2006).

——, "Children's Play as Social Ritual," in *Late Ancient Christianity*, ed. V. Burrus (Minneapolis 2005), 95–116.

Horn, C., and J. W. Martens, *"Let the Little Children Come to Me": Childhood and Children in Early Christianity* (Washington, DC 2009).

Horn, C., and R. Phenix (eds.), *Children in Late Ancient Christianity* (Tübingen 2009).

Humphries, M., "From Emperor to Pope? Ceremonial, Space, and Authority at Rome from Constantine to Gregory the Great," in *Religion, Dynasty, and Patronage in Early Christian Rome*, ed. K. Cooper and J. Hillner (Cambridge 2007), 21–58.

Hunt, E. D., *Holy Land Pilgrimage in the Later Roman Empire 312–460* (Oxford 1982).

Huskinson, J., *Roman Children's Sarcophagi: Their Decoration and Social Significance* (Oxford 1996).

Jalland, T., *The Life and Times of St Leo the Great* (London 1941).

Janes, D., *God and Gold in Late Antiquity* (Cambridge 1998).

Johnson, M. J., "On the Burial Places of the Theodosian Dynasty," *Byzantion* 61 (1991), 330–39.

———, *The Roman Imperial Mausoleum in Late Antiquity* (Cambridge 2009).

Jones, A. H. M., *The Later Roman Empire*, 2 vols. (Norman, Okla. 1964).

Jones, H., "Agnes and Constantia: Domesticity and Cult Patronage in the Passion of Agnes," in *Religion, Dynasty, and Patronage in Early Christian Rome*, ed. K. Cooper and J. Hillner (Cambridge 2007), 115–39.

Kamp, A., "Where Have All the Children Gone? The Archaeology of Childhood," *Journal of Archaeological Method and Theory* 8 (2001), 1–34.

Keay, S. J., "The Late-Antique Complex of Centcelles (Tarragona)," review of Arce's *Centcelles*, *JRA* 17 (2004), 741–43.

Kelly, C., "Empire Building," in *Interpreting Late Antiquity*, ed. P. Brown et al. (Cambridge, Mass. 2001), 170–95.

Kent, J. P. C., *The Divided Empire and the Fall of the Western Parts AD 395–491*, The Roman Imperial Coinage 10 (London 1994).

Kertzer, D. I., and R. P. Saller (eds.), *The Family in Italy from Antiquity to the Present* (New Haven 1991).

Kessler, H. L., "Pictures as Scripture in Fifth Century Churches," *Studia Artium Orientalis et Occidentalis* II (1985), 17–31.

King, M., "Commemoration of Infants on Roman Funerary Inscriptions," in *The Epigraphy of Death: Studies in the History and Society of Greece and Rome*, ed. G. J. Oliver (Liverpool 2000), 117–54.

Kötting, B., *Die Bewertung der Wiederveheiratung (der zweiten Ehe) in der Antike und in der Frühen Kirche* (Opladen 1988).

———, "Univira in Inschriften," in *Romanitas et Christianitas: Studia Iano Henrico Waszink*, ed. W. den Boer et al. (Amsterdam 1973), 195–206.

Krautheimer, R., *Corpus basilicarum Christianarum Romae: The Early Christian Basilicas of Rome (IV–IX Centuries)* (Rome 1937–).

———, *Rome: Profile of a City, 312–1308* (Princeton 1980).

———, *Three Christian Capitals: Topography and Politics* (Berkeley 1983).

Kulikowski, M., and K. D. Bowes (eds.), *Hispania in Late Antiquity: Current Perspectives* (Boston 2005).

———, *Late Roman Spain and Its Cities* (Baltimore 2004).

Kurdock, A., "Demetrias ancilla dei: Anicia Demetrias and the Problem of the Missing Patron," in *Religion, Dynasty, and Patronage in Early Christian Rome*, ed. K. Cooper and J. Hillner (Cambridge 2007), 190–224.

Lavagne, H., "Deux mosaïques de style orientaisant a Loupian (Hérault)," *Monuments Piot* 61 (1977), 61–86.

Lavagne, H., D. Rouquette, and R. Prudhomme, "Les nouvelles mosaïques de la villa gallo-romaine de Loupian," *Revue archéologique de Narbonnaise* 14 (1981), 173–203.

Leader-Newby, R. R., *Silver and Society in Late Antiquity: Functions and Meanings of Silver Plate in the Fourth to the Seventh Centuries* (Aldershot 2004).

Lee-Stecum, P., "Dangerous Reputations: Charioteers and Magic in Fourth Century Rome," *G&R* 53 (2006), 224–34.

Lepelley, C., *Les cités de l'Afrique romaine au Bas-Empire*, 2 vols. (Paris 1979–1981).

———, "Mélanie la Jeune, entre Rome, la Sicilia, et l'Afrique: les effects socialement pernicieux d'une forme extrême de l'ascétisme," in *Atti del IX congresso internazionale di studi sulla Sicilia antica: Kokalos* 43–44 (1997–1998), I.1.15–32.

Leyerle, B., "Appealing to Children," *JECS* 5 (1997), 243–70.

Liebeschuetz, J. H. W. G., *Ambrose of Milan: Political Letters and Speeches* (TTH 43) (Liverpool 2005).

———, *Barbarians and Bishops: Army, Church and State in the Age of Arcadius and Chrysostom* (Oxford 1990).

Lim, R., "People as Power: Games, Munificence, and Contested Topography," in *The Transformation of Urbs Roma in Late Antiquity*, ed. W. V. Harris (*JRA* supp. 38) (Portsmouth 1999), 265–81.

Limberis, V., *Divine Heiress: The Virgin Mary and the Creation of Christian Constantinople* (New York 1994).

Liverani, P., "Victors and Pilgrims in Late Antiquity and the Early Middle Ages," *Fragmenta* 1 (2007), 83–102.

Lizzi Testa, R., "*Augures et pontifices*: Public Sacral Law in Late Antique Rome (4th–5th Centuries)," in *The Power of Religion in Late Antiquity*, ed. A. Cain and N. Lenski (Farnham 2009), 251–78.

Long, J., "Julia-Jokes at Macrobius's Saturnalia: Subversive Decorum in Late Antique Reception of Augustan Political Humor," *International Journal of the Classical Tradition* 6 (2000), 337–55.

Lowden, J., "The Beginnings of Biblical Illustration," in *Imagining the Early Medieval Bible*, ed. J. Williams (University Park 1999), 9–59.

———, "The Beginnings of Biblical Illustration," in *Late Antiquity and Medieval Art of the Mediterranean World*, ed. E. R. Hoffman (Malden, Oxford 2007), 117–34.

Luck, G., *Arcana Mundi* (Baltimore 1985).

Lunn-Rockleffe, S., "Ambrose's Imperial Funeral Sermons," *JEH* 59 (2008), 1–17.

Lütkenhaus, W., *Constantius III: Studien zu seiner Tätigkeit und Stellung im Westreich 411–421* (Bonn 1998).

MacCormack, S. G., *Art and Ceremony in Late Antiquity* (Berkeley 1981).

MacGeorge, P., *Late Roman Warlords* (Oxford 2002).

Mackie, G., *Early Christian Chapels in the West: Decoration, Functions, and Patronage* (Toronto 2003).

———, "The Mausoleum of Galla Placidia: A Possible Occupant," *Byzantion* 65 (1995), 396–404.

MacMullen, R., *Voting about God in Early Church Councils* (New Haven 2006).

Maenchen Helfen, O. J., *The World of the Huns: Studies in Their History and Culture* (Berkeley 1973).

Magnani, A., *Serena: l'ultima romana* (Milan 2002).

Magnou-Nortier, E., "Autour des Constitutions Sirmonidiennes," in *Traditio Iuris: Permanence et/ou discontinuité du droit romain durant le haut Moyen-âge* (Lyon 2005).

La maison urbaine d'époque romaine en Gaule Narbonnaise et dans les provinces voisines. Actes du colloque d'Avignon, novembre 1994 (Avignon 1996).

Marasco, G., "La magia e la guerra," *Millennium: Jahrbuch zu Kultur und Geschichte des ersten Jahrtausends n. Chr.[Yearbook on the Culture and History of the First Millennium CE]* 1 (2004), 83–132.

Marchetta, A., *Orosio e Ataulfo nell'ideologia dei rapporti romano-barbarici* (Rome 1987).

Marcos, M., "Política dinástica en la corte de Teodosio I: Las Imágenes de Aelia Flacia Flaccilla," in *Congreso internacional La Hispania de Teodosio 1995* (Salamanca 1997), 1, 155–64.

Marot, T., "Algunas consideraciones sobre la significacion de las emisiones del usurpador Maximo en Barcino," in *Congreso internacional La Hispania de Teodosio* (Salamanca 1997), II, 569–80.

Mathisen, R. W., *Ecclesiastical Factionalism and Religious Controversy in Fifth-Century Gaul* (Washington, DC 1989).

———, "Sigisvult the Patrician, Maximinus the Arian, and Political Stratagems in the Western Roman Empire c. 425–40," *Early Medieval Europe* 8 (1999), 173–96.

Matthews, J., "Four Funerals and a Wedding: This World and the Next in Fourth Century Rome," in *Tranformations of Late Antiquity: Essays for Peter Brown*, ed. P. Rousseau and M. Papoutsakis (Farnham 2009), 129–46.

Matthews, J. F., *Laying Down the Law: A Study of the Theodosian Code* (New Haven 2000).

———, "Roman Law and Barbarian Identity in the Late Roman West," in *Ethnicity and Culture in Late Antiquity*, ed. S. Mitchell and G. Greatrex (London 2000), 31–44.

———, *Western Aristocracies and Imperial Court 364–425* (Oxford 1975).

Maxwell, J. L., *Christianization and Communication in Late Antiquity: John Chrysostom and His Congregation in Antioch* (Cambridge 2006).

Mazzarino, S., *Stilicone: la crisi imperiale dopo Teodosio* (Milan repr. 1990).

Mazzolani Storoni, L., *Galla Placidia* (Milan 1975, repr. 1981).

McCormick, M., *Eternal Victory: Triumphal Rulership in Late Antiquity, Byzantium and the Early Medieval West* (Cambridge 1986).

McGill, S., "Virgil, Christianity, and the *Cento Probae*," in *Texts and Culture in Late Antiquity: Inheritance, Authority, and Change*, ed. J. H. D. Scourfield (Swansea 2007), 173–94.

McLanan, A., *Representations of Early Byzantine Empresses: Image and Empire* (New York 2002).

McLynn, N., "Christian Controversy and Violence in the Fourth Century," *Kodai* 3 (1992), 15–44.

———, "Theodosius, Spain and the Nicene Faith," in *Congreso internacional La Hispania de Teodosio* (Salamanca 1997), 1, 171–78.

McLynn, N. B., *Ambrose of Milan: Church and Court in a Christian Capital* (Berkeley 1994).

Meyers, C., et al. (eds.), *Women in Scripture: A Dictionary of Named and Unnamed Women in the Hebrew Bible, the Apocryphal/Deuterocanonical Books, and the New Testament* (Boston 2000).

Millar, F., *A Greek Roman Empire: Power and Belief under Theodosius II* (Berkeley 2006).

Miller, M. C., "The Development of the Archiepiscopal Residence in Ravenna, 300–1300," *Felix Ravenna* 141–44 (1991–1992), 145–73.

Moorehead, J., *The Roman Empire Divided 400–700* (Harlow 2001).

Morvillez, E., "Les salles de réception triconques dans l'architecture domestique de l'Antiquité tardive en Occident," *Histoire de l'Art* 31 (1995), 15–26.

Mratschek, S., *Der Briefwechsel des Paulinus von Nola: Kommunikation und soziale Kontakte zwischen christichen Intellectuellen* (Göttingen 2002).

———, "*Multis enim notissima est sanctitas loci*: Paulinus and the Gradual Rise of Nola as a Center of Christian Hospitality," *JECS* 9 (2001), 511–53.

Nagl, A., *Galla Placidia: Studien zur Geschichte und Kultur des Altertums* (Paderborn 1908).

Narkiss, B., *El Pentateuco Ashburnham* (Valencia 2007).

Nelson, J., "Queens as Jezebels: The Career of Brunhild and Bathild in Merovingian History," in *Medieval Women: Studies in Honor of Rosalind Hill*, ed. D. Baker (Oxford 1978), 31–77.

Neraudau, J.-P., *Etre enfant à Rome* (Paris 1984).

Nixon, C. E. V., and B. Saylor Rodgers, *In Praise of Later Roman Emperors* (Berkeley 1994).

Norman, N., "Death and Burial of Roman Children: The Case of the Yasmina Cemetery at Carthage: Part I, Setting the Stage," *Mortality* 7 (2002), 302–23.

———, "Death and Burial of Roman Children: The Case of Yasmina Cemetery at Carthage: Part II, the Archaeological Evidence," *Mortality* 8 (2003), 36–47.

O'Donnell, J. J., *Augustine: A New Biography* (New York 2005).

Oliviero, A. A., *A Time of Rome: The Empress Galla Placidia* (2006).

Oost, S. I., *Galla Placidia Augusta: A Biographical Essay* (Chicago 1968).

———, "Some Problems in the History of Galla Placidia," *CP* 60 (1965), 1–10.

Palmer, R. E. A., *Studies of the Northern Campus Martius in Ancient Rome* (Transactions of the American Philosophical Society 80) (Philadelphia 1990).

Paschoud, F., *Roma Aeterna: études sur le patriotisme romain dans l'occident latin à l'époque des grandes invasions* (Rome 1967).

Pellecuer, C., *La villa des Prés Bas (Loupian, Hérault) dans son environnement. Contribution à l'étude des villae et de l'economie domaniale en Narbonnaise* (PhD thesis, Université de Provence 2000).

Pellecuer, C., and H. Pomaredes, "Crise, survie ou adaptation de la villa romaine en Narbonnaise Première? Contribution des récentes recherches de terrain en Languedoc-Roussillon," in *Les campagnes de la Gaule a la fin de l'Antiquité*, ed. P. Ouzoulias et al. (Actes du colloque Montpellier, mars 1998) (Antibes 2001), 503–32.

Perevalov, S. M., "Bazas 414; la rupture de l'alliance alano-gothique," *Dialogues d'histoire ancienne* 26 (2000), 175–94.

Pernot, L., *La rhétorique de l'éloge dans le monde gréco-romain* (Paris 1993).

Pharr, C., *Christiana Respublica*, 3 vols. (Paris 1997).

——, "The Interdiction of Magic in Roman Law," *TAPA* 63 (1932), 269–95.

——, *Roma Christiana: Recherches sur l'Église de Rome, son organisation, sa politique, son idéologie de Miltiade à Sixte III (311–440)* (Rome 1976).

Pizarro, J. M., *Writing Ravenna: The Liber Pontificalis of Andreas Agnellus* (Ann Arbor 1995).

Price, R., "The Council of Chalcedon (451): A Narrative," in *Chalcedon in Context: Church Councils 400–700*, ed. R. Price and M. Whitby (Liverpool 2009), 70–91.

Price, R., and M. Gaddis, *The Acts of the Council of Chalcedon*, 3 vols. (TTH 45) (Liverpool 2005).

Rasch, J. J., and A. Arbeiter, *Das Mausoleum der Constantina in Rom* (Mainz am Rhein 2007).

Ratti, S., "Nicomacque Flavien sr. et l'Histoire Auguste: la découverte de nouveaux liens," *REL* 85 (2007), 204–19.

Rawson, A., *Children and Childhood in Roman Italy* (Oxford 2003).

——, *Marriage, Divorce and Children in Ancient Rome* (Oxford 1991).

Rawson, A., and P. Weaver (eds.), *The Roman Family in Italy: Status, Sentiment, Space* (Oxford 1997).

Rebenich, S., "Gratian, a Son of Theodosius, and the Birth of Galla Placidia," *Historia* 34 (1985), 372–85.

——, "Gratianus Redivivus," *Historia* 38 (1989), 376–79.

Rebillard, E., *In hora mortis: évolution de la pastorale chrétienne de la mort aux IV et V siecles dans l'Occident latin* (Rome 1994).

Reynolds, P., *Hispania and the Roman Mediterranean, AD 100–700: Ceramics and Trade* (London 2009).

Richlin, A., "Julia's Jokes, Galla Placidia, and the Roman Use of Women as Political Icons," in *Stereotypes of Women in Power*, ed. B. Garlick et al. (Westport, Conn. 1992), 65–91.

Rives, J. C., "Magic, Religion, and Law: The Case of the *Lex Cornelia de sicariis et veneficiis*," in C. Ando and J. Rüpke (eds.), *Religion and Law in Classical and Christian Rome* (Stuttgart 2006), 47–67.

Roberts, M., "Rome Personified, Rome Epitomized: Representations of Rome in the Poetry of the Early Fifth Century," *AJP* 122 (2001), 533–65.

Rossiter, J., "Convivium and Villa in Late Antiquity," in *Dining in a Classical Context*, ed. W. J. Slater (Ann Arbor 1991), 199–214.

Roueché, C., "Acclamations in the Later Roman Empire: New Evidence from Aphrodisias," *JRS* 74 (1984), 181–99.

Rouge, J., "Justine la belle Sicilienne," *Latomus* 33 (1974), 676–79.

———, "La pseudo-bigamie de Valentinien I," *Cahiers d'histoire* 3 (1958), 5–15.

Rouge, J., and R. Delmaire, *Les lois religieuses des empereurs romains de Constantin à Théodose II (312–438)* (SCh 531) (Paris 2009).

Rousseau, P., *Basil of Caesarea* (Berkeley 1994).

Rousselle, A., *Porneia: On Desire and the Body in Antiquity*, trans. F. Pheasant (New York 1996).

Russell, D. A., and N. G. Wilson, *Menander Rhetor: Translation and Commentary* (Oxford 1981).

Sabrié, M., R. D. Rouquette, and Y. Solier, *La maison à portiques du Clos de la Lombarde à Narbonne et sa décoration murale*, *RAN* supp. 16 (Paris 1987).

Sabrié, M., and R. Sabrié, *Le Clos de la Lombarde: Un quartier de Narbonne dans l'Antiquité* (Narbonne 2002), catalog.

——— (eds.), *Le Clos de la Lombarde à Narbonne: Espaces publics et privés du secteur nord-est* (Montagnac 2004).

Sales Carbonell, J., "Teodosi, fill d'Ataulf i Galla Placidia, mai va estar enterrat a Sant Cugat del Valles. Notes de topografia paleocristiana Barcelonesa (1)," *Gausac. Publicacio del grup d'estudis locals de Sant Cugat del Valles*, 24 (July 2004), 53–58.

Salzman, M., "The Christianization of Sacred Time and Sacred Space," in *The Transformation of Urbs Roma in Late Antiquity*, ed. W. V. Harris, *JRA* supp. 38 (Portsmouth 1999), 123–34.

———, *The Making of a Christian Aristocracy: Social and Religious Change in the Western Roman Empire* (Cambridge, Mass. 2002).

Sanchez, G., and M. Sirventon (eds.), *Narbonne 25 ans d'archeologie: Catalogue d'exposition* (Narbonne 2000).

Saradi-Mendelovici, H., "Christian Attitudes toward Pagan Monuments in Late Antiquity and Their Legacy in Later Byzantine Centuries," *DOP* 44 (1990), 47–61.

Scharf, R., "Iovinus-Kaiser im Gallien," *Francia* 20 (1993), 1–13.

Schild, W., *Galla Placidia* (Halle 1897).

Schlunk, H., et al., *Die Mosaikkuppel von Centcelles*, 2 vols. (Mainz 1988).

Schubert, K., "Jewish Traditions in Christian Painting Cycles: The Vienna Genesis and the Ashburnham Pentateuch," in *Jewish Historiography and Iconography in Early and Medieval Christianity*, vol. II, ed. H. Schreckenberg and K. Schubert (Assen 1991), 211–60.

Scott, E., *The Archaeology of Infancy and Infant Death* (Oxford 1999).

Seeck, O. *Regesten der Kaiser und Päpste für die Jahre 311 bis 476 n.C.* (Stuttgart 1919).

Sessa, K., "Domestic Conversion: Households and Bishops in Late Antique 'Papal Legends,'" in *Religion, Dynasty, and Patronage in Early Christian Rome*, ed. K. Cooper and J. Hillner (Cambridge 2007), 79–114.

Shaw, B. D., "The Age of Roman Girls at Marriage; Some Reconsiderations," *JRS* 77 (1987), 30–46.

Shelton, K. J., "The Consular Muse of Flavius Constantius," *Art Bulletin* 65 (1983), 7–23.

Sirago, V. A., *Galla Placidia e la trasformazione politica dell'Occidente* (Louvain 1961).

——, *Galla Placidia: la nobilissima (392–450)* (Milano 1996).

Sivan, H., "Alarico tra Pollenzo et Roma," in *Romani et Barbari: Incontro e scontro di cultura*, ed. S. Giorcelli Bersani (Turin 2004), 259–69.

——, "Alaricus Rex: Legitimizing a Gothic King," in *The Construction of Communities in the Early Middle Ages*, ed. R. Corradini et al. (Transformation of the Roman World) (Leiden 2003), 109–21.

——, "Anician Women, the Cento of Proba, and Aristocratic Conversion in the Fourth Century," *Vigiliae Christianae* 47 (1993), 140–57.

——, *Ausonius of Bordeaux: Genesis of a Gallic Aristocracy* (London 1993).

——, "Between Gaza and Minorca: The Un/making of Minorities in Late Antiquity" (in press).

——, "From Athanaric to Ataulf: The Shifting Horizons of 'Gothicness' in Late Antiquity," in *Humana Sapit: Études d'antiquité tardive offertes à Lellia Cracco Ruggini*, ed. J.-M. Carrié and R. Lizzi Testa (Turnhout 2002), 55–62.

——, "Funerary Monuments and Funerary Rites in Late Antique Aquitaine," *Oxford Journal of Archaeology* 5 (1986), 339–53.

——, "The Last (Prose) Gallic Panegyric: Paulinus of Nola and Theodosius I," *Studies in Latin Literature and Roman History* 7 (1994), 577–94.

——, "On *Foederati, Hospitalitas* and the Settlement of the Visigoths in AD 418," *American Journal of Philology* 108 (1987), 759–772.

——, "On Hymen and Holiness in Late Antiquity: Opposition to Aristocratic Female Asceticism at Rome," *Jahrbuch für Antike und Christentum* 36 (1993), 81–93.

——, *Palestine in Late Antiquity* (Oxford 2008).

——, "Town, Country and Province in Late Antique Gaul: The Example of *CIL* XIII 128," *Zeitschrift für Papyrologie und Epigraphik* 79 (1989), 103–113.

——, "Why Not Marry a Barbarian? Marital Frontiers in Late Antiquity (*CTh* 3.14.1)," in H. Sivan and R. W. Mathisen (eds.), *Shifting Frontiers in Late Antiquity* (Aldershot 1996), 136–45.

Sivan, H., and R. W. Mathisen, "Forging a New Identity: The Kingdom of Toulouse and the Frontiers of Visigothic Aquitania," in *The Visigoths: Studies in Culture and Society*, ed. A. Ferreiro (Leiden 1999), 1–60.

Sodini, J.-P., "Habitat de l'Antiquité tardive," *Topoi* 5 (1995), 151–218, and 7 (1997), 435–577.

Solier, Y., et al., *La basilique paléochrétienne du Clos de la Lombarde à Narbonne: Cadre archéologique, vestiges et mobiliers* (Paris 1991).

Soraci, R., *Ricerche sui conubia tra Romani e Germani nei secoli IV–VI* (Catania 1974).

Sorrell, S., *Galla Placidia: Empress of Rome in a Time of Turmoil (389–450)* (New Orleans 2006).

Sotinel, C., *Identité civique et Christianisme: Aquilée du IIIe au Vie siècle* (Rome 2005).

Sotomayor, M., "La iconografia di Centcelles: Enigmas sin resolver," *Pyrenae* 37 (2006), 143–73.

Stanely, D. J., "New Discoveries at Santa Costanza," *DOP* 48 (1994), 257–61.

Stein, E., *Histoire du Bas Empire*, trans. J. Palanque (Paris 1959).

Stern, H., "Les mosaïques de l'église de Sainte-Constance à Rome," *DOP* 12 (1958), 157–218.

Stickler, T., *Aëtius: Gestaltungsspielräume eines Heernmeisters im ausgehenden Weströmischen Reich* (Munich 2002).

Stroheker, K. F., "Spanische Senatoren der spätrömischen und westgotischen Zeit," *MM* 4 (1963), 107–32.

Teetjen, A. B., *The Life and Times of the Empress Pulcheria* (London 1907).

Thompson, E. A., "The End of Roman Spain," *Nottingham Mediaeval Studies* 20–23 (1976–79), repr. in E. A. Thompson, *Romans and Barbarians: The Decline of the Western Empire* (Madison 1982), 137–229.

———, *Saint Germanus of Auxerre and the End of Roman Britain* (Woodbridge 1984).

———, "The Suevic Kingdom of Galicia," in *Romans and Barbarians: The Decline of the Western Empire* (Madison 1982), 161–87.

Tomlin, R., "Christianity and the Late Roman Army," in *Constantine: History, Historiography and Legend*, ed. S. N. S. Lieu and D. Montserrat (London 1998), 21–51.

Tougher, S., "In Praise of an Empress: Julina's Speech of Thanks to Eusebia," in *The Propaganda of Power: The Role of Panegyric in Late Antiquity*, ed. M. Whitby (Leiden 1998), 105–23.

Traina, G., *428 AD: An Ordinary Year at the End of the Roman Empire* (Princeton 2009).

Treadgold, W., "The Bride Shows of the Byzantine Emperors," *Byzantion* 49 (1979), 395–413.

Trout, D., "*Amicitia, auctoritas*, and Self-fashioning Texts: Paulinus of Nola and Sulpicius Severus," *Studia Patristica* 28 (1993), 123–29.

———, "The Dates of the Ordination of Paulinus of Bordeaux and of His Departure for Nola," *REAug* 37 (1991), 237–60.

———, *Paulinus of Nola: Life, Letters, and Poems* (Berkeley 1999).

Twyman, B. L., "Aetius and the Aristocracy," *Historia* 19 (1970), 480–503.

Urbainczyk, T., *Socrates of Constantinople: Historian of Church and State* (Ann Arbor 1997).

Vanderlinden, E., "Revelatio Sancti Stephani," *REByz* 4 (1946), 178–217.

Van Nuffelen, P., "Gélase de Césarée, un compilateur du cinquième siècle," *Byz.Z* 95 (2002), 621–39.

Vera, D., "Le statue del senato di Roma in onore di Flavio Teodosio e l'equilibrio dei potere imperiali in età Teodosiana," *Athenaeum* 57 (1979), 381–403.

Vilella, J., "Biografía crítica de Orosio," *Jahrbuch für Antike und Christentum* 43 (2000), 94–121.

Volbach, W. F., *Elfenbeinarbeiten der Spätantike und des frühen Mittelalters*, 3rd ed. (Mainz 1976).

Wallace-Hadrill, J. M., "Gothia and Romania," *Bulletin of the John Rylands Library* (Manchester) 44 (1961), 213–37.

Weber, R. J., "Albinus: The Living Memory of a Fifth Century Personality," *Historia* 38 (1989), 472–97.

Weitzmann, K., "Illustration for the Chronicles of Sozomenos, Theodoret and Malalas," *Byzantion* 16 (1942–1943), 87–134.

Wemple, S. F., *Women in Frankish Society: Marriage in the Cloisters* (Philadelphia 1981).

Wessel, S., "The Ecclesiastical Policy of Theodosius II," *Annuarium Historiae Conciliarum* 33 (2001), 285–308.

——, *Leo the Great and the Spiritual Rebuilding of a Universal Rome* (Leiden 2008).

Wickham, C., *Framing the Early Middle Ages: Europe and the Mediterranean 400–800* (Oxford 2005).

Wiedemann, T. E. J., *Adults and Children in the Roman Empire* (New Haven 1989).

Wiemer, H. U., "Akklamationen im spätrömischen Reich: Zur Typologie und Funktion eines Kommunikationsrituals," *Archiv für Kulturgeschichte* 86 (2004), 27–73.

Wilkes, J. J., "A Pannonian Refugee of Quality at Salona," *Phoenix* 26 (1972), 377–93.

Wilkinson, J., *Egeria's Travels to the Holy Land* (Jerusalem 1981).

Wirbelauer, E., *Zwei Päpste in Rom: der Konflict zwischen Laurentius und Symmachus (498–514)* (Munich 1993).

Wolfram, H., *History of the Goths*, trans. T. J. Dunlap (Berkeley 1988).

Wood, I., "The End of Roman Britain: Continental Evidence and Parallels," in *Gildas: New Approaches*, ed. M. Lapidge and D. Dumville (Woodbridge 1984), 1–25.

Woods, D., "On the Alleged Reburial of Julian the Apostate in Constantinople," *Byzantion* 76 (2006), 364–71.

Wormald, P., "The Decline of the Western Empire and the Survival of Its Aristocracy," *JRS* 66 (1976), 217–26.

Zangara, V., "Una predicazione," *AT* 8 (2000), 265–304.

Zecchini, G., *Aezio, l'ultima difesa dell'Occidente romano* (Rome 1983).

Index

Eudoxia, empress, wife of Arcadius, half brother of Galla Placidia, 10, 76–77, 112, 116, 117, 123, 127, 165

Eugenius, usurper defeated by Theodosius I, Galla Placidia's father, 82, 89, 98, 103, 153

Eulalius, contender to the papal throne, 73–79

Eusebia, empress, wife of Constantius II, patroness of Julian, 79, 80, 95, 96, 97, 111, 114, 115, 116, 127

Eustochium, Roman noblewoman, settled in Bethlehem and correspondent of Jerome, 13

Eutyches, abbot at Constantinople, 135–36

Fausta, wife of the emperor Constantine I, 111, 121–22

Faustus, Anicius Acilius Glabrio, senator, prefect of the city of Rome, 97, 124, 127, 150

Felix, military commander under Galla Placidia and Valentinian III, 90, 107n51, 109–10, 117, 152, 160–61

Flaccilla, Aelia, first wife of Theodosius, father of Galla Placidia, 28n78, 55, 112

Flavianus, Nichomachus (the elder), Roman aristocrat and supporter of Eugenius; composed elusive Annals, 82, 100, 103

Flavianus, Virius Nichomachus (the younger), son of the former, official under Galla Placidia and Valentintinian III, engineered the rehabilitation of his father, 98–103

Fravittas, Gothic chieftain favored by Theodosius I, 17–18

Fronto, monk in Spanish Tarragona who stirred locals with accusations of heresy and sorcery, 84

Gaatha, Gothic queen, 23

Galates, son of the emperor Valens, 50

Galla, daughter of Valentinian I and Justina, second wife of Theodosius I, mother of Galla Placidia, 95

Geiseric, Vandal king, 156–57

Germanus, bishop of Auxerre, 154, 167–69

Grata, sister of Valentinian II, aunt to Galla Placidia, 52, 65

Gratian, emperor, half uncle of Galla Placidia, 9, 12, 27, 41, 53, 94, 103, 115, 122, 142, 149, 164

Helena, empress, mother of Constantine I, 2, 33, 53–54, 113–14, 117, 134, 140, 145

Helena, wife of Julian, 144

Helena, Gallic town where Constans, son of Constantine I, was killed, 41

Helion, Master of the Offices and patrician who crowned Valentinian III at Rome, 91–92, 95, 117

Herculanus, Flavius Bassus, husband selected for Honoria, Galla Placidia's daughter, 153, 155–56

Hilarion, holy man, active around Gaza, 84

Hilary (deacon, later pope), 136–37, 159

Honoria, Iusta Grata, daughter of Galla Placidia and Constantius III, sister of Valentinian III, 89, 91, 117, 123, 153–57

Honorius, emperor of the western Roman empire, half brother of Galla Placidia, 2, 6, 9, 11, 12, 13, 19, 21–25, 27–30, 35, 37–39, 45, 47, 50, 52, 58, 60–61, 65–71, 73–79, 82, 84, 86, 88–92, 94, 97, 103–4, 110, 140, 143, 148, 151, 159, 161–64, 168

Huneric, son of the Vandal king Geiseric, intended husband of Eudocia, daughter of Valentinian III and granddaughter of Galla Placidia, 156

Iamblichus, philosopher, on power and empathy, 83

Illryicum, contested region between the eastern and western Roman empires, under papal jurisdiction, 95, 103, 120, 127, 140, 147, 149, 174

Ingenius (Ingenuus), nobleman at Narbonne at whose house Galla Placidia and Athaulf celebrated their wedding, 15–16, 35